Changing New York City Politics

Changing
New York City
Politics

ASHER ARIAN, ARTHUR S. GOLDBERG,
JOHN H. MOLLENKOPF, AND
EDWARD T. ROGOWSKY

ROUTLEDGE

NEW YORK AND LONDON

First published in 1991 by

Routledge
an imprint of
Routledge, Chapman & Hall, Inc.
29 West 35 Street
New York, NY 10001

Published in Great Britain by

Routledge
11 New Fetter Lane
London EC4P 4EE

Photographs on cover: David Dinkins (Photo by Ricky Flores, Impact Visuals, 1989); Rudolph Givliani (Photo by Rich Reinhard, Impact Visuals, 1988); Edward Koch (Photo by Les Stone, Impact Visuals, 1989).

Library of Congress Cataloging in Publication Data

Changing New York City politics / Asher Arian . . . [et al.].
     p.   cm.
   ISBN 0-415-90420-X; ISBN 0-415-90421-8 (PB)
     1. New York (N.Y.)—Politics and government—1951- I. Arian,
Alan.
   F128.55.C46   1991
   320.97471—dc20   91-18735
                                                                   CIP

British Library cataloguing in publication data also available.

This book is dedicated to the memory of

Harold S. Proshansky

President, The Graduate Center
1973–1990

an extraordinary human being who blended into a single whole
academic values, leadership, and humanity

CONTENTS

PREFACE

New York is without doubt a complex phenomenon: it has a complicated political structure, a highly diverse mix of racial and ethnic
groups, and correspondingly complex electoral alignments. Although
an awareness of these complexities informs this book, it does not seek
to fully account for them. Instead, it seeks to shed light on what
motivated the voters of New York City to elect their first black mayor
in the fall of 1989 and why they did so by the closest of margins
with vast numbers of defections from traditional Democratic voting
patterns. At first glance, "race" would appear to be the obvious explanation, but we believe that single word says both too much and too
little.

Race is not a sufficient explanation because important groups in
New York City did not vote along strictly racial lines. A majority of
liberal whites living in cosmopolitan neighborhoods voted for Dinkins
in the primary and stuck by the Democratic candidate during the
general election. Jewish voters favored Koch during the primary, but
a substantial minority of them did vote for Dinkins in the general
election. Even some of the most conservative parts of the city, such as
white Catholic Richmond Hill, Queens, gave Dinkins a quarter of
their votes. Moreover, though it was by no means certain that Latinos
would back Dinkins solidly in the general election, they ultimately

did. A complete analysis of the Dinkins victory must therefore go beyond the simple distinctions of race.

To develop a more complete, if more complicated, answer to why New York voters elected their first African American mayor, though by a slim margin, we have analyzed four bodies of data: a survey on the 1988 presidential election, surveys of primary and general election voters in seven selected assembly districts in the 1989 primary and general elections, exit polls for the 1989 mayoral elections, and actual election returns.

For the 1988 presidential race, the Robert F. Wagner, Sr., Institute of Urban Public Policy at the Graduate Center of the City University of New York supported the authors in designing the New York City Presidential Election Survey (NYCES). In the six weeks before the November 1988 general election, the Survey Research Laboratory of the CUNY Center for Social Research undertook telephone interviews with 1,280 respondents. This survey was parallel to the 1988 National Election Studies (NES) conducted by the Survey Research Center at the University of Michigan, for decades a major source of election research. Our NYCES survey replicated many of the questions used in NES; we were also able to follow national patterns over time because of the pioneering work of the National Election Studies.

For the 1989 mayoral primary and general elections, the Wagner Institute sponsored a survey of a random sample of prime Democratic voters in seven of New York City's assembly districts (ADs). (Prime voters have voted in one or more Democratic primaries over a four-year election cycle.) The ADs were selected to gain diversity in race/ethnicity and political organization. We selected three white ADs, two black ADs, and two Latino ADs that varied according to whether they had a reform orientation or were more aligned with the regular Democratic party organization. Using our questionnaire, Schulman, Ronca, and Bucuvalas, Inc. conducted telephone interviews with approximately 300 prime Democratic voters in each AD before the primary election. They reinterviewed 815 respondents before the general election.

CBS and the *New York Times* conducted exit polls for the 1989 mayoral primary and general elections using a random sample of voters from thirty-nine polling places throughout the city. They interviewed 2,014 Democratic voters and 513 Republican voters as they left polling places during the primary; in the general election, they interviewed 2,109 voters from all parties.

Certain themes regarding the role of race emerged repeatedly in our analysis of these elections. We set them forth here so that the reader will keep them in mind as we travel through the complexities of New York City politics.

First, race was certainly a major factor in these elections, but not primarily in the way that people usually think. Race has manifested itself in our data in three different ways:

- The first aspect can be called "racism pure and simple." That occurs when a person makes a negative judgment about a candidate based solely on that person's race without reference to any other aspect of the person. Such judgments are not likely to change even in the face of excellent performance by the person being judged. We estimate that only about 10 percent of the vote in the 1989 mayoral election was a manifestation of such "racism pure and simple."
- A far more important aspect of race is what we have called "race-based anxiety." This anxiety pivots around the question of whether you trust a candidate of another race to treat persons of your race fairly. Race-based anxiety was widespread during the 1989 mayoral election, affecting, in our estimate, about 39 percent of the voters.
- Finally, "race-correlated agenda items" also affected the vote. The priority that a voter gave to crime on the public agenda as opposed to homelessness, or to drug treatment centers as against constructing more prisons, had an influence on her or his choice. These differences in substantive agenda are aspects of life situations, "haves" versus "have-nots," that are themselves correlated with race.

But one cannot conclude that these three aspects of race—racism pure and simple, race-based anxiety, and racially correlated differences on the issues—constitute unbridgeable racial cleavages. Our second major finding is that large portions of the white New York City electorate describe themselves as "liberal," and that many of these white liberal "haves" articulate policy preferences quite similar to those of "have-a-lot-less" black and Latino New Yorkers. Liberal whites have a long and effective political history in New York and will be a crucial part of multiracial coalitions for some time to come. They provide a crucial bridging role among whites, blacks, and Latinos.

Third, it is a practical as well as a technical mistake to equate blacks and Latinos when describing race in New York City. Although they prefer some of the same policies, their overall policy preferences are by no means identical. Latinos are much more likely to call themselves conservatives. Moreover, Latinos identify much less strongly than blacks with the Democratic party, and when they do it carries less information about their voting behavior than it does for blacks. Latinos thus comprise an available constituency for an astute challenger. If appropriately mobilized, they could become a crucial "swing" vote.

Finally, party identification remains a potent force despite the cross-cutting impact of race. Without that potent force, it is doubtful that David Dinkins could have been elected. The degree to which identification with the Democratic party will remain a potent force among whites is an open question.

So yes, race did matter, in fact a great deal. But it mattered least in its most blatant form, racism pure and simple. It mattered most as race-based anxiety, a condition that a black mayor might well be able to alleviate (or aggravate) through his performance. Indeed, Mayor Dinkins' desire to have white voters perceive him as fair may well constrain his actions toward his core black and white liberal constituencies, much to their consternation. Race also mattered in terms of issues and policy preferences, but these have much more to do with class than with race. Yet whatever their base, how these issues and policy questions are managed will determine the viability of this multiracial and multiethnic metropolis.

As with any large-scale research project, we have accumulated many debts of gratitude in undertaking our work. Under the superb guidance of Dr. Susanne Tumulty, the Survey Research Lab of the CUNY Center for Social Research did a fine job of mounting our 1988 NYCES. Schulman, Ronca, and Bucuvalas also did an excellent job on the prime voter survey in the 1989 mayoral primary and general elections; we especially thank Dr. Mark Schulman. Dr. Kathleen Frankovic of the CBS News polling unit graciously made their exit polls available to us, and Dr. Chris Von Der Haar helped us understand their technical aspects. Ms. Marta Fisch, associate director of the CUNY Data Service, provided invaluable assistance in analyzing these data. Ms. Jean Krasno brought her considerable skills to bear upon our graphics, for which we are very grateful. Ms. Marilyn Stevens did an outstanding job administering the Robert F. Wagner, Sr., Institute of Urban Public Policy, which sponsored our project.

We dedicate this volume to the late Harold M. Proshansky, president of the City University Graduate Center, both for his steadfast support for the Wagner Institute and our other colleagues engaged in urban research and for building a precious institution that delivers on its promise to provide both excellence in teaching and scholarship and access for those from all races, classes, and quarters of the globe who seek it.

1

UNDERSTANDING NEW YORK

It is, indeed, in every possible respect, desirable that every
nation should possess one city in which every interest of man
and of society is adequately represented and cared for.
—Anonymous, 1856

City of the world! (for all races are here, all lands of the earth
make contributions here) . . .
—Walt Whitman, 1865

When the New York City Board of Elections released the official
results of the November 7, 1989, general election, the report showed
that Democrat David N. Dinkins had defeated Republican/Liberal
Rudolph Giuliani by 47,080 votes out of 1.8 million cast, the smallest
margin for a successful mayoral candidate in more than eighty years.
In percentage terms, Dinkins had won 48.3 percent of the total vote
cast for mayor, compared to Giuliani's 45.8 percent.[1] By a margin of
less than three percentage points, Dinkins had become the city's first
African American mayor.

The circumstances that enabled Dinkins to capture the Democratic nomination from the incumbent three-term mayor, Edward I. Koch, and then to narrowly defeat his Republican/Liberal opponent, Rudolph W. Giuliani, the "conservative" candidate, indicate the massive forces that have altered the terrain of local politics in New York City since the 1960s. The social dislocations caused by economic transformation and racial succession, the declining role of political parties, and the rising media dominance of political campaigns have all strongly influenced the conduct of New York City politics. As these forces have altered New York politics, an ever more significant gap has opened between the makeup of the city's resident population and the racial and ethnic backgrounds of its highest elected officials.

Understanding New York City has always been a difficult task. For the "world city" (so named by Le Corbusier in the late 1930s), the period from the 1960s to 1990 witnessed especially dramatic changes in demography, economy, and politics. While the city is still at the center of international attention and interest, a postindustrial revolution has altered the environment for politics in New York City, as it has for the other older cities of the Northeast. To varying degrees, they endured, and even prospered, despite the doomsday prophecies of urban decline during the late 1960s. But in New York, these trends enabled a conservative political coalition to come to power during the 1980s that altered the city's political landscape and reshaped the tenor of political debate.

Writing in the mid-1960s, two sets of analysts foresaw different futures for New York City politics. In the introduction to the 1965 paperback edition of their already classic treatise *Governing New York City*, Sayre and Kaufman affirmed their view that "no single elite dominates the political and governmental system of New York City." The issue of race and the effects of race and other intergroup relations on political attitudes and municipal elections were not central to their description. Rather, they were satisfied that "the City of New York can confidently ask: What other large American city is as democratically and as well governed?"[2] At about the same time, Glazer and Moynihan concluded their study of ethnicity and politics in New York, *Beyond the Melting Pot*, by observing that "religion and race define the next stage in the evolution of the American peoples."[3] Just a few years later, after summer riots in several of New York City's black neighborhoods and the onset of the movement for community control of the public school system, Glazer wrote:

Obviously at this point in time, during New York's primaries and election campaign of 1969, it hardly seems as though religion defines the present, or the future, major fissures in New York life. Race has exploded to swallow up all other distortions.[4]

Just as racial and ethnic cleavages would challenge the prevailing view of New York City as an open and responsive political system, so too would the fiscal crisis of the mid-1970s present a dilemma about the balance of power in municipal politics.[5] The drama of New York City as the nation's prodigal municipality was captured at once in the October 30 1975 *Daily News* front-page headline characterizing President Ford's reply to the city's request for congressional reauthorization of the federal loan guarantees that had helped to rescue New York: "Ford to City: DROP DEAD!"

THE POSTINDUSTRIAL TRANSFORMATION

The context for the shaping of New York City's current political coalitions has been framed by major economic, demographic, and social change and accompanied by basic alterations in governmental structure.[6] The basic local element in this transformation is the massive and irreversible shift of large-scale urban employment from its prior base in manufacturing toward the service sectors of the economy— finance, corporate services, nonprofit social services, and government—with an associated shift from production workers to managers, professionals, clericals, and service workers. Basic changes in capitalism have driven this transformation at the global level: rapid technological change, the internationalization of economic activity, the centralization of financial markets, the increasing importance of finance relative to production, and new patterns of massive migration from third world countries to first world core cities.

New York has been central in propagating these forces and in being influenced by them. The corporate, nonprofit, and public sectors grew rapidly between 1977 and 1987, with sharp increases in employment and earnings, especially in finance. As a result, the number of upper-income, dual-career professional households grew, as did their disposable income. At the same time, dramatic shifts took place in the social makeup of the city. The nature of racial succession changed from native-born blacks and Puerto Ricans replacing whites to a more complex pattern reflecting the upsurge of Caribbean, Latin American, and Asian immigration. Increasing numbers of black and Latino female headed households were excluded from the labor force, increasing the poverty rate. Latinos concentrated in downwardly mobile manufacturing industries, thus suffering declining earnings relative to other groups. The cumulative effect of these forces was to bring about a new racial division of labor, increasing income inequality, and a new mix of cultures, residential patterns, and social distinctions throughout the city.[7] The simultaneous growth of wealth and poverty made inequality a more pressing municipal issue during the 1980s, especially when it took on racial and ethnic dimensions.

As the 1960s began, New York was a relatively well off, white, blue-collar city. By the late 1980s, it had become an economically divided, multiracial and more multiethnic, white-collar metropolis. The city's poverty rate, which was still only 15 percent in 1975 (about 20 percent over the national average), rose to 23 percent (about twice the national average) by 1987. These social trends had disastrous consequences for the old ghetto cores in the 1970s and early 1980s, exemplified by the South Bronx as a national symbol of urban decay. As many neighborhoods were burned to the ground, the loss of housing pushed the black and Latino populations outward. The settlement of new immigrants into the city's neighborhoods also produced new communities, some on the boundaries of the old ghetto cores, and exerted added demographic pressure on former white working- and middle-class areas.

In many cases, white ethnics retreated into old and new neighborhoods at the city's periphery, such as Canarsie and Bensonhurst in Brooklyn, Howard Beach and Bayside in Queens, and Riverdale in the Bronx. Some vigorously resisted the integration of their schools or the building of housing for low-income tenants. Divisions over neighborhood transition thus joined patterns of economic inequality as an underlying fault line in the city's political life. Housing units disappeared by the thousands, the school system abruptly lost its once-perceived ability to educate the children of the poor and immigrants into employability, the health care system was stressed well beyond capacity, and, by the 1980s, the epidemics of drugs, crime, and AIDS and the collapse of the city's physical infrastructure threatened to demoralize the civic spirit.

The magnitude of the changes in the makeup of the population can be seen in Table 1.1: the 10.4 percent decline in the overall population between 1970 and 1980, as enumerated by the census, continued the downward trend of the two previous decades. New York's population became less white and more black and Latino, as it had previously. But in contrast to the 1950s and 1960s, it also became more foreign born. Waves of southern black and island-born Puerto Rican migrants no longer replaced white ethnics. In the 1970s and 1980s, the native-born black and Puerto Rican cohorts, like white ethnics, began to decline in absolute as well as relative terms. By the 1980s, racial succession meant that West Indians, Dominicans, Latin Americans, Chinese, and other Asians were displacing not only whites, but also native-born blacks and Latinos.

The 1977–1987 economic boom reversed the city's population decline. The 1990 census showed a population increase. Projecting from vital statistics on birth and death rates, public and private school enrollments, Social Security recipient rates, and other indicators, Emanuel Tobier has estimated the city's population actually rose to 7.74 million, substantially more than the official figure.[8]

A key problem in enumerating New York City's population is the number of undocumented aliens, a group whose presence is acknowledged but difficult to count officially. The 1980 tally of just under 1.7 million foreign-born would have exceeded 2 million if all undocumented aliens had been counted in the census.[9] Overall, immigration is acknowledged as *the* contributing factor in the city's population growth. The estimated net growth of more than half a million new

Table 1.1

Census Profile of New York City, 1970–1990

	1970	1980	1990
Total population	7,894,862	7,071,639	7,322,564
Non-Latino white population	4,972,509	3,668,945	3,163,125
Non-Latino black population	1,525,745	1,694,127	1,847,049
Latino population	1,278,630	1,406,024	1,783,511
Puerto Rican	846,731	860,552	963,000*
Non–Puerto Rican	476,913	545,472	820,000*
Asian and Pacific islanders	115,830	300,406	489,851
Foreign-born	1,437,058	1,670,199	2,270,000*

Source: 1970, 1980, 1990 census; *estimated on the basis of 1988 CUNY survey

immigrants since 1980 includes Caribbean blacks (approximately one-third of the total), Asians (one-quarter), and Latinos (one-fifth).[10]

These populations and demographic changes, taking place in the context of economic transformation, provide evidence of New York City's increasing polarization. Though some have used the term "dual city" to describe this process, the fragmentation of this process of polarization is more complex than any metaphor of the dual city can capture.[11] Many blacks, Latinos, Asians, and women have entered the economic mainstream as white males have departed from the labor force due to aging, outmigration, and death. At the same time, others have been consigned to long-term welfare dependency, incarceration, or homelessness. The enduring inequalities of the thirty-year period from 1960 to 1990 have thus become more pronounced. This and other patterns have contributed to the increasing disparity between the city's resident population and those who participated in its elections.

FISCAL CRISIS

The municipal budget rose faster than revenues from 1960 to the 1970s. This expansion was financed during Robert F. Wagner, Jr.'s, third term (1962–1965) and John Lindsay's two terms as mayor (1966–1973) by rising taxes, extensive borrowing, and, for a while, expanding federal aid. It was during this period that a municipal maxim was enshrined and devoutly practiced: "A good loan is better than a bad tax." These sources fed growing demand for housing and human services until back-to-back national recessions reduced local revenues and Nixon-era retrenchment curtailed federal aid. By mid-1975, New York City, with in excess of $5 billion in short-term debt and facing closure in the capital markets, found itself in the throes of fiscal crisis. Rescue efforts enacted by the state government—the Municipal Assistance Corporation ("Big Mac," as it came to be known) and the Emergency Financial Control Board—restructured the debt and saved the city from bankruptcy, but compromised local government autonomy and reduced the number and compensation of city employees.

By the late 1970s and early 1980s, tight fiscal management and promoting private investment had displaced responding to urban social problems at the top of New York City's political agenda. Not only were a series of legal requirements and fiscal monitors put in place, but all major forces on public opinion, ranging from the *New York Times* editorial board to the leaders of municipal unions, were united in agreeing on these ends. Previous proponents of increased social spending, such as liberal Democrats and officials of the poverty program, were on the defensive, while their social base had been demobilized. The policies of the Lindsay administration, and the electoral coalition that had given it power, were in disarray.

POLITICAL PARTIES, ELECTIONS AND GOVERNMENT

Politically and electorally, New York City has long been regarded as a "one-party town" in which Democratic nominees generally won public office.[12] There is substantial evidence for this image. On inauguration day in January 1990, Democrats comprised all three citywide officials (mayor, city council president, and comptroller), four of the five borough presidents, thirty-four of thirty-five city councilpersons, all five of the county district attorneys, fifty-eight of the sixty state assemblypersons, eighteen of the twenty-four state senators, and eleven of the twelve U.S. congresspersons from districts wholly or partially within the city. Registration figures underscored this one-party dominance. In 1989, 69 percent of New York City's three million registered voters were self-enrolled Democrats; independent voters (registered but not enrolled in a political party, and thus unable to vote in party primaries) accounted for 15 percent of the electorate, and Republicans 14 percent. Enrollment in the Liberal, Conservative, and Right to Life parties totaled only 1.8 percent; the remainder of the registered electorate were voters whose party preference was "void or missing."

Yet despite their meager numbers, the Liberal and Conservative parties have each occasionally played an important role by cross-endorsing Democratic or Republican candidates or by nominating their own standard bearers, thereby splitting votes from major party candidates. (The Liberal party had been formed in 1944 by garment union leaders who were uncomfortable with the extent of Communist party influence in the American Labor party. The Conservative party was formed in 1962 by right-wing Republicans disgruntled by Governor Nelson Rockefeller's centrist/liberal policies). The manipulation of Liberal or Conservative party endorsement by their own party leaders or the anticipation of their support by candidates in Democratic or Republican primaries has, from time to time, provided an interesting sideshow in local politics. More importantly, Liberal endorsement of a Republican reformer such as La Guardia or Lindsay has been a critical ingredient in creating a fusion movement for reform.

The election of a mayor in New York City is the most visible and symbolic municipal contest. In 1969, when John Lindsay was seeking reelection as the Republican/Liberal (fusion) incumbent, an examination of the prior forty-year history showed that in the previous eleven mayoralty contests, the Democratic candidate, sometimes with third- or minor-party support, was the victor six times, while Republicans, *always* with the endorsement of other parties, won four times. Only once did an "independent" candidate prevail, when Lindsay was re-elected in 1969 as a Liberal and independent party candidate, having been defeated in the Republican primary.[13] Since that time, Democrats have dominated mayoral elections. Lindsay himself switched party enrollment in a notably unsuccessful try at the 1972 Democratic presidential nomination.

Underneath this pattern of persistent, if sometimes fragmented, one-party domination, important changes have occurred in the dynamics of municipal politics. These include the declining role of political parties, the development of candidate-centered campaigns heavily dependent on mass media, and the attendant heightened importance of raising massive campaign funds. At one time, as recently as Mayor Wagner's ascent in 1953, the major county leaders could meet in the proverbial "smoke-filled room" and choose the Democratic nominee for mayor and the other two citywide offices. In doing so, they sought to balance their ticket both ethnically, to reflect the Irish, Italian, and Jewish voting blocs that were the heart of their party, and geographically, paying tribute to the dominant county organizations in Manhattan, Brooklyn, and the Bronx.

Although usually referred to as "Tammany Hall" (the name for the Manhattan Democratic party organization), New York's Democratic party is in fact an amalgam of the five separate county (borough) organizations. State election law carefully details the nature of political parties at the county level, and each county organization adopts its own rules. State law does not require that there be a citywide unit of party organization. All that prevailed was the necessity and willingness of the county leaders to agree among themselves, thereby augmenting their own power. Their endorsement of a candidate and their subsequent ability to "deliver" the support of the local assembly district clubs in their boroughs by collecting nominating petition signatures and getting out the vote on primary day would, in turn, be the basis for their claim on the mayor for patronage and other favors.

The campaign of 1961 marked a watershed in New York City mayoral elections and local party politics. In declaring for a third term, incumbent mayor Robert F. Wagner, Jr., decided to run against his own record and the county leaders who had supported his previous candidacies. Wagner's father had been an eminent U.S. senator from New York who was instrumental in bringing about New Deal reforms in labor and housing. Wagner himself had been the Manhattan borough president and chairman of the New York City Planning Commission prior to his first election as mayor in 1953. Carmine DeSapio, the Greenwich Village district leader who became the first Italian American to lead Tammany Hall, had supported Wagner against the incumbent mayor, Vincent R. Impellitteri, an independent, and Wagner had in turn made DeSapio his "political agent."[14]

Although he was not regarded as charismatic, Wagner's family heritage of political prominence and his social awareness and political skills enabled him to achieve significant gains in middle-income housing, address education and health problems, and put civil rights issues on the table. Wagner was also credited with modernizing the civil service, recognizing public employee unions, increasing the size of the police force, and creating the office of city administrator. With Liberal endorsement, he had carried the 1961 elections by a large margin.

Sensing the importance of the emerging reform movement as embodied in its defeat of Tammany leader DeSapio, who thus became more of a liability than an asset, Wagner changed courses in 1961 and ran against his own record and the "regular" party organization that had spawned him. In this effort he turned to Alex Rose, Liberal party boss, to be his new political agent. This campaign gave the issue of "bosses and reformers," an enduring theme in New York political history, its contemporary incarnation. Wagner's primary campaign against State Comptroller Arthur Levitt (the reluctant candidate drafted by the county leaders) also helped to launch the political career of Edward I. Koch, the young reformer who defeated DeSapio's attempt to regain his district leadership in Greenwich Village.

Led by such notables as Eleanor Roosevelt and Governor Herbert Lehman, the reform movement had developed strongly in Manhattan's Upper West Side, the East Side, and the Village. It stimulated the formation of many new independent local clubs whose origin can be traced, in part, to the dissatisfaction of would-be party activists with the closed system of local party organization they encountered when they attempted to become involved in campaigns for progressive candidates.[15]

Directed against internal party rules that kept control in the hands of a few leaders, the reform movement sought to "democratize" the inner workings of the party, especially in candidate selection. There were motivational, ideological, and generational components to the effort. Reformers tended to be younger and more professional than the "regular" party leaders whom they sought to depose; they also tended to be more "liberal" in their politics and to regard political participation as a civic duty rather than a means for gaining tangible rewards or a way of maintaining organizational control *per se*. During the 1960s and 1970s, the movement took hold in Brooklyn and the Bronx, with less significant incursions into Queens and Staten Island.[16]

Along with his alliance with the reform movement and the choice of Liberal party boss Alex Rose as a major political adviser during his third term, Wagner also received strong support from the newly established municipal labor unions whose recognition Wagner had engineered.[17] Wagner's 1961 success in running against the county organizations laid the basis for opening up the process of mayoral nominations. The county leaders and their local organizations did not disappear, but the lesson was clear: it was possible to appeal over the heads of the bosses directly to the primary electorate within the Democratic party, and, with the support of volunteers, new recruits into political activity, and some fledgling local clubs, it was possible to win.[18] As one observer put it, "If the 1961 mayoral election suggested the embarrassing decline of the power of the Democratic organization, the next contest glaringly exposed its feebleness."[19] In 1965, Wagner decided against seeking an unprecedented fourth term, hoping instead to seek future statewide office and perhaps fulfill his dream to become a U.S. senator from New York. As a result, the Democratic party field was wide open.

The other two citywide officeholders in Wagner's third term, City Council President Paul Screvane from Queens and Comptroller Abraham Beame, a product of the Brooklyn Democratic organization, dominated the fray in the Democratic primary; the hotly contested primary gave Republicans an opening as well. Encouraged by Governor Nelson Rockefeller and other Republican leaders, John Lindsay, the four-term liberal congressman from Manhattan's Upper East Side "silk stocking" district, entered the race. The cagey Alex Rose supported him, launching a Republican/Liberal fusion candidacy that evoked memories of Fiorello La Guardia.

Tall, charismatic, and eager, Lindsay pushed forward the evolution of electoral dynamics in New York City. Two dimensions became crucial: the candidate's ability to communicate via television and, taking a lesson from Democratic reformers, the ability to launch and sustain a genuine grassroots campaign organization. With a network of storefront headquarters that overshadowed the regular party local clubhouses in the liberal neighborhoods of Manhattan and in primarily Jewish as well as some black and Puerto Rican districts in the other boroughs, Lindsay waged a dazzling campaign to defeat his general election opponents, Democratic nominee Abe Beame and Conservative party candidate William F. Buckley. (Buckley intended to siphon votes away from Lindsay, but postelection analysts concluded that he actually drew more conservative Democratic votes from Beame, an early indication of the emerging shift in the ideological preferences of New York's white Catholic Democratic voters.)

Major upheavals marked Lindsay's mayoralty. Upon taking office on January 1, 1966, he faced a paralyzing citywide transit strike led by veteran New York labor leader Michael Quill of the Transport Workers Union. Openly defying both the mayor (whose name he regularly mispronounced as "Lindslay") and the judicial system, Quill declared: "Let the judge drop dead in his black robes, we're not going back to work!" After much acrimony, the strike was eventually settled; as the opening act of Lindsay's first term it was, however, a barometer of things to come. The turbulence of social protest and governmental change that would be the tenor of the next several years was in stark contrast to the label "Fun City" Lindsay coined for New York.

Lindsay's execution of the municipal chief executive role helped to advance the mayoralty to the center of New York life in the arts and cultural arenas as well as on the local and national governmental scene. Lindsay became a national spokesman for the dilemmas and crises of urban America. He brought the Rand Corporation to the city to improve agency management and undertook a series of ambitious policy innovations.[20] This variety of mayoral initiatives, combined with the expectations that Lindsay aroused, added to the centrality of the office in the minds of New Yorkers whether they agreed with the mayor or were opposed to his initiatives.[21]

Among the many heated controversies that would occur during Lindsay's eight years in office, including scattered site housing proposals, strikes by major municipal unions, confrontations with Governor Rockefeller, demands for greater citizen participation, the movement for community control of the school system, and summer riots and looting in black and Puerto Rican neighborhoods, one episode stands out as a turning point. Just as Lindsay's 1965 election heralded the triumph of reform and his 1969 reelection the emergence of a liberal biracial electoral coalition, the 1966 referendum on a civilian complaint review board marked the entrance of overt racial divisions onto the electoral stage.[22]

Civilian review of the police had been a controversial issue in New York City for some years. In 1964, in response to frequent and intense charges by black and Puerto Ricans of police brutality, civil rights groups proposed that civilians be added to the Police Department's Civilian Complaint Review Board. (The word *civilian* in the name of the police review board described the source of the complaints brought before the board, not the composition of its membership.) The presence of civilians on a board investigating complaints of brutality would, it was argued, strengthen the confidence of the citizenry in the impartiality of the review. During his 1965 campaign, Lindsay proposed adding four civilians to the three deputy commissioners on the department's board. His proposal seemed modest in contrast to the one demanded by the major civil rights organizations calling for a completely independent civilian board with black and Puerto Rican membership. Black and Puerto Rican votes had helped to elect Lindsay, and it was generally believed that this support was in some measure the consequence of his commitment to civilian review.

In May 1966, Lindsay fulfilled his campaign promise by issuing an executive order creating a new Civilian Review Board (CRB). This action touched off one of the most bitterly fought electoral battles in New York City's history and signaled the emergence of a continuing crisis in the city's politics. All sides immediately criticized the CRB. The NAACP and CORE attacked the new board because they did not believe it had strong enough powers to alleviate minority community suspicion of and hostility toward police justice and policemen. But the strongest reaction came from the Patrolmen's Benevolent Association (PBA), which challenged the mayor's authority to promulgate the executive order and vowed continued opposition to the board unless it was approved by the voters in a referendum.

The furies unleashed in the campaign for or against the CRB prompted Daniel P. Moynihan to observe: "At the risk of over-generalizing, the Civilian Review Board was a proposal that originated in the liberal upper middle-class white community of the city as a measure to control the behavior of less liberal, lower middle-class white city employees toward members of the black and Puerto Rican community of varying social classes."[23]

In July 1966, the PBA filed petitions with 51,852 signatures placing a referendum on the general election ballot to render the mayor's CRB illegal. New York voters rendered a decisive verdict in November. Some 63 percent voted yes on the referendum measure to abolish the review board. Table 1.2 shows that the CRB aroused an unusually high degree of voter interest. Nearly 85 percent of the city's voters in the 1966 gubernatorial election also cast their ballot on the CRB referendum, as contrasted with the more typical 57 percent who voted on a lottery referendum.

As expected, areas with heavy concentrations of blacks and Puerto Ricans favored the board; most of these districts were in Manhattan, the only borough to produce a majority in favor of the board. Clearly,

Table 1.2

Participation in the 1966 Gubernatorial Election and
Referenda on CRB and State Lottery

	New York City Vote	Percent of Gubernatorial
Gubernatorial Election	2,464,894	
CRB Referendum	2,078,629	84.3%
State Lottery Referendum	1,395,888	56.6%

Source: David W. Abbott, Louis H. Gold, and Edward T. Rogowsky, *Police, Politics and Race* (Cambridge: Harvard-MIT Joint Center for Urban Studies, 1969)

the liberal electoral coalition that had elected Lindsay was in full retreat before this issue. As one study observed:

The magnitude of the outcome was stunning. For years, the white electorate of New York City had been dominated by a coalition of liberal forces—a coalition that had been especially willing to support the demands of blacks and other minority groups. In addition to giving clear and consistent support to a string of liberal candidates for state and national offices, these electoral groupings had rallied behind the symbols of liberal reform in both the 1961 and 1965 mayoral elections. Yet, in the 1966 referendum, the presumed liberalism of white voters could not be translated into support for the Review Board. For the first time in recent years, white New Yorkers turned their backs on a clearly articulated liberal cause, and civil rights forces suffered their worst defeat.[24]

Moreover, despite Lindsay's reelection, the dissolution of the liberal biracial coalition and the rise of a conservative alternative were also apparent in 1969.

First, Lindsay was denied the Republican nomination when conservative John Marchi, a veteran state senator from Staten Island, defeated him in the primary. Lindsay's Liberal party endorsement protected his access to the ballot, and his volunteer organization was able to secure the needed independent party petition signatures, gathered by law after the September primaries, to provide an additional line for the November general election. (Candidates who feel that many voters could not or would not bring themselves to vote on the leading party line often seek this feature.)

Seven contenders, including then–Bronx borough president Herman Badillo, the first serious Puerto Rican candidate to seek the mayoralty, and conservative Mario Procaccino, the incumbent comptroller, crowded the Democratic party primary field. Procaccino was able to win with little more than 30 percent of the vote. While a majority of Democratic primary voters appeared to favor one or another of the more liberal alternatives, the plurality of conservatives ruled the outcome. (The following year, the state legislature adopted a law requiring a runoff primary requiring that if no candidate gained at least 40 percent for any of the three citywide offices, the two top vote-getters would hold a runoff ten days later.)

The 1969 mayoral election was thus notable for two central reasons. First, a liberal, biracial electoral coalition did win the day. Many Democratic elected officials and the citywide organization of Democratic reform clubs bolted their party to support Lindsay's reelection bid. Even the "regular" county organization leaders did not actively support their party's official candidate. Aided by a masterful campaign theme describing the New York mayoralty as "the second toughest job in America," Lindsay spent the campaign apologizing to the voters for mistakes made, particularly for the Sanitation Department's lack of preparedness for a heavy and unexpected snowstorm in early 1969 that almost totally shut down Queens, and promising to do better in his second term. Toward the end of the campaign, Lindsay added stops at major Jewish centers, especially in Queens, in order to directly confront voters' concerns about what they deemed to be his excessively liberal and problack policies.

Though Lindsay was skilled at handling these and other confrontations, his opponents' inept campaign was also a great help. While Republican/Conservative John Marchi was no better than bland, Democrat Procaccino's malapropisms were glaringly shocking when not downright comical. Campaigning on the streets of Harlem in an attempt to identify common cause with area residents, he said: "My heart is as black as yours." Abe Beame, who had been comptroller in Wagner's last term and the unsuccessful Democratic nominee against Lindsay in 1965, was returning to political combat as Procaccino's running mate for comptroller. At a party unity dinner late in the campaign, Procaccino attempted to remark on the affability of Frank O'Connor, the other member of the slate (candidate for city council president) as a running mate with whom he had not been too familiar: "He grows on you—like a cancer." The stunned silence of the crowd in reaction to this pathetic attempt at joviality was, unfortunately, lost on the candidate.

But despite Lindsay's charisma and organization and the ineptitude of his opponents, he was barely able to win. As in the 1966 CRB referendum, conservative candidates won the majority of the vote. Lindsay gained only 42 percent of the vote. Because his two opponents divided the remainder, Lindsay won, but the city's liberal majority electoral coalition had come apart.

In his first term, Lindsay had been an activist mayor seeking to foster change in both public policy and governmental structure. If he was daring, it was often to challenge the hold of municipal labor unions, whose leaders he termed "power brokers," or to direct the governmental system to serve the needs of the growing numbers of black and Latino New Yorkers. Whether in response to shifting currents in public opinion or merely to advance his political career, after 1969 Lindsay settled into a more tempered moderator/broker style of leadership.

After changing his party enrollment to Democrat in 1971, he made an attempt at the party's 1972 presidential nomination. Haunted by some New Yorkers who followed his campaign to Florida for that state's presidential primary with taunts about his record in New York City, Lindsay's poor showing put an early end to that effort. "The presidential campaign diverted the attention of the mayor and his top aids. His defeat in the early primaries led to a loss of political prestige and probably made his retirement from office at the end of 1973 inevitable."[25] By 1973, he decided to retire, leaving no white liberal heir apparent in his wake.

The 1973 mayoral election applied the new runoff procedure to candidates for citywide office. In a wide-open Democratic primary, incumbent comptroller Abe Beame led the field but fell short of the 40 percent needed to win the nomination. Bronx congressman Herman Badillo came in second. Their runoff confrontation was both a contest between the regular and reform factions of the Democratic party and the first test of a serious minority challenge for the mayoralty. Badillo had narrowly lost the endorsement of the New Democratic Coalition, the citywide federation of reform clubs, to West Side assemblyman Al Blumenthal. Blumenthal's poor showing in the primary left Badillo as the de facto reform candidate in the short runoff campaign. A remark by Queens County Democratic leader Matthew Troy captured the racial tension that also emerged during this brief campaign:

Three days before the election the white middle class will wake up and realize that Badillo represents a real threat to their existence. They'll turn out in droves in Brooklyn and Queens because this guy isn't a Democrat who just happens to be a Puerto Rican. He'd be a Puerto Rican mayor, and the whites don't have to be told that under Badillo, welfare could bankrupt the city.[26]

Troy's comment not only reflected the outer-borough reaction to the Lindsay years, but also suggested how ideological and racial factors were redefining and realigning elements of the Democratic party electorate. A survey also revealed an age difference among white primary voters. Younger Jewish voters between twenty and thirty years old favored either Blumenthal or Badillo over Beame. It was not surprising that this group was more liberal, less religious, and better educated than older Jewish voters, given the life experience of the baby boom generation. But observers did find the extent and apparent depth of their political difference with their parents' generation surprising.[27]

The electoral verdict was that neither majority nor young white liberal voters constituted anything like a majority in 1973. Beame's substantial victories in the runoff and general elections returned the Democratic party organization to power, for he was preeminently a party "regular." Less than a year after he was inaugurated, however, the fiscal crisis overwhelmed the city and abruptly drew power away not only from the party leaders but from the entire municipal government. Governor Carey, the Municipal Assistance Corporation, the Emergency Financial Control Board, the federal government, bankers, and the municipal labor unions became the dominant actors in the city's governmental life. As decision-making moved away from City Hall, matters of basic service delivery and municipal survival overshadowed intergroup political tensions.

CONCLUSION

The stage was thus set in 1977 for a rather different kind of election than had dominated New York City since Robert Wagner's victory in 1961. The alignment of forces assembled by Wagner and Lindsay had favored the growth of public spending, the widening of municipal responsibilities for social services, and the participation of new groups such as municipal unions, blacks, and Latinos in the formation of city policy, and led to the defeat of the regular party organizations. With the backing of the broad traditionally Jewish electorate that formed the great middle of the Democratic electorate, a new generation of reform activists had led these forces into participation and influence, if not always power. Their success was predicated on overcoming and reducing the salience of racial differences, and they reinforced their position by expanding the role of city government.

By 1977, however, economic, social, and political trends, had turned the tables on this approach. New York City's economy had suffered a catastrophic decline that erased one-sixth of the city's jobs, income, population, and housing. The pace of racial change had increased, making the dwindling white ethnic population feel deeply embattled in their neighborhoods, in the job market, and as beneficiaries of public policy. For blacks and Latinos, the inability of New York City's economy and policy to generate as much upward mobility for them as it had for earlier ethnic immigrants created genuine grievances.

Racial polarization over minority demands, the Lindsay administration's policy responses, and the perception among whites that they had contributed to the fiscal crisis discredited Lindsay-style reform and undermined the electoral coalition that had made them possible. By 1966, and certainly by 1969, the outlines of a conservative alternative to the Lindsay coalition were readily apparent. The fiscal crisis was a devastating blow not only to liberal reformers but also, when combined with the reformers' earlier political successes, to the regular Democratic organizations, which might have served as a bulwark against a conservative shift. The institutional forces that organized New York's New Deal–oriented, liberal political establishment were thus in extreme disarray. It was in this environment that Edward I. Koch began, in 1977, to build a new kind of conservative dominant coalition.

2

THE EVOLUTION OF THE KOCH COALITION

GAINING POWER

The 1975 fiscal crisis and Mayor Abraham Beame's resulting decline in public opinion drew myriad candidates into the 1977 Democratic mayoral primary, just as Lindsay's departure had in 1974. Five "independent" candidates challenged Beame in his search for vindication at the ballot box. In addition to Edward I. Koch, who had risen from Village district leader and city councilman to U.S. congressman from the Upper East Side Manhattan district that had elected John Lindsay, they included Mario Cuomo, Governor Carey's secretary of state;

Bella Abzug, the first woman to seek the mayoralty and a highly visible liberal congresswoman and feminist leader; Percy Sutton, the Manhattan borough president and a prominent leader in the black community; and Congressman Herman Badillo, who was still the most popular Latino in New York politics despite his loss in 1973. Although not yet current, the phrases "rainbow coalition" and "gorgeous mosaic" certainly described the ethnic and racial diversity of the Democratic field—three Jews ranging across the ideological spectrum (the "regular" Beame, the middle-of-the-road Koch, and the liberal activist Abzug), an Italian (Cuomo), an African American (Sutton) and a Latino (Badillo).

The political era in New York City politics that will bear the name of Ed Koch did not spring fully formed from the racial conflict, fiscal crisis, and political dynamics of the decade that led up to the 1977 mayoral elections. To the contrary, it was not obvious that Koch would be elected or that he would prove to be a relatively conservative mayor. Other candidates initially stood higher in public opinion polls and, while Koch had criticized a low-income housing project in Queens and favored the death penalty, he was a Village reform Democrat who had compiled one of the most liberal records in Congress. Koch's campaign theme (like Lindsay's, a David Garth creation) captured the sense of what had become of party politics: "After eight years of charisma and four years of the clubhouse, why not try competence?" His ultimate success resulted from hard political work, fortuitous timing, and an ability to project values that tapped into and drew out latent but powerful feelings among the city's white middle-class voters, particularly its Jews. In so doing, he changed not only how he defined himself, but how his constituency defined themselves. The coalition that narrowly enabled him to win office in the primary and general elections of 1977 differed greatly from those which reelected Mayor Koch in 1981 and 1985. Only after he took office did Mayor Koch articulate the positions that reshaped his administration's electoral base. In 1977, however, it was not so clear what form the Koch coalition would ultimately take.

On September 8, 1977, Democratic primary voters put Mayor Abraham Beame out of office and made Congressman Koch the front-runner to win office as his successor.[1] The wide array of competitors and the closeness of the race had drawn voters from every ethnic background to the polls in record numbers. Given a Securities and Exchange Commission report on the eve of the primary that accused Mayor Beame of misleading investors about the city's financial condition and widespread looting in black neighborhoods during a July electricity blackout, it was perhaps not surprising that voters turned away from Mayor Beame. Beame got only 17 percent of the vote, an emphatic repudiation of his stewardship and of the regular party organization that had supported him.

More surprising was the fact that Congressman Koch narrowly led the other challengers with 20 percent of the vote, only ten thousand votes ahead of Secretary of State Mario Cuomo. In early polling, Bella Abzug had led the other candidates, only to fall behind as they became better known. Chief among these was Mario Cuomo. Governor Hugh Carey strongly backed Cuomo's candidacy. Known previously for his successful mediation of the Forest Hills subsidized housing dispute in Queens, Cuomo received the endorsement of the *New York Times*, the Queens Democratic organization, and a number of public employee unions. He had raised almost $1 million in campaign contributions, half again as much as Koch. Cuomo counted the Catholic vote as his base, while hoping that his three Jewish competitors would sufficiently split the Jewish vote to enable him to place first.

The campaign was not marked by sharp differences on most issues, and the CBS/*New York Times* exit poll suggested that Koch's and Cuomo's supporters had broadly similar views. Regular Democrats leaned toward Cuomo, while reformers leaned slightly to Koch, despite his turn toward conservatism. Conservatives favored Beame, while liberals, who made up about 20 percent of the Democratic electorate, leaned toward Ms. Abzug; Koch and Cuomo divided the middle.

Though he had been one of the most liberal members of the House, Koch had begun to differentiate himself from his Manhattan reform Democratic roots in the early 1970s. While he eventually endorsed the compromise Mario Cuomo fashioned in the dispute over the construction of subsidized housing in Forest Hills in 1972, he initially backed the project's opponents and had appeared alongside their openly reactionary leader. His primary campaign counted on support from his traditional Manhattan base, but Koch sought to deepen his appeal outside Manhattan and to distinguish himself from Cuomo and his other opponents by emphasizing his support for the death penalty (which Cuomo opposed), his determination to engage in hard bargaining with civil service workers, and his desire to crack down on welfare abuses and "poverty pimps" in the community action program.

These appeals evidently succeeded in winning him support in the more conservative Jewish neighborhoods outside Manhattan, especially in Brooklyn, Mayor Beame's home turf, as Table 2.1 suggests. Koch mounted an increasingly aggressive campaign through the summer, denying Abzug endorsement by the liberal, reform New Democratic Coalition and pulling himself out of last place. A substantial media effort in the last weeks of the campaign also enabled Koch to pick up a disproportionate share of undecided voters. Despite starting from the back of the pack, Congressman Koch was able to get 180,248 votes against 170,560 for Cuomo and 163,719 for Beame. (Sutton and Badillo together garnered 263,525, while Abzug took 150,719.)

Since Koch failed to win 40 percent of the total, he had to face Cuomo in a runoff primary held eleven days later. Both candidates sought to swing three "available" constituencies: the more conservative Jews who had supported Beame, the liberals who backed Abzug, and the supporters of the black and Latino candidates, Percy Sutton and Herman Badillo. A liberal strategy might win Abzug supporters and those of Sutton and Badillo, but a more conservative pitch to established Democratic regulars might be able to gain support from Beame's regular constituency as well as a considerable number of blacks and Latinos. Koch chose to present himself not only as one who could "make tough decisions and say 'No,' " but as a friend of regular Democratic organization leaders in the Bronx and Brooklyn and the black establishment in Harlem. Given that a preponderance of the available voters were Jewish, Koch could also emphasize his ethnic background.

Koch was largely successful in this strategy. Bronx county party leader Pat Cunningham and his key operative and successor, Deputy Mayor Stanley Friedman, backed Koch immediately after the primary. Friedman also helped convince Mayor Beame to endorse Koch. Koch successfully solicited Herman Badillo's support as well and ultimately named Badillo to be a deputy mayor in his administration. Badillo and the Bronx regular organization both encouraged Puerto Ricans in the South Bronx and elsewhere to back Koch. Although Queens County leader Donald Manes endorsed Cuomo, a Queens native son, he allowed his district leaders to split along ethnic lines; most Jewish district leaders backed Koch, who had won several of the most Jewish assembly districts in the first primary.

Brooklyn was a more problematic situation. Here, in the home of the largest number of Democrats, Manhattan-based Koch had come in third, after Beame (a product of the Brooklyn regular organization) and Cuomo (who appealed to the borough's many Italian voters). Meade Esposito, the county party leader, was a machine boss in exactly the mold that Koch made his career fighting. Yet on Sunday, September 11, Koch met in the basement of Esposito's mother's house in Canarsie to ask for his endorsement, something Cuomo declined to do. At the urging of Friedman and Canarsie district leader Tony Genovesi, Esposito agreed to back Koch. The only condition Koch set was that he keep this endorsement secret.[2]

A few days later, Koch also met with members of the Manhattan black political establishment, led by Congressman Charles Rangel. Koch promised to name more minority officials than the two previous mayoralties combined and to give blacks jobs at the highest level of the administration. He also promised not to use the phrase "poverty pimp" any more and not to dismantle the poverty program. (Carl McCall and Congressman Major Owens, present at the meeting, had led the poverty program during the Lindsay administration.) On this basis, Rangel, the *Amsterdam News*, and all but a few Brooklyn black leaders endorsed Koch. Koch also won support from Rupert Murdoch and the *New York Post* by promising an influential post for Edward Costikyan. (Fifty of the *Post*'s sixty reporters later submitted a grievance petition to Murdoch complaining of "slanted news coverage" in favor of Koch.)[3]

On the other end of the ideological spectrum, Abzug and many of her backers favored Cuomo. He was able to win the endorsement of Victor Gotbaum of District Council 37, AFCSME, as well as the transit workers and the firefighters. From his base in the Italian parts of Staten Island, Brooklyn, and Queens, Cuomo sought to expand support to middle-class, ethnic Jewish neighborhoods as well as among blacks and Latinos. Governor Carey weighed in with renewed support for Cuomo. Cuomo sought to bolster his position by running a controversial television ad that showed Koch's face dissolving into that of former Mayor John V. Lindsay. He also fought the perception that the campaign might have degenerated into a conflict between Catholics and Jews.

In the runoff primary, as Table 2.1 shows, Koch proved to have put together the broader range of support, defeating Cuomo by 432,000 to 355,000 votes. Koch's somewhat improbable winning coalition spanned the white reform precincts of Greenwich Village and the Upper West Side of Manhattan to more conservative outer borough Jewish neighborhoods such as Canarsie, Sheepshead Bay, and Forest Hills. Koch also picked up a majority in black and Puerto Rican districts in Harlem, the South Bronx, and Brooklyn. Cuomo once more did best in white Catholic areas of the city. While both Koch and Cuomo were perceived as middle-of-the-road candidates and "fresh faces,"

Table 2.1

Shift from 1977 Primary to Runoff by AD Primary Winner

	Primary Vote	Koch %	Runoff Vote	Koch %	Vote Falloff
Koch (10 ADs)	168,732	31.0%	158,871	65.9%	5.8%
Beame (10 ADs)	197,632	23.9%	185,995	63.9%	5.9%
Abzug (3 ADs)	67,230	23.8%	47,193	66.3%	29.8%
Cuomo (19 ADs)	225,068	18.1%	213,388	37.8%	5.2%
Sutton (14 ADs)	152,809	10.3%	94,996	54.4%	37.8%
Badillo (9 ADs)	98,303	8.6%	68,250	55.6%	30.6%
Total	909,774	19.8%	768,693	55.3%	15.5%

Source: John Mollenkopf, *A Phoenix in the Ashes* (Princeton: Princeton University Press, 1992), Chapter 5.

the formerly liberal Koch was seeking to project himself in a more conservative light, attacking liberal ideologues, black "poverty pimps," and municipal unions. Cuomo, from a culturally conservative background, was seeking support from liberals and labor. While each had support across the ideological spectrum, Koch was ultimately able to construct a broader coalition of outer borough Jews, Manhattan liberals, blacks, and Puerto Ricans, thus recreating the traditional liberal coalition. He spent a total of $1.2 million against Cuomo's $1.5 million, both using media heavily in the interprimary period.

Normally, this would have insured Koch a mayoral victory. But he still faced a November general election against state senator Roy Goodman, a Manhattan liberal Republican, and also Mario Cuomo, who was still running hard on the Liberal party line despite the defection of Governor Carey and Victor Gotbaum. Cuomo attacked Koch as "no longer a 'traditional' Democrat but a conservative who has made 'deals' with politicians."[4] He also commented on a "reversal of roles" from the initial situation in which he had been viewed as the candidate of the establishment and Koch the outsider, a sentiment reinforced by endorsements Koch received from Carey, Vice President Mondale, Senator Patrick Moynihan, Bella Abzug, Percy Sutton, and even the New Democratic Coalition. The *New York Times* once more endorsed Cuomo.

Yet, as Table 2.2 shows, Koch's margin in the general election proved to be closer than in the runoff primary. Koch received 712,976 votes, or 50.2 percent, compared to Cuomo's 587,257 (41.4 percent). The Republican and Conservative candidates garnered the remainder, only 119,093 votes. Koch's 30 percent margin in the late September polls had shrunk to 9 percent in the November actual results. Koch's pollsters attributed this to the electorate's distrust of anyone favored by the establishment, but it seems more likely that Cuomo kept his base among white Catholic Democrats and expanded it to independents and Republicans who saw him as the only viable alternative to the Democratic nominee.

Edward I. Koch thus became the 105th mayor of New York City by a relatively narrow margin produced partly by a runoff primary that pitted only two candidates against each other, insuring that one

Table 2.2

Shift from 1977 Runoff to General by AD Primary Winner

	Runoff Vote	Koch %	General Vote	Koch %	Vote Increase
Koch (10 ADs)	158,871	65.9%	290,070	57.2%	82.6%
Beame (10 ADs)	185,995	63.9%	291,211	58.1%	56.6%
Abzug (3 ADs)	47,193	66.3%	87,750	65.7%	85.9%
Cuomo (19 ADs)	213,388	37.8%	466,318	31.4%	118.5%
Sutton (14 ADs)	94,996	54.4%	170,467	62.0%	79.4%
Badillo (9 ADs)	68,250	55.6%	109,613	62.1%	60.6%
Total	768,693	55.3%	1,415,429	50.4%	84.1%

Source: Same as Table 2.1

would win a majority of the votes. His coalition encompassed three competing parts of the Democratic electorate: relatively liberal Manhattan professionals who provided part of the social base for reform politics; more conservative Jews from working-class and managerial backgrounds living in Brooklyn, Queens, and the Bronx who provided the social base for the regular Democratic organizations; and black and Puerto Rican voters. It excluded one part: white outerborough Catholics who had also provided the basis for machine politics.

Koch recognized the tenuous nature of his electoral coalition and its potential for hampering his ability to govern by appointing seven deputy mayors, including Badillo and prominent black attorney and former New York secretary of state Basil Paterson, a widely respected labor mediator. But the inner tensions of his 1977 coalition were also revealed in squabbling, policy differences, and personality clashes among these deputy mayors. By 1979, only three remained; Badillo and Paterson left the administration.

Race, class, ethnicity, religion, life-style, and political culture divided the 1977 Koch coalition. A particular tension had existed between reformers and regulars; Koch had grown up among the reformers but needed regular support to win and to govern. Another tension existed between blacks and Puerto Ricans and the white political establishment. Blacks and Puerto Ricans were struggling against whites for greater influence within the system, but, more often than not, the regular Democratic organizations had absorbed blacks and Latinos who did win office.[5] Koch had served as a civil rights lawyer in the South, but he had also sided with whites who opposed subsidized housing projects on racial grounds.

In 1977, he "did business" with powerful black elected officials like Charles Rangel and Percy Sutton to get their support, yet as a reformer, he had helped depose the regular organization with which these black leaders were allied and had attacked how the Beame administration had used the community action program as a form of political patronage in black and Puerto Rican neighborhoods.

Given his relatively narrow margin of victory and the divisions within his coalition, Mayor Koch had to find ways both to broaden his base and to hold its disparate parts together. He also had to convert an electoral coalition into a governing coalition. Moving to the left offered relatively little gain: Cuomo had received some liberal support, but much the greater part of his base was conservative. Moving to the right might appeal to white Catholics without leaving much room for the parts of Koch's coalition that might be inclined to defect: white liberals, blacks, and to a lesser extent, Latinos.

Perhaps it was inevitable that Mayor Koch would seek to redefine his coalition in a more conservative, business-oriented direction in response to racial tensions that had been brewing for more than a decade, his political center of gravity in New York's Jewish, outer-borough middle class, the city's recent fiscal crisis, and Koch's conviction that Lindsay-style liberalism was dangerously wrong. The challenge was to win more votes than he lost in the course of taking this direction and to prevent those who were disaffected from uniting against him.

REDEFINING THE DOMINANT COALITION: 1981

Having risen to power without the backing of identifiable, organized political forces (either reform or regular), Mayor Koch had to forge

new alliances and accommodations to govern the city. First, he continued his rhetorical attacks on ideological liberals, blacks, and municipal
unions, making him increasingly popular not only with the white
Jewish ethnics who voted for him in 1977, but with the white Catholic
Italians who had voted for Cuomo. More importantly, he cemented
this popularity with two organizational alliances: one with the regular
Democratic county party organizations outside Manhattan (which
controlled four of the eleven votes on the Board of Estimate; Koch
himself had two votes), and a second with the Manhattan corporate
elite, especially the intertwined world of large real estate developers,
investment bankers, and lawyers.[6]

Mayor Koch consummated these alliances by granting regulars,
especially Bronx and Queens county leaders Stanley Friedman and
Donald Manes, access to patronage, while fostering a positive climate
in taxation, finance, and real estate regulation for the Manhattan corporate elite. In turn, these two forces not only backed him strongly in his
reelection campaigns in 1981 and 1985 but aided him in accumulating
power within the city's political system. As Shefter points out, Koch
probably did not require these two sources of support in order to win
election over a possible regular challenge, but they certainly relieved
him of the burden of such challenge, guaranteed he would win against
anyone else, and strengthened his ability to govern.[7]

The tenor of Koch's first term was dominated by the constraints
of the fiscal crisis and the need to hold down city spending in order to
balance the budget. He was outspokenly critical of municipal labor
unions. Along with the unions and "ideological liberals," Mayor Koch
took no pains to endear himself to the black political establishment.
Though he had made specific commitments to black leaders in order
to win endorsement, he reneged on some of them and carried others
out in a way that leaders did not like. He reorganized and retrenched
the poverty program, producing considerable outcry from black and
Puerto Rican elected officials. He also closed Sydenham Hospital in
Harlem despite a belief among many black elected officials that he had
promised not to do so and despite vocal opposition from Harlem
residents. In retrospect, and despite his subsequent ability to attract
sizable vote percentages from black voters, the black community

viewed the Sydenham closure as a major turning point in their attitude toward Koch and his toward them.

Though Koch had named Basil Paterson, an ally of Charles Rangel and Percy Sutton, deputy mayor for labor relations, Paterson had soon left the administration. Koch did not clear his other black appointments with the Harlem political establishment but recruited them instead from foundations, law firms, and similar sources. "Every bit as important as these deeds," Shefter notes, "were Koch's words. When he was denounced in hyperbolic language by black political leaders, the mayor replied in kind."[8] Koch's popularity with white ethnic voters outside of Manhattan rose as he championed the "middle class." He parlayed his role as the city's leading "cheerleader" into national political prominence.

Mayor Koch first tested the strength of his strategy for building electoral dominance in 1981. Riding the crest of popularity in white ethnic constituencies, he engineered an unprecedented bipartisan endorsement for his 1981 reelection bid. A group of dissident white liberals backed Assemblyman Frank J. Barbaro, a little known labor-oriented populist who represented a conservative Italian American district in Bensonhurst, Brooklyn, to oppose Koch in the Democratic primary. Black leaders, however, neither generated their own candidate nor backed Barbaro with any great enthusiasm. Public employee unions, which desired to make up the income losses they suffered in the fiscal crisis, were also not inclined to join a merely symbolic challenge of the incumbent mayor. (The reversal of these two factors would later prove to be highly consequential in the 1989 mayoral primary.)

Mayor Koch, meanwhile, had so successfully redefined himself as a conservative that he was able to win endorsement from the five Republican county leaders and received the Republican nomination for mayor. His only challenge thus came from within the Democratic primary. Here his political adviser, John LoCicero, worried that Koch's political repositioning and the disaffection he had aroused among blacks might open the way for a serious challenge.

He need not have worried. The mayor raised a substantial campaign war chest, largely from real estate developers, investment bankers, and lawyers, many of whom did business that was subject to city government regulation or approval. Assemblyman Barbaro was unable to raise funds or mount an extensive campaign. The 1981 Democratic mayoral primary was marked by a low turnout heavily favoring Koch. He won 64 percent of the 581,072 votes cast, the smallest total vote in a Democratic mayoral primary since World War II.

Koch dominated in virtually every sector of the population, including blacks and liberals. Most importantly, as Table 2.3 shows, he received strong support from white Catholic ethnics, including Italian Americans, against a white Catholic opponent. Four years earlier, these constituencies had voted for Mario Cuomo. By the 1981 race, Koch had cemented his appeal to white Catholics, enabling him to widen his base beyond the Jewish outer-borough districts that had previously provided his white middle-class base. Koch beat Barbaro not only in Barbaro's home assembly district, but on his own block. Two previously divergent segments of the white middle class thus were united.

In the general election, only the Liberal party, which had given its line to Barbaro, prevented Koch from achieving a grand slam. Endorsed by the Republicans as well as the Democrats, Koch received an overwhelming and historic 75 percent of the vote in the general elec-

Table 2.3

Shift from 1977 Runoff to 1981 Primary by AD Primary Winner

	1977 Runoff Vote	Koch %	1981 Primary Vote	Koch %	Vote Falloff
Koch (10 ADs)	158,871	65.9%	105,750	70.9%	33.4%
Beame (10 ADs)	185,995	63.9%	134,397	71.6%	27.7%
Abzug (3 ADs)	47,193	66.3%	46,033	51.4%	2.5%
Cuomo (19 ADs)	213,388	37.8%	139,456	62.5%	34.6%
Sutton (14 ADs)	94,996	54.4%	94,175	37.0%	0.8%
Badillo (9 ADs)	68,250	55.6%	57,641	46.6%	15.5%
Total	768,693	55.3%	577,941	59.5%	24.8%

Source: Same as Table 2.1

tion. Fueled by this success and egged on by the *New York Post*, Mayor Koch sought to capitalize on this popularity by running for governor to succeed Hugh Carey in 1982.

Once more he faced Mario Cuomo, now lieutenant governor. In contrast to 1977, Mayor Koch was the heavy early favorite in the polls and fundraising. Sources of political funds in the real estate and investment banking industries now understood that Koch would remain a pivotal figure whether or not he won the governorship. This period produced a famous photograph of Mayor Koch flanked on the steps of City Hall by four Democratic party county leaders or "bosses," Stanley Friedman of the Bronx, Donald Manes of Queens, Meade Esposito of Brooklyn, and Nick LaPorte of Staten Island, who provided his first endorsements. (The first three were subsequently convicted of corrupt political practices.) This tableau was particularly important because it showed that Manes and the Queens regular organization had shifted their support from Cuomo to Koch.

Once more, as in the 1977 races, the Koch-Cuomo race proved to be close. Assisted by a *Playboy* interview in which Koch had disparaged suburban and rural lifestyles, Cuomo won the race statewide and lost the city to Koch only by a narrow four-thousand-vote margin. Koch beat Cuomo by two to one in his core areas of outer-borough Jewish support, but he only matched Cuomo in liberal areas like the Upper West Side of Manhattan and Brooklyn's Park Slope and lost heavily to Cuomo in predominantly Italian American areas like Bensonhurst and Staten Island; he also lost by two to one in black neighborhoods like Harlem and central Brooklyn. Despite Friedman's and Manes's support, Koch took the Bronx and Queens each by only a thousand votes. Brooklyn provided Koch his largest margin of support, fourteen thousand votes; he lost Manhattan by eight thousand votes and Staten Island by four thousand.

This race, like the 1977 mayoral primary and general elections, showed that a suitable Catholic challenger could attract white liberal, black, and white Catholic votes away from the mayor's electoral base. Nonetheless, even against such an attractive competitor, Mayor Koch's electoral base still constituted a majority. As before, his most intense levels of support could be found in the apartment houses occupied by lower-middle-class Jews in the outer reaches of Brooklyn and in the single-family homes occupied by upper-middle-class Jews in Queens.

TRIUMPH OF THE NEW DOMINANT COALITION: 1985

The 1982 loss, coming on the heels of the smashing 1981 victory, did not harm Koch's popularity within the city. He retrospectively rationalized it by saying that the voters had pulled the lever for Cuomo because they really wanted him to remain mayor of the city. In any case, the New York City economy was extremely strong during the early and mid-1980s, despite the national recession of 1982, and city revenues and expenditures could and did rise rapidly, enabling the mayor to declare that the fiscal crisis was behind the city and the problem was now how to restore the level of services and repair capital facilities.

Budget increases meant that the mayor and the political establishment could grant more contracts to nonprofit service providers and private construction firms. The mayor agreed to wage settlements that exceeded the inflation rate, enabling city workers to recoup the losses they experienced in the fiscal crisis. Finally, his administration actively promoted the office-building boom occurring in Manhattan. This recovery of governmental capacity gave community-based organizations, municipal workers, and private developers an economic incentive to be responsive to the administration's political interests.

In the mid-1980s, therefore, Mayor Koch was at the height of his governmental and electoral power. At the same time, however, the seeds of challenge were being sown, though in the 1985 mayoral elections they appeared to have fallen on barren ground. In particular, Mayor Koch became even more combative toward the black leadership and white liberals. Both of these attitudes crystallized around the 1984 Democratic presidential primary in which Jesse Jackson first sought the nomination.

The black political establishment had become estranged from Mayor Koch by 1979. This disaffection only partly coalesced around the potential Jackson candidacy, however. Many black leaders, such as Congressman Rangel, did not support Jackson in 1984, preferring to ally themselves with Walter Mondale's candidacy and the national Democratic political establishment. Nevertheless, Mayor Washington's 1983 victory in Chicago had roused New York City's black community, and some black leaders, particularly the Brooklyn insurgents led by Assemblyman Al Vann, enthusiastically supported Jesse Jackson's 1984 Democratic presidential primary campaign. Vann himself intended to run for Brooklyn borough president in 1985. The Jackson campaign gave the insurgents a reason to mount a rigorous minority voter registration campaign that produced large gains in registration against a background of white apathy.

By the April 1984 presidential primary, more than 125,000 new voters had been registered in minority districts compared to 1982 (about 91,000 blacks and 34,000 Hispanics). This registration gain significantly tilted the Democratic party registration base toward the city's black and Latino populations. While Mondale received heavy support in New York City, Jesse Jackson attracted 34 percent of an electorate of about three-quarters of a million voters despite his catastrophic "Hymietown" comment. This gave black leaders the hope that a coalition with Latinos, labor unions, and liberal whites around a less divisive candidate could lead to a successful challenge to Mayor Koch in 1985. Map 2.1 shows where black, Latino, mixed minority, and white populations are concentrated across the New York City's sixty ADs.

Beginning in July 1984, a group of forty black political leaders, chaired by Vann, began to search for a consensus candidate to oppose Koch. The group, called the Coalition for a Just New York, grew out of an earlier, unsuccessful effort to pressure the mayor to appoint a black, Dr. Thomas Minter, chancellor of the school system. The coalition's first choice was a widely respected former secretary of state and former deputy mayor, Basil Paterson. However, Paterson withdrew from consideration because he had a heart condition and would soon have bypass surgery.

After these developments, the coalition had great difficulty identifying a candidate for mayor that it could support. City Council Presi-

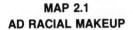

MAP 2.1
AD RACIAL MAKEUP

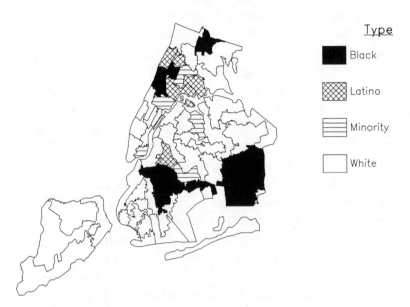

Source: John Mollenkopf, *A Phoenix in the Ashes* (Princeton: Princeton University Press, 1992), Chapter 5.

dent Carol Bellamy presented herself as a reform critic of Koch; however, she had earlier supported him for governor because she would succeed him as mayor if he won. Bellamy had first held elective office as a Brooklyn reformer and had forged ties with Manhattan reformers, though she had also sought support from the Brooklyn regular Democratic organization. Bellamy did not have a strong record of backing minority candidates, was not inclined to support Vann's bid for the Brooklyn borough presidency, and was not black. She was also committed to the race regardless of whom the coalition endorsed. The coalition, therefore, rejected the idea of endorsing her.

Another possibility was offered by Herman Badillo, former Bronx borough president, former congressman, and former Koch deputy mayor. Badillo had, however, run for mayor and lost in 1974 and 1977. More importantly, he had failed to support black candidate Percy Sutton as black leaders had expected before the 1977 mayoral primary.

He was also regarded as erratic and weak on organization. Nor did he have unanimous backing from other Latino leaders. On the other hand, Al Vann supported him because he anticipated the need to win Latino votes in his quest for the Brooklyn borough presidency. Just when it seemed that the coalition had no alternative but to back Badillo despite his flaws, coalition member and Manhattan party leader Herman "Denny" Farrell offered himself to the group, winning its endorsement. Thus the Badillo candidacy never get off the ground. Farrell's candidacy in the primary proved to be in name only. He raised very little campaign money, had no organization, and had a hard time articulating his positions or his rationale for making the race.

While the coalition's choice may have been rational in that Farrell was more acceptable to its members' immediate constituencies than were the alternatives, it created a storm of criticism that reflected the deep tensions within the black political leadership stratum and between it and its potential allies. It caused the coalition to be criticized for excluding women, even though a third of the black state legislators were female. It exacerbated the tension between the Manhattan black establishment and insurgents who felt that supporting Badillo was important if blacks were ever to win Latino votes for a black candidate. Several members, including Calvin Butts, executive minister at Adam Clayton Powell's Abyssinian Baptist Church, resigned from the coalition in protest. It did nothing to build solidarity with Latino and public employee union leaders, who were not party to the deliberations and did not support the coalition choice. Indeed, some Latino elected officials showed up at Farrell's announcement session to harass him.

In the primary, as Table 2.4 shows, the mayor routed both his white liberal and black challengers. Koch won 63.3 percent of the vote, holding his two opponents to the same percentage that the weaker Barbaro campaign had attracted four years earlier. Bellamy got 19 percent and Farrell only 16 percent. Moreover, the mayor won 75 percent of the white vote, 70 percent of the Latino vote, and 37 percent of the black vote. Among non-Hispanic whites, the Mayor appeared to do even better among Irish and Italian Catholics than he did among Jews (85, 83, and 75 percent, respectively).[9] The 1985 primary thus consolidated the position that Koch had developed in the 1981 primary.

Table 2.4

Democratic Primary Vote, Registration, and Turnout by AD Type

	11/82	4/84	September 1985			
	Koch	Jackson	Votes	Koch	Farrell	Latinos[a]
Black	39.3%	75.2%	129,464	41.0%	32.7%	23.9%
Latino	50.4%	40.4%	55,353	62.4%	17.8%	43.3%
Mixed	44.0%	51.1%	54,131	58.2%	19.8%	39.5%
Liberal	50.6%	16.2%	147,000	59.2%	6.4%	16.6%
Catholic	50.0%	14.6%	122,456	73.6%	6.1%	15.6%
Jewish	62.3%	11.8%	180,150	77.6%	5.6%	12.0%
All ADs	51.1%	33.7%	688,554	63.3%	13.0%	20.1%

Source: Same as Table 2.1
[a]Vote for three Latino candidates as percent of total vote cast for city council president.

His core supporters, Jews, amounted to 29 percent of the electorate. He had once more cemented the support of white Catholics, particularly Italian Americans, who constituted another 25 percent of the electorate.

More important, Koch added to this core large portions of the constituencies anticipated to be supporters of his opponents, namely blacks, white liberals, and Latinos. Koch won ten of the thirteen majority black assembly districts and piled up substantial minorities even in the three ADs won by Farrell. While Koch got 37 percent of the black vote, Farrell got only 41 percent, with 20 percent going to Bellamy. Mayor Koch won 44 percent of the votes of feminists who supported the ERA, while Carol Bellamy, a strong feminist, took only 45 percent of that vote. Koch systematically outpolled the more liberal Bellamy among those taking liberal positions on a variety of controversial positions.[10]

On the surface, the 1985 primary demonstrated the practical hegemony of the Mayor's electoral coalition. (Bellamy, like Barbaro and Cuomo before her, remained on the November general election ballot as the Liberal party nominee but ran only a perfunctory campaign. Koch was overwhelmingly reelected, but by a slightly less wide margin than four years earlier.) Not only did he consolidate a core of white

MAP 2.2
1985 PRIMARY VOTE FOR KOCH

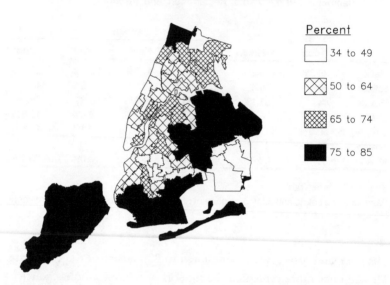

Percent

☐ 34 to 49

▨ 50 to 64

▩ 65 to 74

■ 75 to 85

Source: John Mollenkopf, *A Phoenix in the Ashes* (Princeton: Princeton University Press, 1992), Chapter 5.

middle-class support, but he generally beat his black and white liberal opponents or fought them to a draw on the terrain most favorable to them. Map 2.2 shows that Koch's strength was centered in the heavily Jewish assembly districts on the city's periphery and that black areas gave him the least support (compare with Map 2.1). Yet he drew a substantial minority of the vote in black areas, while white liberal and Latino areas also gave him substantial support.

SEEDS OF CHANGE

Even in the midst of this debacle for the mayor's black and white liberal opponents, the black political leadership made two important gains. The first had been the increase in black and Latino registration that began before the Jackson campaign and continued into 1985. This altered the terrain upon which future contests would be fought. The other was the election of David N. Dinkins as borough president of Manhattan.

Dinkins "came up" through the Carver Democratic Club in Harlem, the regular black club run by the legendary J. Raymond Jones.[11] Dinkins had been elected an assemblyman, and he had been named a deputy mayor in the Beame administration in 1973 but had been unable to take the position when it became known that he had not filed his income taxes in the preceding years. He subsequently held patronage positions as head of the Board of Elections and city clerk. While holding these positions, he ran three times for Manhattan borough president. He lost badly in 1977 but failed by only 1 percent of the vote in 1981.

Some have argued that by selecting Farrell the Manhattan black political establishment deliberately nominated a weak citywide black candidate so as not to draw any strength away from Dinkins's run for the borough presidency in 1985. In any case, since Andrew Stein, who had narrowly beaten Dinkins in 1981, was moving on to the city council presidency, Dinkins was ideally positioned to make the 1985 race. Though he had been Jackson's 1984 coordinator for Manhattan, Dinkins did not ask Jackson to campaign for him in 1985. Instead, he ran a campaign appealing to white liberals, Jews, and Latinos as well as blacks. The NBC exit poll showed that Dinkins won 91 percent of the black vote, 79 percent of the Latino vote, and 50 percent of the white vote against a white liberal opponent.[12] This breakdown held much more potential for a citywide candidacy than did Farrell's dismal performance. Al Vann, in the meantime, lost badly in the Brooklyn borough president race, in which the incumbent was also challenged by two relatively strong white candidates. In contrast to Dinkins in Manhattan, Vann could take only 60 percent of the black vote, only 28 percent of the Latino vote, and a mere 6 percent of the white vote, removing him as a threat to the hold of the Manhattan black leadership in the city.

Finally, Mayor Koch's third inauguration in January 1986 was soon overshadowed by yet another source of eventual difficulty for him: the exposure and ultimate downfall of two of his most important supporters, Stanley Friedman of the Bronx and Donald Manes of

Queens. A federal investigation of corruption in Chicago had inadvertently led back to Manes, who had been taking bribes in return for awarding contracts to collection agencies that would pursue those who failed to pay their parking tickets. This in turn led into a web of corrupt activities that would ultimately lead to a large number of indictments, convictions, and resignations. The unfolding investigations and trials became a daily political soap opera that consumed public attention for some twenty months. Several commissioners, two borough presidents, judges, two congressmen, party leaders, state legislators, and City Hall aides were variously indicted, convicted, or forced out under a cloud, thus weakening the mayor's organizational support and his standing in public opinion.

Although most people never seriously believed that Koch was personally dishonest, the effect of the scandals, when added to the outspoken, aggressive, and sometimes outrageous traits that he had exhibited throughout the years, produced a growing civic sentiment of "enough already!" By January 1989, only 39 percent of those surveyed by the *Daily News* approved of the way Koch was handling his job and the city; 47 percent said they definitely would not support him for reelection, and an additional 23 percent said they probably would not. Undaunted, Koch maintained his intention to seek an unprecedented fourth term.

Thus, though the 1985 election was a resounding victory for the mayor, it brought with it the seeds of its own undoing. While only dimly visible in 1985, these seeds became more apparent in the 1988 presidential primary in New York. As he had four years earlier, Jesse Jackson once more appealed deeply to New York City's black voters. In contrast to 1984, however, support from local black officials was almost unanimous and the Jackson campaign was much more professionally organized. By the time of New York's April primary, the national race had narrowed; Jackson was running strongly against Michael Dukakis and Albert Gore, Jr.

Mayor Koch refrained from endorsing a candidate until late in the New York campaign, but when he did, it was Gore rather than frontrunner Dukakis. To many it seemed that Koch was more intent upon throwing a roadblock in the path of an accelerating Jackson campaign

MAP 2.3
JACKSON IMPROVEMENT OVER FARRELL

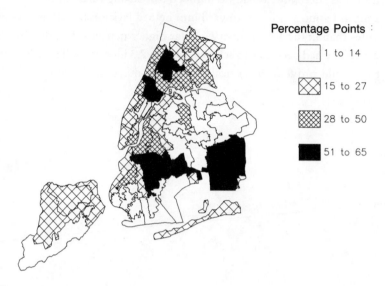

Percentage Points :

☐ 1 to 14

▨ 15 to 27

▩ 28 to 50

■ 51 to 65

Source: John Mollenkopf, *A Phoenix in the Ashes* (Princeton: Princeton University Press, 1992), Chapter 5.

than advancing the cause of his endorsee. In particular, Koch's admonition that Jewish voters "would have to be crazy" to vote for Jackson made front-page headlines and stirred up strong black/Jewish antipathies. The furor Koch created by his opposition to Jackson added to the turmoil that characterized his third term.

Though he lost the state to Dukakis, Jackson won the New York City primary with over 40 percent of the vote. This stunning outcome was taken by many, especially within the black leadership, as a ringing signal of future political developments. Jackson's campaign enabled major municipal labor unions to coalesce in an insurgent campaign, including Teamsters Local 237, Local 1199 of the Drug, Hospital and Health Care Employees, and Local 1180 of the Communications Workers union. Although the city's largest municipal union, the 120,000 member District Council 37, AFSCME (American Federation of State, County and Municipal Employees) did not make an official endorsement, its president, Stanley Hill, was a major leader in the

Jackson campaign. And while minority registration efforts were not nearly as successful as had been hoped for, strong black turnout and a shift in Latino sentiment toward him helped Jackson to roll up bigger votes than in the 1984 primary and far higher margins than the Farrell candidacy had been able to achieve, as Map 2.3 illustrates. These factors too would prove to be critical in the 1989 mayoral election.

3

THE 1988 PRESIDENTIAL
ELECTION IN NEW YORK CITY

THE PRESIDENTIAL PRIMARY

By 1988 the municipal corruption scandals, the disaffection of black
public opinion, and the coalescing of previously divided opponents
finally began to challenge the coalition that Mayor Koch had put
together during the first ten years of his tenure. Koch had been able to
unite his own coalition and keep his opponents divided partly by
articulating middle-class values (held by those of all ethnic backgrounds, but especially his Jewish constituents) and partly by capitaliz-
ing on and reinforcing the many strands of ethnic and geographic

competition within the city. The 1988 Democratic presidential primary played an important role in beginning to shift this balance.

Koch had been hurt by (although not personally implicated in) the scandals that felled many of his political friends and appointees. Moreover, the Wall Street crash of October 1987 signaled an end to the decade-long boom and eroded the optimism of the market and the money-managers overnight. For the first time, Koch encountered mounting criticism not just from his bitter enemies among the black political establishment and the white left. The press began to question him aggressively about the scandals, and even established figures who had been his allies distanced themselves from him. Public opinion seemed to have grown tired of his outspokenness. As the rise of property values, incomes, and city revenues slowed to a halt in the wake of the market crash, racial tension, never far below the surface in New York City, reappeared with a vengeance. The New York Democratic presidential primary, held on April 18, 1988, heightened citywide attention to racial cleavages.

Previous primaries in 1988 had narrowed the Democratic field, leaving Michael Dukakis the likely nominee with Jesse Jackson as his only substantial symbolic challenger. For Jackson, New York was a chance to do well in a northern state. He thus campaigned vigorously in New York City. Ed Koch reacted strongly to Jackson's effort, provoking bitter controversy by saying that Jews "would have to be crazy" to vote for Jackson. Koch justified his statement on the grounds of Jackson's embrace of the leader of the Palestine Liberation Organization, Yasir Arafat, Jackson's endorsement of a Palestinian homeland, his acceptance of support from the Muslim activist Louis Farrakhan, and the furor Jackson had created four years earlier by referring to New York as "Hymietown." These stands, combined with the left-oriented substance of Jackson's campaign, produced an emotionally charged attack from Mayor Koch.

The *Amsterdam News*, a Harlem weekly, responded with a front-page editorial on April 9, 1988, calling for Koch's resignation. It carried statements by Rabbi Alexander Schindler, calling Koch's comments "extremely unfortunate," and exhorted Koch to remember that "he is the Mayor of the city; not just of New York Jewry." Then–Manhattan

Borough President David Dinkins was quoted as expressing "distress" and "disappointment" with the remarks and saying that they were "not helpful to our efforts to create an atmosphere whereby [racial] tensions can be eased. . . . Loose language such as that used by the Mayor to describe Jackson does not contribute positively to this cause."

The paper's editor-in-chief, Wilbert A. Tatum, characterized Koch as "a morally corrupt human being" and reminded its readers of the ethics investigations that continued to plague City Hall. "Remember all the slights and code words," Tatum wrote of Koch's supposed racial biases.

Remember the unheated houses, and the high rents, and the mayor who bows and scrapes before the rich while shoving his jackboot into the groin of the poor. . . . Also remember that this is not new. Those who head major Jewish organizations who disagree violently with Edward I. Koch have been coerced into silence by the knowledge that Koch can be vindictive . . . [Their] organizations find themselves hampered in their fundraising efforts because the "grapevine" has been activated against them, they believe, by Edward I. Koch.

It is no overstatement to say that Jesse Jackson embodied the self-esteem of black America more than any other single person. Residents of various New York neighborhoods welcomed Jackson as "a celebrity, not just another candidate." The April 10, 1988, *New York Times* reported on the intensity of emotion even a promise of Jackson's appearance could rouse:

They poured out of their homes. They leaned from windows, lined streets, ran down sidewalks exclaiming: "Jesse's here!" trying to glimpse him, snap his picture, or touch him. . . . "This one I'm not going to wash," said Sonia Findley in the Bedford-Stuyvesant section of Brooklyn, gazing at the hand that had just brushed against the candidate. . . . At the Pilgrim Cathedral Baptist Church in Bedford-Stuyvesant, 2,000 people waited for seven hours on Saturday, unaware that an overscheduled campaign had canceled the stop, until Jesse Jackson Jr. came and told them his father could not make it."

The New York City Presidential Election Survey (NYCES) asked, among many other things, how the respondent felt about Jesse Jackson.[1] The polarization that characterized the city is captured by the display in Figure 3.1: for every twenty blacks who felt favorable toward Jackson, only one black was unfavorable; for every nine Jews feeling unfavorable toward him, only one felt favorably disposed.[2]

Mayor Koch responded to Jackson's popularity among blacks and his low standing among Jews not by opting for Michael Dukakis but by endorsing Senator Albert Gore of Tennessee. Neither Gore nor Dukakis was a match for Jesse Jackson in New York City, however. Jackson's manpower was overwhelmingly supplied by New York's biggest municipal labor unions, the members of which are mostly minorities. He enjoyed additional strength among black ministers whom he had cultivated during the 1984 campaign and maintained throughout the second Reagan term. One Brooklyn newspaper, the *Phoenix*, reported in early March that Jackson had already filed multiple slates of delegates in all the Brooklyn congressional districts, outstripping the legendary Dukakis campaign in advance organization.

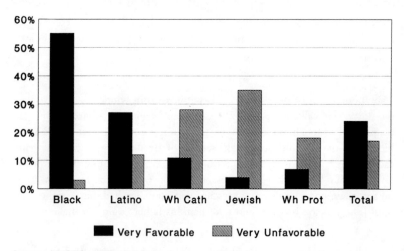

FIGURE 3.1
FEELINGS TOWARD JESSE JACKSON
by Group

Source: NYCES, 1988
$N = 1,280$

By contrast, Senator Albert Gore had a full slate of delegates in only two Brooklyn CDs, partial slates in another two, and no candidates at all in one district.

Gore, the third party in the two-way race between Jackson and Dukakis within the city, was attempting to play the spoiler in order to keep his candidacy alive. His entire presidential campaign had been based on the narrowly selective strategy of bypassing Iowa and New Hampshire to campaign long and hard in the South, where he was a favorite son, on Super Tuesday. He continued on that heading in New York by focusing almost exclusively on the Jewish vote, which had cast 23 percent of the state total in 1984.

He was well-positioned to get this vote. Facing the liberal Governor Dukakis and the pro-Palestinian Jackson, Gore could claim a strong pro-Israel record. He was associated with conservative stands on issues of public morality. His wife, Tipper Gore, had spearheaded a movement to force record companies to label their rock albums with parental advisories about lyrics referring to, among other things, devil-worship and drug use; Gore had conducted Senate hearings on the subject. These issues were often close to the hearts of middle-class Jews, many of whom prided themselves on their traditional values.

A great many Jews considered Jackson anti-Semitic and would vote on the single issue of who could beat him. Unfortunately for Gore, he needed 20 percent of New York's delegates to continue to qualify for federal matching campaign funds, not to mention further private donations. If he did not achieve that margin, it was widely expected that he would throw in the towel, having incurred millions of dollars in debts. Dukakis, on the other hand, was leading in polls throughout the city and nationwide. He was the front-runner in state delegates to the national Democratic convention. He, not Gore, was the clearer choice to beat Jackson.

The candidates debated twice on television in the ten days before the primary, mostly without incident. "Yesterday's combatants fought with rhetorical pillows," said the *New York Times*. Within a few days of their arrival in the city, it seemed as though the candidates were waging separate campaigns. Gore went to the Jewish sections, Jackson to black and white liberal neighborhoods, and Dukakis split his time among the Greek area of Astoria, Latino neighborhoods, and white middle-class neighborhoods.

The hardest-fought contest was for the Latino vote, where Dukakis's fluent Spanish was a persuasive argument in his favor. Jackson received the unanimous support of New York's Latino elected officials, but as late as April 13 a survey showed him behind by almost 10 percent of Latino voters with about 20 percent undecided. Puerto Rico's delegates had decided to endorse Dukakis in spite of the fact that Jackson had won the island's nonbinding primary. New York's Latino population, although increasingly diverse, was still predominantly Puerto Rican in origin.

Jackson, however, did have several points in his favor. The Puerto Rican median family income in New York, $8,913 in 1980, was nearly $2,000 a year lower than that of an African American family. Jackson's attack on poverty appealed to this population. Jackson also had higher visibility than Dukakis, having campaigned heavily in these Puerto Rican neighborhoods four years before, and had regularly made headlines since.

As the campaign advanced, Jackson began to retaliate indirectly for Koch's continued jibes, as well as remarks by other prominent New Yorkers such as Geraldine Ferraro, the 1984 Democratic vice presidential nominee. Koch had called Jackson the "Teflon candidate," saying that reporters and politicians were afraid to criticize Jackson because they would be called racists. Ferraro had contrasted Jackson's candidacy with her own, asserting that his race had insulated him from questions about his qualifications for the presidency.

Jackson replied to these remarks by telling the American Society of Newspaper Editors in Washington, D.C., that New York City had created the racial "hysteria" of the campaign. "We went across the South on Super Tuesday without a single catcall or boo, without a single ugly sign at a mass meeting. It was not until we got North to New York that the litmus tests for race and religion spouted from the mouths of public officials without any significant media challenge. . . . They're making hysteria while I'm making history."

On April 15 Koch endorsed the underdog, Al Gore. Predictably, he based his support on Gore's record on Israel. "A much-talked-about issue in New York's primary has been the nature of each candidate's commitment to continuing America's strong support for Israel," read Koch's three-page opening statement. "On this issue, Senator Gore is head and shoulders above his rivals. . . . There is no ambiguity on where he stands."

The *New York Times* described Koch's endorsement news conference as "a vintage performance" and noted the mayor's overweening dominance of the microphone. However, many questioned the potential impact of the endorsement. Gore had never been shown to hold more than 9 percent of New York's Democrats; despite Koch's insistence to the contrary, he was sure to draw any improvement on his part away from Dukakis's majority. There was no question that Gore would lose New York, only whether or not his candidacy would continue. Koch's endorsement might help Gore win the vital 20 percent that would fill his empty campaign coffers with federal matching funds. "It's kept him alive over the weekend," commented city council member Robert Dryfoos. "If [Koch] had endorsed Dukakis, Gore would have disappeared."

The announcement profoundly disappointed Dukakis. Skepticism that the Jewish vote might be swayed in his direction had emerged from his refusal to rule out a Palestinian homeland or the return of Jerusalem. But Dukakis reacted strongly to the news of Koch's endorsement. "There's no ambiguity on where Dukakis stands," he said. "There's no ambiguity in my support for Israel, or for peace in the Middle East. It's a position I've had for 25 years and I'm very proud of it." In the final analysis, however, Ed Koch suffered the most from his endorsement of Gore, whose approval rating first rose to 13 percent but then dropped back down to a predicted 9 percent before the primary. Koch had not only backed a loser, but his most devoted constituency, New York's Jews, had ignored his advice, as Table 3.1 shows.

Jackson won the Democratic presidential primary in New York City with 45.2 percent of the vote, closely followed by Michael Dukakis, who got 44.8 percent. Combined with his much larger margins elsewhere in the state, Dukakis could claim an important victory. Dukakis received his strongest support in the city's outer-borough

Table 3.1

1988 Democratic Presidential Primary in New York City
(percentage distribution by assembly district type)

	Votes	Jackson	Dukakis	Gore	Turnout
Black	227,879	88.2	9.5	1.8	48.3
Mixed Minorities	69,069	71.4	23.6	5.0	39.8
Latino	67,740	63.5	31.8	4.7	39.4
Liberal White	188,946	27.8	59.3	12.9	44.7
Catholic	150,710	22.7	63.8	12.5	40.5
Jewish	222,689	17.7	66.3	16.0	49.7
Citywide	927,060	45.3	44.8	9.1	45.0

Source: John Mollenkopf, *A Phoenix in the Ashes* (Princeton: Princeton University Press, 1992), chapter 7.

Jewish ADs. Gore, meanwhile, won only 9.1 percent of the citywide vote, gaining only one in six votes even in outer-borough Jewish ADs. The race was even more racially polarized than Table 3.1 suggests, since ADs are always ethnically mixed, whatever their dominant characteristic. The CBS/*New York Times* exit poll suggests that Jackson received only 17 percent of the votes cast by whites and only 9 percent cast by Jewish residents of New York City.[3] In stark contrast to the 1985 mayoral primary, or even the 1984 presidential primary, Jackson was the winner in this contest and Koch the loser.

THE ATTITUDINAL CONTEXT

The primary furor had an influence on how people voted in the general election, as may be seen in Figure 3.2. It shows how much of the vote went to Dukakis within each demographic group, controlling for how much influence the respondent thought Jackson would have on Dukakis, if he were elected. The pattern is interestingly complex and remarkably consistent across the groups. Blacks showed almost no variance. But in all the other groups, those who thought that Jackson would have "some" influence on Dukakis were more likely (and usually substantially more likely) to prefer Dukakis than either those who

FIGURE 3.2
VOTE FOR DUKAKIS
by Amount of Influence, Jackson on Dukakis

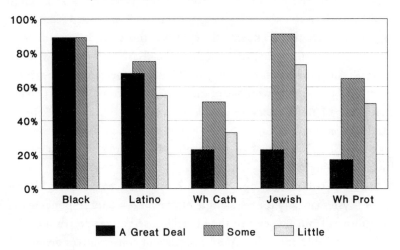

A Great Deal   Some   Little

Source: NYCES, 1988
N = 1,280

thought that Jackson would have "a great deal" of influence or those who thought that Jackson would have "little" influence.[4]

This pattern reflects an ambivalent position among whites. On the one hand, they had an anxiety about the Jackson agenda rooted in some mix of racial mistrust and genuine policy disagreement about the proper role of government in people's lives. At the same time, they were concerned that the policy agenda should not exclude the interests of blacks and other disadvantaged groups. In each white demographic group, mistrust dominated the thinking of some, while concern for their fellow human beings and fear of deteriorating race relations was most important for others. This matrix of interracial mistrust and the desire for interracial harmony proved to be the pivotal dimension along which the 1989 New York City mayoral election was played out.

While it is obviously relevant to analyze elections on the basis of demographic groups, it is also customary to discuss New York City politics along the liberal-conservative continuum. People outside of

New York City tend to view it as a "liberal" city, and indeed more of its residents identify themselves as "liberal" and fewer as "conservative" compared to the rest of the nation. In the 1988 National Election Studies (NES), twice as many people nationwide identified themselves as conservative than as liberal; the split was more nearly even in New York City, slightly favoring the liberals.[5] Based on the New York City Presidential Election Survey (NYCES), 49 percent of the sample identified themselves with one of the three liberal responses, 44 percent with one of the conservative categories, and 8 percent were in the middle (see Figure 3.3).[6] So, while the median position in the city is more liberal than that of the nation, New York is by no means overwhelmingly liberal.

The distribution of opinion on a number of central issues clearly varies systematically for the sample of New York City respondents as one moves from one end of the liberal-conservative spectrum to the other (see Table 3.2). New York liberals and conservatives generated

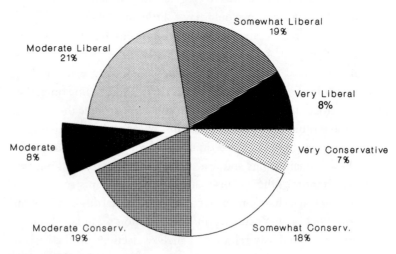

FIGURE 3.3
LIBERALS AND CONSERVATIVES
in New York City

Somewhat Liberal
19%

Moderate Liberal
21%

Very Liberal
8%

Moderate
8%

Very Conservative
7%

Moderate Conserv.
19%

Somewhat Conserv.
18%

Source: NYCES, 1988
N = 1,280

Table 3.2

Political Profile of New York City Respondents
(Beliefs as a Function of Position on a Liberal-Conservative Scale)[a]
(percents)

	Total Respondents	"Very Liberal" Respondents				"Very Conservative" Respondents		
N	(1,280)	(89)	(209)	(239)	(92)	(208)	(202)	(81)
Feel close to:								
Blacks	(68%)	87	73	71	61	62	61	56
Latinos	(67%)	81	69	66	69	61	61	61
Unions	(47%)	62	50	48	50	42	40	35
Feminists	(42%)	63	57	47	32	37	35	21
Homosexuals	(28%)	60	34	35	17	20	23	10
Business	(62%)	38	57	57	65	71	76	79
Believe Reagan policies hurt groups respondent feels close to	(42%)	79	57	53	33	26	24	20
Believe government should help fund daycare	(62%)	62	66	59	49	42	36	47
Believe government should help minorities	(72%)	89	83	76	69	66	58	53
Believe government is responsible to see that everyone has a job and a good standard of living	(67%)	83	78	66	70	63	56	48
Prefer Dukakis	(55%)	85	76	70	58	39	35	30

Source: NYCES, 1988
[a]Categories are as in Fig. 3.3, above.

mirror-image patterns when asked whether they "feel close to" labor
unions on the one hand and business on the other. Regarding "feeling
close to" blacks and Latinos, conservatives were clearly different from
liberals, but more than 50 percent of the "very conservative" reported
feeling close to these groups. This may be higher than might have been

expected, but it is consistent with the fact that the median position in New York City was more liberal than in the nation as a whole.

For all items in Table 3.2, those calling themselves "very liberal" were markedly different from the next most intense category of liberal respondents. Though few in number (about 7 percent of New York City voters), these "very liberal" New Yorkers have exerted a strong influence on the politics of the city, partly because of their long activity in "reform politics" and partly because the direction of their opinions was consistent with the much larger liberal category, for which they set the tone.

Interestingly, "very liberal" New Yorkers did not have a markedly different demographic profile from New Yorkers in general (see Figures 3.4, 3.5, and 3.6), the exception to this generalization being the higher rates of education among the "very liberal." This characteristic probably affected their levels of political activity and their effectiveness.

Liberals in general, and this "very liberal" group in particular,

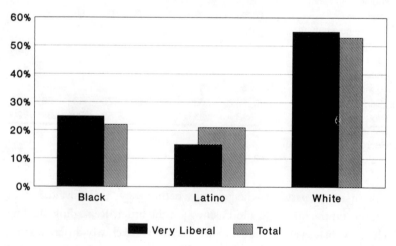

FIGURE 3.4
GROUP PROFILE
of Very Liberal and Total Samples

Source: NYCES, 1988
$N = 1,280$

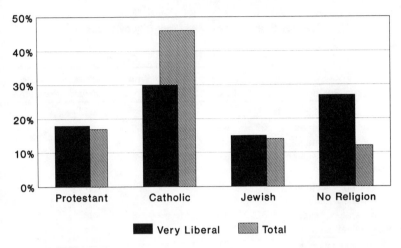

FIGURE 3.5
RELIGIOUS PROFILE
of Very Liberal and Total Samples

Source: NYCES, 1988
N = 1,280

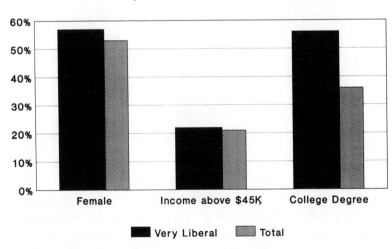

FIGURE 3.6
SELECTED SOCIAL CHARACTERISTICS
Very Liberal and Total Samples

Source: NYCES, 1988
N = 1,280

Table 3.3

Policy Preferences in New York City by Group

Issue Position	Total	Black	Latino	White Catholic	White Jewish	White Protestant
				Group		
Increase education spending—% agree	98	99	97	99	97	98
Reduce government services—% disagree	82	83	83	80	87	78
Reduce defense spending—% agree	76	79	65	71	87	81
Government-funded day care—% agree	52	63	61	38	46	33
Government should help minorities—% agree	72	85	86	54	66	59
Government responsible for jobs and standard of living—% agree	67	80	79	58	59	40

Source: NYCES, 1988

become pivotal in multiracial coalitions in the city because their opinions on the issues that most divide the city are much closer to those of blacks and Latinos than they are to more conservative white ethnic voters (compare Tables 3.2 and 3.3).

ISSUES AND THE PRESIDENTIAL VOTE

To study the 1988 presidential general election in New York City might seem an exercise in the obvious. This overwhelmingly Democratic city both in registration (70 percent Democrat to 14 percent Republican in 1988) and self-identification (Democrats outnumbered Republicans by more than two to one in 1988) also preferred the Democratic candidate, Michael Dukakis, over George Bush, the Republican, by a margin of two to one in 1988. So, why study this phenomenon?

Two concerns are germane: the first was how the preference for president varied across the racial and ethnic groups that comprised the complex mosaic of this city. The second was a desire to discover how the choice of candidates within and across these groups related to the kinds of issues that voters thought were important.

The demographic groups varied substantially in their preferences regarding the candidates (see Figure 3.7). Bush ran ahead of Dukakis among white Catholics, for example, while white Protestants produced an essentially even split. Indeed, among non-Latino whites, only Jews behaved in the traditional Democratic manner, going better than two to one for the Democratic candidate. The Latino preference was also strongly in the Democratic tradition, favoring Dukakis by two to one. The black preference for the Democratic candidate, by contrast, ran at better than five to one. Thus when issues or candidates reduce turnout among blacks, Latinos, and Jews, or pit these groups against one another, a competent Republican candidate might face a genuine political opportunity, as Rudolph Giuliani certainly did in the fall of 1989.

Our analysis of how issues influenced the way New Yorkers voted for president in 1988 was based on questions in the 1988 National Election Studies (NES) augmented by topics germane to an urban population such as New York City's (crime, drugs, welfare, minorities, and government spending).[7] The issues included:

- Level of government spending on education
- Cutting government services
- Level of defense spending
- Method of funding day care
- Government aid to minorities
- Governmental responsibility for jobs and a good standard of living

All of the demographic groups held consistent attitudes on the first three of these issues within the New York City sample, as Table 3.3 shows. That is not the case, however, with regard to the last three

FIGURE 3.7
1988 PRESIDENTIAL CHOICE
New York City

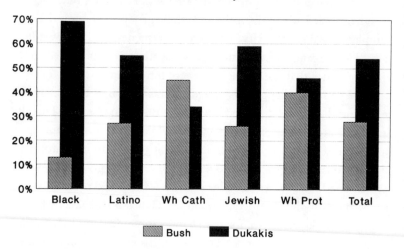

Bush ▨ Dukakis ■

Source: NYCES, 1988 (N = 1,280)
No decision and no answer not reported

issues. The three consensus issues—spending on education, government services, and defense—entail transfers of resources to the city as a whole. But the last three—funding day care, government aid to minorities, and the role of government in jobs and a good standard of living—imply a differential allocation of resources in favor of certain groups. The disagreement about these issues clearly falls along racial and ethnic lines that reflect such differential allocation, with blacks and Latinos most likely to agree with a stronger role for government.

More subtle and perhaps more profound and revealing issues may be involved here than income transfers, however. The last issue is the most divisive; to appreciate what may underlie that division, it is important to consider the wording of the actual questionnaire item:

Some people believe that it is the responsibility of the government in Washington to see to it that every person has a job and a good standard of living. Do you agree or disagree with that position?

Blacks and Latinos were much more likely to agree than were any of the other groups (see Table 3.3). This should not be interpreted as a consciously socialist position on the parts of blacks and Latinos; it may simply reflect their life experiences. A considerably higher proportion of these groups is employed by government or not-for-profit agencies dependent on government than is true of their white counterparts. For many in these groups, their experience of job discrimination, nondiscrimination, and affirmative action may make government an employer of first resort. Moreover, since poverty is far more prevalent among blacks and Latinos, they are far more likely to have seen government intimately involved with their lives from earliest childhood.

New Yorkers disagree over the locus of responsibility for individual economic well-being. If they have similar disagreements about who is responsible for other matters, such as one's physical and mental health, one's intellectual development, and the health and socialization of one's children, this may indeed be a serious cultural division. The size of the gap on whether government should ensure economic well-being implies a potential for major cleavage.

ISSUES AND CANDIDATE EVALUATION

However much groups may agree or disagree about policy positions on a given set of issues, that pattern of agreement and disagreement matters in a given election only if those issues come to play a large role in how voters evaluate the candidates. In conceptualizing the relationship between voters and candidates with regard to issues, we draw upon the model developed by Anthony Downs that places the voter and the candidate in the framework of rational utility theory.[8]

The relevant aspect of Downs' model is his notion that the voter will be drawn to the candidate whom the voter perceives to be closer (given a two-candidate race) to his or her most preferred position on the issue in question. In a multi-issue situation, Downs sees the voter as drawn to that candidate who would yield the voter the greater expected utility based upon how important each issue is to that voter and upon how "distant" each of the candidates' positions is from the voter's most preferred position on each of those issues.[9]

The concept of issue-distance guided the way we defined the questions in our survey. For each of a series of issues, we asked the respondent what he or she perceived to be the policy position of George Bush, then of Michael Dukakis, and finally what his or her own position was on each of those issues. For each issue, we then created a variable called "candidate issue differential" (CID). This measured the differences between the two candidates on that issue in terms of their proximity to the respondent's preferred position.[10]

This approach allows us to ask how, if at all, issues and voters' perceptions of the candidates' differences on them, informed their decision about how to vote in the 1988 presidential election. Put another way, we can ask whether New Yorkers' overall evaluations of the candidates were consistent with their perceptions of how the candidates stood on specific issues. Table 3.4 suggests that there was a fair amount of consistency but it was not uniform across groups.

To assess how the distance between the voter and the candidates on the various issues related to the voter's overall evaluation of the candidate, we developed a five-point position scale from the NYCES data, including a neutral center, for each central issue. Following Markus, we located the candidates' positions on each issue at the mean of where respondents perceived they stood on it.[11] This minimized the effect of a respondent's "pulling" a candidate liked on some other basis "toward" the respondent's preferred issue position.[12] (For operationalization of the variables, see Appendix C.)

The candidate evaluation question allowed us to develop a five-point scale (very favorable, somewhat favorable, neutral, somewhat unfavorable, very unfavorable—coded, respectively, $+2$, $+1$, 0, -1, -2) that was quite highly correlated with vote intention ($r = .72$). By arbitrarily assigning equal intervals to the degree of like or dislike, we could use linear regression, with its readily interpretable regression coefficients (b's and beta's) and multiple correlation coefficients (R^2's), to analyze the relevant relationships.[13]

With the exception of the bottom row, the numbers in Table 3.4 are simple correlation coefficients. When squared, they provide a measure of how much information the state of one variable contains about the state of another. For example, if one knew nothing about a respondent in this sample but wanted to guess that respondent's score on the Candidate Evaluation Differential (CED), one could use the whole sample's mean score on that item as a rough approximation. But if one knew that respondent's score on Candidate Issue Differential (CID) for Defense Spending, one could use the mean CED for the subsample with that respondent's CID on defense to reduce one's error about the hypothetical respondent by about 29 percent on average across a series of such guesses. (The simple correlation in question between CED and CID-Defense is .54; therefore $r^2 = .2916$, meaning the anticipated error reduction is 29 percent.)

We ran linear regressions for the full sample and for each of the demographic groups to assess the consistency or lack of it between issue consistency and overall candidate evaluation. As the multiple correlation coefficient (R^2) at the bottom of the first column of Table 3.4 shows, knowing the respondent's CID on the full set of issues reduces errors in assigning the Candidate Evaluation Differential for the full sample by more than half. Greater or lesser degrees of error reduction were also evident for each of the population groups.

We may therefore reasonably infer that these issues had a substantial impact on how New Yorkers evaluated Bush and Dukakis. This impact was not equal across all groups, however. Whites' candidate evaluations were more consistent with issue positions than were those of either blacks or Latinos. While knowledge about issue distances reduces uncertainty about blacks' and Latinos' candidate evaluations by a respectable 41 percent and 30 percent respectively, they still deviate from the higher rate for white groups. It is not clear why this is so. While one might suppose that differences in education account for this result, the analysis in Chapter 8 does not sustain this explanation. Other possible causes might be that: blacks and Latinos had other bases for evaluating candidates besides their stands on the issues; concern among black and Latino respondents with issues not raised in the questionnaire; or even the randomness that might stem from more uninvolved respondents. The failure of blacks and Latinos, a sizable portion of the electorate, to conform to a model generally accepted

Table 3.4

Correlations Between Issue-Distance and Candidate Evaluation Differential by Group[a] (Very Likely Voters Only[b])

Issue Position	Total	Black	Latino	White Catholic	White Jewish	White Protestant
Spending on education	.46	.33	.42	.47	.53	.41
Reduce government services	.40	.16	.28	.46	.57	.36
Defense spending	.54	.27	.41	.57	.58	.60
Government-funded day care	.37	.25	.10	.44	.43	.35
Government help minorities	.37	.39	.23	.28	.49	.37
Government responsible for jobs and standard of living	.36	.23	.27	.39	.37	.31
Drugs[c]	.67	.62	.50	.66	.75	.68
Adjusted R^2	.56	.41	.30	.63	.65	.54

Source: NYCES, 1988

[a]Cell entries are Pearson's r's, except for the last row, which provides the multiple correlation coefficients, resulting from simultaneous application of all of the independent variables listed.

[b]80 percent of the sample.

[c]The drug issue was not a true issue-distance variable. Because the candidates had not articulated clear policy differences on this issue, respondents were simply asked, with regard to each candidate, how good a job that candidate would do with drugs. This variable is thus susceptible to the "pulling" syndrome.

among students of electoral behavior is troubling and demands a reassessment of the completeness of that model.

Voting (or, in this case, candidate evaluation) may be consistent with issues and yet not driven by them. Studies have found that at least two other factors also have a direct impact on voting behavior: the respondent's party identification (i.e., self–identification with a party, as opposed to registration as a party member) and the perception of candidate personality characteristics.[14] In order to understand how issues stood up against these other factors in determining how New

York City's likely voters in the 1988 presidential election evaluated the candidates, we calculated linear regression equations using the CIDs, the respondent's party identification, and candidate personality differentials on leadership ability, knowledgeability, and honesty as independent variables and the candidate evaluations as the dependent variable.

In asking how much a given independent variable "drives" a dependent variable, one is not asking how much information the independent variable contains about the dependent variable; that question is answered by the r^2. Instead, we are asking what amount of change in the dependent variable is associated with a unit of change in a given independent variable. That relationship is measured by the regression coefficient, which is the slope of the regression line.[15]

The standardized partial regression coefficients, or betas, resulting from a series of multiple regression analyses are reported in Table 3.5.[16] It shows clearly that, with the notable exception of drugs, issues did not strongly drive candidate evaluations. This does not mean that they were of no account. Were that so, the issue-candidate evaluation consistency described earlier could not be explained. Rather, the impacts of the issues were subsumed under the stronger impacts of other variables, specifically party identification and candidates' personality traits.

Several other interesting points emerge from Table 3.5. First, the drug issue played a lesser role in the white Catholic group than it did in any of the others. Instead, other issues showed significant impact within that group. Second, the perception that a candidate was a strong leader counted heavily with this group, as it did with the black segment, although these two groups obviously differed on who was strong. Indeed, 25 percent of the white Catholics thought the term "strong leader" described Bush "very well," while only 16 percent of that group described Dukakis that way. By contrast, only 14 percent of the blacks thought that "strong leader" described Bush "very well," while 35 percent thought it described Dukakis "very well." Spending on education proved to be a significant issue (beyond party identification and candidates' personality traits) for Latinos, who greatly need such spending in the New York City environment.

Finally, it is worth noting that party identification, normally a significant variable in presidential elections, appears to have had virtu-

Table 3.5

Relative Impacts (Partial Betas[a]) of the Independent Variables
on Candidate Evaluation Differential by Group
(Very Likely Voters Only)

Independent Variable	Total	Black	Latino	White Catholic	White Jewish	White Protestant
				Group		
Spending on education	d	d	.19^c	d	d	d
Reduce government services	.05^c	d	d	.12^b	d	d
Defense spending	.10	d	d	.17	d	d
Government-funded day care	d	d	d	.10^c	d	d
Government help minorities	d	d	d	d	d	d
Government jobs and standard of living	.06^c	d	d	d	d	d
Drugs	.23	.35	.33	.15^b	.31	.41^b
Party identification	.15	d	d	.17	.19^b	.50
Strong leader	.18	.31	d	.24	.19^b	d
Knowledgeable	.10	d	d	,12^c	d	d
Honest	.16	.20^b	.20	.13^c	.22	d
Adjusted R^2	.66	.56	.32^c	.76	.76	.67

Source: NYCES, 1988
[a]All betas reported are significant $p < .001$ unless otherwise noted.
[b]$p < .01$
[c]$p < .05$
[d]Coefficient not significantly different from zero.

ally no impact in either the black or Latino groups. Less than 6 percent of the black respondents in New York City identified as Republican; accordingly, there was little variation in party identification to influence the dependent variable in this group. Among Latinos, on the other hand, 26 percent identified to some degree as Republican, so there was ample opportunity for this variable to have an impact; yet it did not. It would appear that party identification means something different to Latinos than it does to non-Latino whites in New York City. This suggests that a major component of the Latino segment—

potentially one-fifth of the New York City electorate—is up for grabs, or at least open to persuasion.

Latinos are a key factor in the political future of New York City. It is imperative to note that Latinos differ significantly from blacks in their attitudes and electoral preferences. They are much less Democratic than blacks, but also have a political orientation (as measured by the spatial model of candidate evaluation and issue voting) that differs from that of the city's whites. A group this size will obviously be crucial in mayoral contests, as we shall see.

INTERGROUP PERCEPTIONS

Given the divisiveness of some of the issues raised in Table 3.3, one might almost take comfort in the fact that issues played such a small role in determining how New York City's voters cast their ballots in the 1988 presidential election. However, the group differences on these issues suggest that real divisions undergird the politics of the city. The dynamics of these differences can be explored through a series of NYCES questions on intergroup relations. As the potentially racially polarizing primary and general election campaigns unfolded in 1989, the basic feelings each group held about the others took on greater importance. We asked each respondent whether she or he felt close to or did not feel close to blacks, whites, Latinos, and Jews. Table 3.6 reports the extent to which members of each of these groups reported "feeling close" to the other groups.

A central point stands out. Blacks and Latinos both reported feeling close to whites at nearly the same rate that they reported feeling close to each other. But whites did *not* reciprocate these feelings of closeness. The data confirm the popular impression that the white/nonwhite cleavage was a major potential fault line in the "gorgeous mosaic" which was New York City. The data also indicate a real basis for the perception among blacks and Latinos that their affective relations with whites are asymmetric. In plain words, whites are not as fond of them as they are of each other.

Table 3.6

Feeling of "Closeness" to Other Groups

Percentage of *Group A* reporting "feeling close to" *Group B* was:

A	B	
blacks	feeling close to whites	77%
whites	feeling close to blacks	53%
Latinos	feeling close to whites	83%
whites	feeling close to Latinos	49%
blacks	feeling close to Latinos	80%
Latinos	feeling close to blacks	76%
blacks	feeling close to Jews	68%
Jews	feeling close to blacks	52%
Latinos	feeling close to Jews	50%
Jews	feeling close to Latinos	42%

SUMMARY

The 1988 presidential primary and general elections in New York City had a number of fundamental implications for the approaching 1989 mayoral elections. First, they showed that a popular and effective black candidate could assemble the magic number of votes in a Democratic primary, namely a plurality over 40 percent. Such a margin would avert a two-person runoff campaign that a black might not win and, for the first time in the city's history, send a black Democratic nominee into the general election. Jesse Jackson's victory in New York City set off a flurry of think-pieces and political strategy discussions among the would-be supporters of David Dinkins for mayor.

Just as important, the 1988 Jackson campaign in New York City united previously divided forces. In the electorate, Jackson increased his standing among all segments over his 1984 performance and vastly outdistanced what Farrell had accomplished in 1985. Most important, he increased his margin in predominantly Latino assembly districts by 31 percentage points to 71.4 percent. Despite the racially polarizing aspects of the campaign, he also increased his margin in white liberal ADs to 27.8 percent. At the same time, the 1988 presidential primary heralded the pattern of political mobilization in 1989; black and Jewish

ADs were highly mobilized, followed by white liberal ADs. As in 1988, the 1989 primary would be a major contest over which group was going to provide the Democratic party's center of gravity.

The 1988 Jackson campaign also united previously divided political elites who would provide the organizational core for the challenge to Mayor Koch in 1989. In 1984 and 1985, black and Latino elected officials had been highly fragmented and competitive with one another. The 1988 campaign brought virtually all of them together, bridging over even the division between those blacks and Latinos identified with the county party organizations and the insurgents who had been challenging them. Moreover, a number of large public employee unions with strong political operations joined to provide the campaign with its organizational infrastructure. These working relationships and the extensive resources they could tap could be carried over directly into a 1989 political campaign.

Just as important, the 1988 primary campaign seemed not only to have weakened Mayor Koch, who backed a loser whom he could not convince his own core constituency to support, but to have turned black and to a lesser degree Latino sentiment more firmly against him. Koch had won a large majority of Latino votes in 1985 and more than a third of the black votes. Though he would have been elected without them, his ability to go over the heads of the black and Latino leaders who opposed him and get support from their constituencies was a prime ingredient in his perceived invincibility. The alienation of this support greatly weakened his position in the 1989 election.

The 1988 elections and our survey of New York City's voters also revealed the underlying differences in political orientation and affinity for other groups that would shape the 1989 mayoral elections. Although the political center of gravity among New Yorkers was more liberal than that of the nation at large, and although New Yorkers had a consensus on certain liberal premises such as spending more on education and less on defense, they clearly divided on racial and ethnic lines about how resources should be redistributed within the city and where they located responsibility for individual economic well-being. Our research also showed an asymmetry in feelings of closeness among groups along white/nonwhite lines.

While New Yorkers' preferences for president in 1988 were consistent with which candidate they thought was closer to their own stand on the issues, the *divisive* issues did *not* have the major impact on the outcome of the election. Concern about drugs, party identification, and candidate personality characteristics had far stronger impact.

Yet the issue cleavages were real, as the pattern of empathy or lack of it across racial and ethnic lines confirms. When activated, these cleavages may be quite difficult to bridge. On the other hand, whites seemed to be deeply ambivalent about the political influence of blacks; this is clearly indicated by the degree to which the vote for Dukakis was a function of anxiety that Jesse Jackson might have a lot of influence, on the one hand, and that he might not have enough to allay racial tension, on the other. Whites who most favored Dukakis clearly wanted some black influence but not too much. How would such voters react when faced with the choice of a black mayoral candidate? How might the racial and ethnic gaps be bridged?

The two groups who could bridge the gap between blacks and whites were those describing themselves as "very liberal" and Latinos. Our research clearly shows that Latinos have different attitudes and electoral behavior than blacks, but also operate with a different political mindset than white groups. This group is on the bottom of the income distribution and identifies with blacks; at the same time, it is predominantly Catholic and identifies itself as relatively conservative. In 1988 Jesse Jackson was able to bring it into his electoral fold. The "very liberal" also hold political attitudes that in some cases more closely resemble those of blacks. Of all the white groups, they gave Jackson the strongest support, though Dukakis was clearly their favorite in 1988. As subsequent chapters will show, the "very liberal" and the Latinos enabled Dinkins to beat Koch in the primary and Giuliani in the general election.

4

THE 1989 MAYORAL PRIMARIES

The political force of the electoral and governing coalition organized by Mayor Ed Koch had steadily mounted since 1977, peaking in 1985. But by 1989 the appeal of his search for an unprecedented fourth term was tarnished, and there were signs that his electoral coalition had eroded substantially. Indeed, the 1989 Koch coalition was the mirror-image of the one he had constructed in 1977. Starting from a base among white liberals and minorities, he had become most attractive to the more conservative, white, ethnic outer-borough elements of the Democratic party.

In retrospect, the demise of the Koch era seems overdetermined.

But in the heat of the political battle, the mayor gave no quarter. He unequivocally stated his intention to run and win, and only the naive or self-deluded would underestimate his skills and strengths. Yet many in the electorate were troubled by the corruption and scandal around the mayor, weary of his abrasive style, and ready for a change. The alternative of a mild-mannered, establishment Democratic candidate in the person of David Dinkins would put Koch's electoral skills to a supreme test. Dinkins was not only not a threatening political figure like Jesse Jackson, he was also the recognized leader of a group that had surpassed Jews as the single largest fraction of the Democratic party electorate. Could Mayor Koch reinvigorate the broad base of his previous coalition? Could Dinkins expand beyond his black base to fashion a majority of the Democratic primary voters? These were the key questions posed in the 1989 Democratic mayoral primary.

THE CANDIDATES

The post-1986 scandals had not only deposed the two strongest Democratic county leaders who were Mayor Koch's close allies, but had caused several of his senior commissioners to resign in disgrace. The scandals had tarnished Bess Meyerson, who had added crucial glamor to Koch's 1977 victory, and they had caused him to remove two of his closest confidants and advisers in City Hall, Victor Botnick (who had lied about his credentials) and Joe DeVincenzo (Koch's chief dispenser of jobs, who was discharged for running a patronage operation in the guise of an affirmative action effort and destroying records in a coverup attempt.) Meanwhile, Dinkins's 1985 victory for the Manhattan borough presidency and Jackson's 1988 primary campaign had positioned Dinkins and his allies to make a serious challenge to the mayor. With his party organizational support in disarray, Koch would have to appeal above their heads directly to the electorate.

According to a *Daily News* poll taken eight months before the primary, however, Koch fell short with every group.[1] Sixty-three percent said they definitely would not or probably would not vote for Koch. His fortunes were sagging even among Democrats: 42 percent said they definitely would not support him, and an additional 23 percent said probably not. Jews, Koch's ethnic constituency, gave him no greater encouragement. Among Jews, 39 percent said they would definitely not or probably not vote for him.

Though Dinkins was perhaps the most logical person for New York's political elites to embrace as an alternative to Koch, Dinkins kept the city guessing regarding his intentions. He was anxious to determine that the unions and elected officials who were critical of Koch could raise sufficient campaign funds and would not change their mind and return to Koch's camp after Dinkins announced his candidacy. He sought to win the support not only of his core backers, but of party leaders anxious to dump a failing Koch and latch on to a new winner. Dinkins's strategy of forcing others to make a commitment before he made his own worked. On February 1, 1989, many big political players who had always backed Koch attended a huge fund-raising event for Dinkins at the Tavern on the Green, at which he made his intentions clear. His formal announcement came at a Valentine's Day press conference at his Municipal Building office.

Dinkins was not the only candidate to be drawn into the fray by Koch's decline in the polls. Two other white, Jewish candidates also presented themselves to the Democratic electorate: Harrison J. Goldin, the smart, knowledgeable, sometimes abrasive sixteen-year incumbent of the comptroller's office, and Richard Ravitch, who had distinguished himself as a builder, the savior of the state's Urban Development Corporation during the fiscal crisis, the head of the Metropolitan Transit Agency, and the president of the Bowery Savings Bank, but who had no electoral experience. Since election required that the winner of the Democratic primary receive at least 40 percent of the vote, both were hoping to be the second person in a runoff election, preferably against Dinkins.

On the Republican side, Koch's weakness drew another formidable candidate into the race, former U.S. Attorney for the Southern District of New York Rudolph W. Giuliani. Giuliani had begun his career prosecuting corrupt cops in New York in the late 1960s and had gone on to be an assistant attorney general and famed prosecutor of mafia dons, Wall Street insiders, and corrupt Democratic politicians.

To an electorate concerned with crime and drugs, he would exert a potent appeal, though he too had no previous electoral experience. However, Giuliani was at odds with Republican U.S. Senator Alphonse D'Amato, who backed Ronald S. Lauder, heir to a cosmetics fortune who had served as a patronage appointee as U.S. ambassador to Austria, to counter Giuliani in the Republican primary. Lauder had virtually unlimited funds with which to attack Giuliani as a "closet liberal," anathema to New York's few but resolutely Reaganite Republican voters.

Giuliani had entered the campaign with great media fanfare. But after an insensitive reply to a reporter's question regarding abortion, his support plummeted by fourteen points between May and the end of July, according to a *Newsday* poll.[2] Still, the poll found Giuliani leading Lauder by a margin of 62 points to 22. Giuliani tried to put a positive spin on his slippage in the polls by pointing out that his rating remained high despite Lauder's spending $8 million on what Giuliani saw primarily as negative advertising against him.

THE CAMPAIGN

The lines of the fall campaign had already become obvious by the spring of 1989. On the Democratic side, it shaped up as a two-person race, as neither Goldin nor Ravitch could convince voters he was a compelling alternative to Mayor Koch. And on the Republican side, few other than Lauder himself considered him anything more than an instrument for intraparty infighting against Giuliani.

Campaigns are a matter of tangibles and intangibles. The tangibles include the candidate, money, and organization; the intangible factors in successful campaigns are timing, momentum, and luck. In the primary, Dinkins was not only reasonably well financed, but he had strong support from the organizational bases of the black community, especially its churches and elected officials, and the organizational clout of the labor unions.[3] Timing, momentum, and luck seemed to be on his side in the primary, if not in the general election. Dinkins and Koch both benefited from exposure in the "free media," since, as frontrunners and prominent officeholders, their appearances and utterances were widely covered.

A 1989 campaign finance reform helped Dinkins and put Koch at a disadvantage, however. The new law limited candidates' expenditures to $3.6 million per election and limited the amount they could receive from any given contributor to $3,000. In return, the law provided public matching funds. The provisions of the law were voluntary and applied only to candidates who chose to comply with its provisions, but all the Democrats felt compelled to participate in the new rules.[4]

Accepting public funds meant limiting the amount spent on television commercials, which had been an expensive mainstay of Koch's previous campaigns. Television was the costliest but preferred means of reaching voters; an average series of thirty-second spots on prime time television cost $300,000 a week. According to filings at the Campaign Finance Board at the end of June, Koch had already spent close to $500,000 on his media consultant (David Garth) and television buys. By that time, Koch's total expenditures were $1,025,722, compared to Dinkins's $365,580. All the candidates were making sharp inroads into the $3 million ceiling with the whole summer before them. Goldin had already spent $765,424 by the end of June, and Ravitch $573,638. (Among the Republicans, Lauder did not accept public funds in order to spend his large resources, thus releasing Giuliani, who had spent $958,133, from the spending limits.)[5]

While television ads are enormously costly, it is less easy to demonstrate their effectiveness. In total, all candidates spent about $13 million on television advertising, but Lauder accounted for most of that, spending an amazing $8 million in the six months before his loss in the September primary. Dinkins, on the other hand, spent only $1.2 million on television, but won the primary. Koch spent almost twice as much—nearly $2.4 million—but came in second.[6]

One measure of the effectiveness of television advertising and the debates was provided by a poll of 607 registered voters reported by the *New York Observer*. Those who had seen commercials for the candidates were asked to rate these advertisements on a scale of minus five to plus five as a reason to vote for or against a candidate. More than two out of three of those interviewed had seen the advertisements for Dinkins, and three out of five in that group thought they presented good reasons to vote for him. Only one in ten reported finding negative reasons. Using this method of judging television commercials, Dinkins's overall score was 1.9.

Ed Koch did not start his television campaign until after the others, on the Fourth of July. His commercials were seen at the same rate as Dinkins's, but one in five found reasons *not* to vote for him in them, giving him an average rating of 0.5. Yet despite their more mixed impact, it seemed that the ads for Koch orchestrated by David Garth were instrumental in Koch's gaining ground on the front-running Dinkins in the polls.

Both Goldin and Ravitch spent less on television, about a million dollars each, and their small investment seems to have brought them very little. Goldin ended up with an overall score of 0.1, while Ravitch's million bought him even less, since he ended up with a 0.0 overall score.

Lauder clearly lost the most. He ultimately spent $12 million of his own money on the primary campaign, mostly for television spots. Nonetheless, only 58 percent of the respondents reported seeing his commercials, and two out of three thought they provided good reasons not to vote for him or that they had no effect. Lauder's overall score was minus 0.7. Giuliani went on the air latest, beginning only on August 23, but a week later 58 percent of the sample reported that they had seen his ads; two-fifths had a positive impression, with an additional fifth finding reason to vote against him, and another third unaffected. His overall score was 0.7.

The public was exposed to five debates by the four Democratic candidates.[7] The first Democratic debate, on July 26, 1989, sponsored by the *New York Post*, featured both acrimony among the candidates and evidence of efforts among the white candidates not to come down too hard on David Dinkins. As the front-runner, Dinkins was attacked from the beginning (and again in the general election) for his failure to pay income taxes between 1969 and 1972. (These troubles had kept him from accepting the post of deputy mayor in 1973.) Comptroller Harrison H. Goldin said after the first debate, "Let's face it. If I hadn't paid my taxes, I wouldn't be running for mayor. I wouldn't be comp-troller." *Newsday* reported, "As the crowd milled about afterward, some interviewers asked Goldin if he meant a black candidate could get away with misconduct that would destroy a white. Goldin said he did not."[8] By contrast, Goldin accused Koch of being "mean, petty, and nasty."[9] Dinkins called Koch "Alibi Ed," while Koch cited his experience and said he had already accomplished more than the others said they would do. Koch kept plugging away on these themes and was only seven points behind Dinkins in the *Newsday* poll by the end of July.[10]

Eagerly awaited by the politically interested, the debates were ignored by the majority of the population. Fewer than a third of the registered voters (to say nothing of those not registered) reported seeing any of the debates. Of those, however, 74 percent reported that what Dinkins said and how he said it were good reasons to vote for him, while 55 percent felt that way about Koch. For Goldin the percentage was 44, and for Ravitch only 41.[11]

By early August, some experts felt that Koch might be headed for reelection. Campaign commercials lauding his experience were catching hold, and the media had played up Dinkins's past financial indiscretions to Koch's advantage. Koch stressed the enormity of the task of overseeing a city whose budget, at $26 billion, was larger than the budget of many countries, while Dinkins seemed unable to stir enthusiasm beyond black or white-liberal districts.

But then, on August 23, a shocking event changed the mood of the city and the momentum of the campaign. A pack of forty white youths in the Bensonhurst section of Brooklyn chased sixteen-year-old Yusuf Hawkins and two other black youths, shooting and killing Hawkins. On August 27, five white youths were arraigned in criminal court in Brooklyn on charges stemming from the murder. This sense-less murder seemed to change the dynamics of the primary race and focused attention on racial tension.

After being a source of pride in their mayor for many years, Koch's argumentative style seemed to grate on many, and the murder reminded people of how divisive Koch's personality had become. On August 30, just two weeks before the primary, 7,500 people participated in a "Day of Outrage" march in the predominantly white Catholic Bensonhurst, and some thirty police officers and demonstrators were injured. The campaign would never be the same.

THE DEMOGRAPHY OF THE VOTE

Four questions dominated the campaign's progress: (1) Would any candidate win the 40 percent needed to capture the Democratic nomination? (2) Could Koch retain the Jewish vote against efforts by two other Jewish candidates (Goldin and Ravitch) to draw it away? (3) Would Latinos, socially lower than blacks in terms of income and status but more conservative than blacks in attitude, be attracted to a black candidate? Similarly, would white liberals support Dinkins? (4) Would more conservative white, outer-borough, Catholic Democrats rally strongly to Koch's support?

Before the 1989 primary, two million of New York City's three million registered voters signed up as Democrats (see Table 4.1). Forty percent of the city's adult population were white Catholics and Jews, but these groups made up 47 percent of the total registered voters and 46 percent of the Democrats. (All whites made up about 56 percent of the registered voters and 52 percent of the Democrats.) Blacks were the largest single demographic group in the Democratic party, however, representing 29 percent of the total. Moreover, this disproportionate enrollment in the Democratic ranks gave blacks better representation there than in the adult population. Latinos were underrepresented at all levels, however. With 22 percent of the adult population, they made up only 17 percent of the registered voters and accounted for 18 percent of registered Democrats. (We do not discuss Chinese and other Asian voters because our samples of these voters were too small for statistical reliability.)

Dinkins won the primary by constructing an impressive coalition of black, Latino, and white voters. Dinkins and Koch each won more than the 40 percent needed to avert a runoff, but Dinkins soundly beat Koch by 50.7 percent to 42 percent of the vote. Ninety-four percent of black primary voters supported Dinkins, as did 56 percent of Lat-

Table 4.1

Demography of the New York City Electorate, 1989

	Non-Latino Black	Latino	Non-Latino White			Total Number
			Catholic	Jews	Other	
In population						
(18 and above)	21%	22%	27%	13%	17%	5.30m
Registered to vote	20%	17%	30%	17%	16%	3.02m
Registered Democrats	29%	18%	25%	21%	7%	2.07m

Source: Wagner Institute Calculations

inos.[12] The key to Dinkins's success, however, was that he won a third of the votes cast by white Democrats, a level of support not achieved by any other black candidate for mayor except Tom Bradley in Los Angeles (see Figure 4.1). Despite the fact that he was running against three Jews, Dinkins won 33 percent of the votes of Jews who participated in the Democratic primary.

Dinkins achieved this almost unprecedented level of support by convincing white voters they could trust him. Unlike Jackson, Dinkins did not trigger the negative side of the white ambivalence toward a strong black candidate. The nonthreatening nature of his campaign defused the potential dynamite of the racial factor. Three of every four voters viewed Dinkins favorably, including many who did not vote for him. Koch, on the other hand, was viewed unfavorably by every second respondent. Over half of all Koch voters held a favorable view of Dinkins, whereas 84 percent of Dinkins voters held an unfavorable view of Koch (see Figure 4.2). For Koch, how one felt about him was a good indicator of whether one voted for him. Those who voted for him liked him (91 percent), and those who did not lacked a favorable opinion of him (84 percent).

Koch voters were also much less intense about their preference than Dinkins voters were, according to the *New York Times*/CBS exit poll: 48 percent of Koch voters but 63 percent of Dinkins voters stated that they strongly favored their candidate. Moreover, 41 percent of Koch voters expressed reservations about their candidate, compared

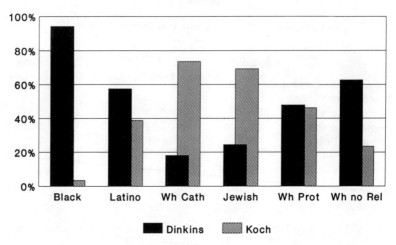

FIGURE 4.1
VOTE IN DEMOCRATIC PARTY
1989 by Group

Source: *New York Times*/CBS exit poll
N = 1,950

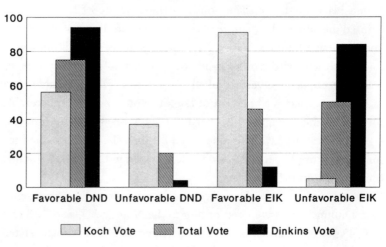

FIGURE 4.2
OPINION OF CANDIDATES BY VOTE
1989 Democratic Primary

Source: *New York Times*/CBS exit poll
N = 2,014

with only 28 percent of those who chose Dinkins. Those who voted for Dinkins generally disapproved of Koch's performance as mayor.

It was inevitable that race would be a major factor in the outcome of the primary. And so it was, particularly for blacks, who voted virtually as a block. But race was not the only important correlate of the vote: gender, age, and union membership also had an important impact. Women favored Dinkins more than men by 54 percent compared to 46 percent. This was crucial because many more women (57 percent of the total) voted in the primary than did men. In the Republican primary, women and men were equally represented and each group gave Rudolf Giuliani 68 percent of their vote.

Generational differences were also important. Over time, the white population has aged, while the black and Latino populations are much younger. These trends affected the Democratic primary. Voters under forty-five (47 percent of the total) gave more than 60 percent of their support to Dinkins, while voters over the age of sixty (32 percent of the total) gave Koch almost 60 percent of their vote.

A key base of support for the Democratic party is the labor unions of the city. Increasingly, as manufacturing has left the city, the unions representing public employees, hospital workers, and the telephone company have become more influential. That Mayor Koch failed to win their support was evident in the voting results. Among the 37 percent of the voters in the Democratic primary who were union members, 61 percent voted for Dinkins, a third for Koch, and the rest for the other two candidates. Among those employed by New York City (17 percent), 59 percent voted for Dinkins; of the 10 percent who were schoolteachers, 54 percent supported Dinkins.

ISSUES IN THE PRIMARY

Koch had to struggle with a number of impediments, beginning with his incumbency. While incumbency is usually desirable because it puts resources at the command of the candidate and facilitates media coverage, it also inevitably generates opponents over time. The incumbent bears the responsibility of the acts committed and omitted during the years of incumbency. And Ed Koch, with twelve years behind him, had a heavy burden to shoulder.

The economy had also soured after the Wall Street crash of October 1987. In 1975, the city had gone through a wrenching fiscal crisis; now, after a decade of economic expansion, a new round of retrenchment seemed to be in the offing. It was clear that difficult times were ahead as the tax base shrank, financial houses laid off workers, and employment and earnings leveled off. Added to these economic troubles were the woes associated with homelessness, the AIDS epidemic, the deteriorated school system, and rampant crime, all of which had welled up during Mayor Koch's watch, deepening the misgivings aroused by the municipal scandals.

When the exit poll asked Democratic primary voters, 34 percent said they thought that Koch was to blame "a lot" for corruption in his administration. Another 44 percent said that he bore "some" blame, while 22 percent said that he was "not much" to blame. Not surprisingly, 53 percent of the Dinkins voters and only 6 percent of Koch voters said that Koch was "a lot" to blame. Among blacks, 53 percent put the blame on Koch, compared with 28 percent of Latinos and 23 percent of the whites.

The rate at which exit poll respondents mentioned the issues that influenced their vote is reported in Table 4.2. More respondents, 30 percent, mentioned drug abuse than any other issue in both Democratic and Republican primaries. Only 11 percent of Democratic primary voters chose corruption as an important issue. (For Republicans, corruption seemed somewhat more important, with 18 percent mentioning it.) The widespread sense of unease about the mayor and his performance was generalized rather than attached to a specific issue area, as can be seen in Table 4.2.

This sense of generalized unease with Koch surfaced when voters were asked to describe the major qualities that motivated their vote. Koch's voters praised his outspokenness (36 percent) and his experience (25 percent), while Dinkins's voters mentioned Dinkins's honesty and integrity (43 percent) and his ability to be fair to all kinds of people (38 percent). Black voters held monolithic negative views of Koch. Din-

Table 4.2

Koch, Corruption, and Issues in the Democratic Primary, 1989

	Drug Abuse	Education	Homeless	Crime	Race Relations	Affordable Housing	Corruption	City Taxes	AIDS
Mentioning issue	30%	20%	17%	16%	15%	14%	11%	5%	2%
Non-blacks who blame Koch for corruption (25%) mentioning issue	20%	13%	19%	12%	20%	15%	20%	4%	1%

Source: *New York Times*/CBS exit poll

kins did much better with white voters, with 67 percent of them having a positive evaluation of the black contender.

In addition to corruption, Koch had to struggle with the perception that he was unfair to blacks. For many, Koch had come to symbolize the racial polarization that seemed to have settled over New York City. Two-thirds of black voters felt that Koch favored whites over blacks. Only one in five thought that he had been fair to all. A large majority of Democratic voters (67 percent) believed, by contrast, that if Dinkins were elected, he would not favor blacks over whites. Even a majority of white voters (56 percent) felt this way, as did 89 percent of black voters, and two-thirds of Latino voters. As we shall see in greater detail, Dinkins's ability to allay race-based mistrust among whites was crucial to his victory, for these whites supported him by much greater margins than did others.

As with corruption, race and racial conflict were not direct issues, although they provided the backdrop for the campaign. Race was a diffuse feature of the electoral atmosphere, but few admitted that the race of the candidates motivated their own votes. But what they would not admit about themselves, they were not hesitant to ascribe to others. Half of the voters who favored the two main candidates thought that race was the main reason other people voted against the candidate they personally preferred.

While the Bensonhurst incident certainly had an impact on the momentum of the campaign and the mood of the city, it is harder to measure its precise impact on the electorate. Two-thirds of the voters said that this event had not affected their choice in the primary. But more than a quarter of all voters in the Democratic primary said they were affected by that incident. Most of those said that the Bensonhurst event had made them more sure of their vote. The incident and its aftermath gave more motivation to Dinkins voters than to Koch voters. Thirty-eight percent of Dinkins voters either changed to Dinkins or became more sure of their vote for him, while only 15 percent of Koch voters were motivated to vote for the incumbent because of Bensonhurst.

On the Republican side, Giuliani's argument that he could fight crack, crime, and corruption scored well. Those three issues worked for him in the Republican primary, although his landslide victory makes it hard to know how effective any single issue was. As we have seen, drugs was the issue most cited among Republican voters as important in deciding their vote. Corruption was mentioned by 18 percent of the Republicans, compared to 11 percent of the Democrats.

Crime was the second most frequently mentioned issue among Republican voters, with 22 percent citing it. This group voted heavily for Giuliani. Sixteen percent of Democrats named crime; this issue worked better for Koch than for Dinkins. Of Democrats who said crime was an important issue determining their vote, 56 percent went for Koch, 35 percent for Dinkins. In the November election, the crime issue helped Giuliani capture some of Koch's supporters in the primary who chose not to switch to Dinkins.

THE PRIMARY ELECTIONS RESULTS

The primary election marked a historic turning point in the political history of New York City. By a fairly substantial margin, the Democratic party selected a black nominee as its leader for mayor for the first time. The black community, which had overwhelmingly supported him, and Dinkins's other supporters appropriately saw the victory as a major achievement. They had worked hard for their opportunity.

Their efforts are obvious in the rate at which they supported Dinkins and at which they turned out for the primary vote (see Table 4.3). Using an array of assembly districts (ADs), which we analyze in depth in chapter 7, we see that black ADs were extremely supportive. Table 4.3 presents the ADs in descending order of support for Koch, ranging from the 80 percent support in the heavily Jewish Brooklyn 45th AD of Midwood/Manhattan Beach, to only 5.2 percent in Harlem (the 70th AD) which gave Koch only 5.2 percent of its vote.

Equally informative is the turnout rate in the various districts, especially in comparison to the turnout rate of the 1985 mayoral primary. Then Denny Farrell, a black politician, competed with Mayor Koch, and lost badly. In general, black ADs turned out at extremely

Table 4.3

Turnout in the Democratic Primary, 1989 and 1985
and Percentage for Koch for Selected Neighborhoods

Assembly District	Neighborhood	% Koch Vote 1989	% Turnout 1989	% Turnout 1985	Difference 1989–1985
45	Midwood, Manhattan Beach	80.0	58.4	39.6	18.8
31	Richmond Hill	67.5	44.9[a]	29.1	15.8
67	Upper West Side	43.2	52.5	37.6	14.9
53	Bushwick	34.6	41.5	27.2	14.3
73	South Bronx	26.8	47.2	33.3	13.9
43	Crown Heights	10.6	59.1	27.8	31.3
70	Harlem	5.2	54.3	27.8	24.4
citywide maximum value		81.4	62.7	43.4	35.8
citywide minimum value		4.5	39.7	22.7	18.2
citywide average value		44.0	50.7	32.5	18.2
standard deviation		23.4	5.5	5.6	6.7

Source: New York City Board of Elections
[a]Underlining indicates under the average turnout.

high rates in the 1989 primary. More surprisingly, Latino ADs also turned out at rates that, though lower than in black or many white ADs, were still much higher than in the past and higher than the citywide figure. By contrast, the white Catholic ADs had extremely low turnout in the primary; Richmond Hill (the 31st AD) was five points below the citywide average.

Note that the citywide turnout rate in 1989 was on average 18.2 percentage points above the 1985 rate. Thus most districts posted higher turnout rates in 1989 than in 1985. But their relative positions differed in the two elections. The Jewish 45th and the Upper West Side white liberal ADs were above the mean on both occasions. The white Catholic 31st and the Latino-black Bushwick Assembly District 53 were below the mean in both races. The two heavily black districts, the 43rd and the 70th, were both below the mean turnout rate in 1985, but much above it in 1989. (The South Bronx 73rd AD, made up of Latinos and blacks, was the only district in this group that went from above the mean in 1985 to below it in 1989.) In general, ADs with large Latino populations turned out much better in 1989 than they had in 1985 or 1988. Turnout obviously favored Dinkins, although Jewish districts also turned out at high levels, as they historically tended to do. White Catholic districts turned out at low levels, depriving Koch of needed votes and setting the stage for the Dinkins-Giuliani shoot-out.

Blacks overwhelmingly favored Dinkins, and they made their decisions early. Almost three-quarters of blacks made their decision more than a month before the election. In contrast, only 58 percent of whites and Latinos decided that early. In the last month, 21 percent of whites, 15 percent of Latinos, and 11 percent of blacks made their decision. In the last few days of the election, only 5 percent of blacks made their decision, compared to 11 and 12 percent of whites and Latinos, respectively.

Dinkins won the primary handily, with more than 50 percent of the vote (see Figure 4.3). Mayor Koch also won more than 40 percent of the vote, despite fears that the two other Jewish candidates would draw from Koch's strength. As Figure 4.4 shows, Dinkins won handsomely in the black 70th and 43rd ADs, did well in the mixed black and Latino 53rd and 73rd ADs, and fought Koch to a draw in the Upper West Side (67th AD) by winning substantial numbers of Jewish voters. Koch did best in the outer-borough Jewish 45th AD and well (but not well enough) in the white Catholic 31st AD.

The Republican contest was more lopsided. Whereas more than a million Democrats voted in their primary, only 112,000 voters participated in the Republican contest (see Figure 4.3). Giuliani won two-thirds of the vote, although Lauder outspent him four to one. In the assembly districts we tracked, Giuliani did best where Dinkins did worst. In ADs that favored Dinkins, not only were there few Republicans, but Giuliani made appeals that were interpreted as similar to the ones put forward by Koch. Two quite different candidates had thus won their respective primaries, setting the stage for a massive confrontation in the general election.

Of the four questions posed at the outset of this chapter, the electorate answered the first question of whether any candidate would

FIGURE 4.3
RESULTS OF PRIMARIES
New York City 1989

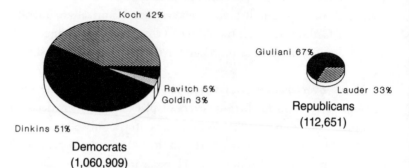

Democrats
(1,060,909)

Republicans
(112,651)

Source: New York City Board of Elections

FIGURE 4.4
DEMOCRATIC PRIMARY RESULTS
in the Study Assembly Districts

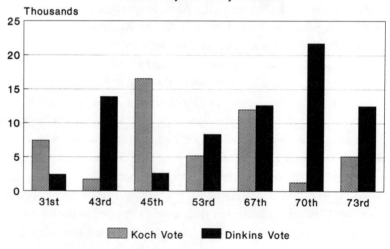

Source: New York City Board of Elections

get enough votes to avoid a runoff by giving Dinkins more than 40 percent required. But the electorate also gave a negative answer to the second question, whether Goldin and Ravitch would draw votes from Koch by giving Koch more than 40 percent as well. The election thus turned on the answers to the other two questions: would Latinos stay with Koch? and would white Catholics turn out for him in large numbers?

Latinos moved away from Koch in two different respects: not only did they abandon their previously overwhelming support for Mayor Koch by giving Dinkins 56 percent of their votes, but they turned out in much greater numbers than they had in 1988 and 1985. (White liberals also gave Dinkins more than half their votes, a far more ringing endorsement than Jackson had received the year before.)

At the same time, white Catholics answered the final question by failing to turn out for Koch and giving a far higher proportion of their votes to Dinkins than they had to Jackson or Farrell. White Catholic outer-borough ADs had an unusually low turnout in the 1989 primary. Though they generally favored Koch, they did not do so by nearly as strong a margin as in 1985, averaging only 61.4 percent for him. In short, they sat on their hands for Mayor Koch even though he had spent much of the 1980s bringing them into his electoral coalition. Instead, they were waiting to support one of their own, Rudolph W. Giuliani.

5

THE 1989 GENERAL ELECTION

THE MOOD

A majority of the voters in the Democratic primary had decreed an end to the Ed Koch era. The promise (or threat, depending on one's outlook) of actually electing a black mayor had finally arrived. For New York City politics, this was both ordinary and extraordinary.

The general election was ordinary because major Democratic party leaders, strategists, and advisers did what any party group anxious to retain power would do: they coalesced behind the winner of their primary in order to win the general election. They were determined to overcome the dissonance that was created by the race issue. They were fortunate because David Dinkins epitomized mainstream New York City Democratic organization politics. In his origins and in his nonthreatening demeanor, Dinkins was universally regarded as a "nice" person. While his positions were to the left of center, he was in tune with much of the New York City electorate; not less important, his style was not confrontational. He was quiet and careful; a conciliator, a healer. In an arena that had spawned the confrontation between Jesse Jackson and Ed Koch, many welcomed the promise of these traits.

But the primary results and the general election were also extraordinary, because New York City was finally poised to join the other American cities where substantial black populations forged multiracial coalitions with a reasonable shot at electing a black mayor (see Figure 5.1). This had first occurred in Cleveland in 1967 and subsequently in Los Angeles, Chicago, Detroit, Philadelphia, and Atlanta, all among the ten largest American cities. New York was the last to join this group.

FIGURE 5.1
GROUPS IN NEW YORK CITY
Mayoral Election 1989

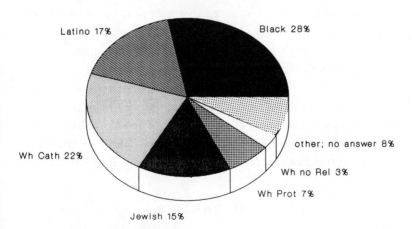

Source: *New York Times*/CBS exit poll
N = 2,109

Having quietly informed the fight in the Democratic primary, the race issue would also be a major, if largely unspoken, theme in the general election. A majority of the New York City Democratic primary electorate had supported the emerging coalition that had gathered around Dinkins. But African Americans were the largest single group in this electorate. Would the larger general electorate, where whites were a larger proportion, follow suit?

David Dinkins had won a surprisingly strong victory in the primary against incumbent Mayor Ed Koch. Though Jews had previously supported Koch in overwhelming numbers, Dinkins had won a third of the Jewish votes in the primary. In the first glow of victory, the Democratic party seemed to have fielded a winning candidate, since blacks and Jews constituted the two largest elements of the general electorate. The color of the candidate was not regarded as a negative factor—and some saw it as an asset.

On closer reflection, however, racial lines had clearly been drawn. The incidents of interracial assault had heightened tensions in the city. Each confrontation had led to violence and two resulted in death. The Howard Beach and Bensonhurst murders and the Central Park assault raised basic questions about the level of civility and evoked strong emotional responses. What was feared had become reality, with newspaper headlines, trials, and street marches pitting white against black.

If the primary was a retrospective judgment on Mayor Koch's performance, the general election would be a prospective decision about who the city's new leader should be. Serious questions were raised about both major candidates. Would Rudolph Giuliani's toughness wear well in a racially divided city? Would Dinkins's loose manner in handling his personal finances spill over into the management of a city vexed by corruption and facing renewed fiscal problems? These basic questions would be fought over in the lattice of ethnic and ideological trenches that make up the city's electoral battlefield.

THE PARTIES

Two sentiments dominated the outlook of the Democratic leadership after the Dinkins victory in the September primary. One was euphoria, because the primary produced not only a clear victory for the insurgents, but also a display of unity orchestrated by the losing mayor himself, Ed Koch. In early October, Dinkins led Giuliani by twenty-four points in public opinion polls. The second, which quickly overcame the euphoria, was a note of caution. No one could be certain of victory, and the downside of pride in having nominated the first black Democratic candidate for mayor was a fear that many white New York voters would not support a black candidate for mayor, regardless of sharing his party identification. David Dinkins was neither a charismatic personality nor a dynamic speaker. Moreover, the opposing campaign was sure to pick up his lapses regarding taxpaying and financial record-keeping.

Even on primary election night, before Dinkins appeared on television or Koch could mount his unity effort, all the networks covered Jesse Jackson speaking at length from the Dinkins victory party. The campaign had previously kept Jackson to a low profile because Dinkins strategists knew that his presence would trigger a strong negative reaction among Jewish voters. Although Jackson took the stage as one of many who were introduced before David Dinkins arrived, he held it the longest. It appeared that Dinkins and his managers lacked either the ability or the will to displace him.

New York's Democratic party had never been a single, integrated machine. Five decades of reform had weakened the ability of county party chairmen to maintain and field a large network of dependent loyalists, and the corruption scandals had thrown two of the five county party organizations into disarray. Even the strongest regular clubs were relatively few and operated with less vigor and discipline than they had a generation earlier.[1] Straight patronage was less available, and the positions still open, such as laborers in the highway department, did not attract the kind of people whose talents would enable a political organization to operate effectively. Political workers were more likely to come out of labor union political operations, reform political clubs, and qualified public job holders who had gotten their positions with some political sponsorship.

Essentially, the Democratic party in 1989 was a loose, latent, citywide network of organizations that might be activated by a strong candidate. Its day-to-day operation rested heavily on the goodwill of elected officials, county leaders, and club stalwarts in the five boroughs of the city. As the central actor in the city's political system, the mayor could build alliances with each of its parts and, when necessary, try to unite them.

What happened after the primary was unusual in recent New York City politics, because the Dinkins organization pulled these disparate elements together as if, in fact, the party had a vibrant organization in place. With a paid central campaign staff of several dozen people, including several lent by labor unions, the campaign combined and gave direction to efforts by existing organizations, especially the public employee unions and black churches.

As chapter 3 suggested, these organizational and coalition-building efforts built upon connections made during Jesse Jackson's 1988 presidential primary campaign in the city. Given Mayor Koch's vitriolic attacks on Jackson, however, the decision by him and the city's other white Democratic leaders to get behind David Dinkins was as remarkable as it was potentially crucial. Koch found himself supporting a candidate who described Jesse Jackson as an "old and dear friend." As the city's highest Democratic elected official, Koch was the party's symbolic leader. It was quite out of character for him to declare, with apparent conviction, that unity was the most important thing. He put aside the attacks that he made against David Dinkins during the primary and sought to rally the traditional party faithful to the cause.

The Republican party had weathered an extremely expensive and divisive primary in which Ronald Lauder spent over $13 million attacking Rudolph Giuliani. Giuliani had been distracted by having to respond to Lauder's charges that he was too liberal to be the Republican standard bearer. The Giuliani campaign had initially expected Koch to win the Democratic primary, and so had decided to position Giuliani the prosecutor as the critic of the corrupt Koch administration. When Dinkins won, Giuliani had to reposition his campaign. He had to be cautious about being perceived as taking advantage of his opponent's race without allowing the issue to intimidate his campaign, as it had Koch's. In contrast with the primary, Giuliani had to appeal not only to registered Republicans and Independents but to the white voters who had participated in the Democratic primary. Essentially, Giuliani had to recreate the former Koch coalition, this time along somewhat more conservative, white, Catholic, Republican lines.

Ultimately, Giuliani decided not to mention race, party, or ideology, but to concentrate instead on hammering Dinkins's perceived financial shortcomings and trying to tie them to past corruption among the Democrats. Of course, his initial denial that race was an issue in the campaign reminded white voters that there was a racial difference between candidates. For many Italian American and Jewish Democratic voters who had seen Jesse Jackson dominate the platform on primary night, this was a poignant reminder.

Along with the dwindling group of WASPs, the Republican party in New York City is predominantly made up of the white ethnic Catholics (particularly Italians) who had both cooperated with and competed against Jews to succeed the Irish as the dominant force in city politics between 1930 and 1960. While many had once been Democrats or came from Democratic families, the liberal and pro–civil rights bent of the Democratic party had disaffected many of these people since the 1960s. While white ethnic Catholics once too had been perceived as an outside minority, they were not happy that the Democratic party had moved to build up its voting strength among the new black and Puerto Rican population that had migrated into the city since World War II. This shift was played out against a backdrop of racial and ethnic transition in which blacks and Puerto Ricans moved into white ethnic neighborhoods whose former residents were forming new enclaves, such as Canarsie, on the city's periphery.[2]

The relatively small number of Republican elected officials from New York City and the party's control of only one of the three statewide power bases, the state senate, gave the city's Republicans a much smaller institutional base than the Democrats. Only when they had been successful at electing a governor had the city enjoyed substantial power and patronage, but it had been twenty years since that had happened (and then only because of Nelson Rockefeller's personality, drive, and family resources).

Although far more conservative than Democrats, New York City's Republican voters remain more to the center and even more liberal than their national counterparts. National Republican leaders were therefore marginally relevant to the campaign. U.S. Senator Alphonse D'Amato, a strong presence in the state Republican party, had helped to generate the Lauder candidacy and gave less than lukewarm support to Giuliani in the general election. D'Amato had been angered by Giuliani's slowness in deciding whether he would run for Democratic Senator Daniel P. Moynihan's seat. (Giuliani finally allowed D'Amato to learn of his decision from the press.) Giuliani had also resisted D'Amato's choice as his successor as federal prosecutor; D'Amato may also have felt vulnerable to Giuliani's criticism of his relationship with the Department of Housing and Urban Development during the Reagan years.

President Bush came into the city only when his presence proved necessary to finance the last stage of the Giuliani campaign. It is generally not in a president's interest to get involved in local or state elections since he may be embarrassed by a loss. Unlike the races for Congress, there is also no clear legislative advantage to be gained in local elections, although political and symbolic issues are clearly at stake.

THE RESULTS

As the campaign came to a close, it was apparent that Dinkins's margin was falling and Giuliani's rising, despite tracking polls that indicated Dinkins would still win by roughly ten percentage points. In the end, the margin was far more narrow; indeed, Dinkins had only 47,080 more votes than Giuliani out of 1.8 million ballots cast. Despite the identification of the vast majority of the city's voters with the Democrats, the Democratic candidate won the general election by just over two percentage points. Almost 30 percent of self-identified Democrats thus defected from the Democratic ranks to vote for Republican Rudolph Giuliani. We shall examine this phenomenon in greater detail in chapter 6. For now, we concern ourselves with the bases upon which the voting choices were made.

RACIAL ANXIETY

On the face of it, the answer seems quite simple. After all, 71 percent of the white vote went to the white candidate and 91 percent of the black vote went to the black candidate. The simple answer to why people voted as they did would appear to be race. But if one accepts that answer, a number of interesting questions follow. First, if the basis of the vote division was race, were the vote decisions themselves racist? If so, was the black vote (91 percent for the black candidate) more racist than the white vote (only 71 percent for the white candidate)?

One could argue, of course, that blacks were simply following a time-honored tradition of rallying about one of their own at a critical historical moment, as had the Irish, and the Italians, and the Jews before them. But if one is persuaded that blacks were not being racist but simply rallying around one of their own, should not one accept the same argument for the 75 percent of those of Italian ancestry who voted for Giuliani, the candidate of Italian ancestry, or for the 81 percent of Republicans who voted for the Republican candidate?

Moreover, what does one make of the *New York Times*/CBS poll of June 11–16, 1989, that found that 51 percent of the white respondents said "yes" when asked if there was a potential candidate for mayor for whom they would not vote? When asked who that was, however, 46 percent named Koch, 41 percent named Lauder, 12 percent named Giuliani, and only 12 percent named Dinkins.[3] When asked what effect electing a black mayor would have on the city, 16 percent of whites and 22 percent of blacks thought it would make things better, while 10 percent of whites and 5 percent of blacks thought it would make things worse. Most, including 64 percent of whites and 52 percent of blacks, thought it would make no difference.

When asked if they would be more or less likely to vote for a candidate for mayor if that person were black, 86 percent of whites and 86 percent of blacks said that it would make no difference. While 38 percent of whites and 40 percent of blacks did think that race was the main reason people voted against their preferred candidate, 50 percent of whites and 52 percent of blacks thought that race was *not* the reason.

All of this suggests that "race" is too simple an explanation for the vote division and that other potential bases for candidate preference also warrant examination in this biracial contest. This is not to say that race played no part. After all, 10 percent of the whites and 11 percent of the blacks did indicate in the *New York Times*/CBS poll that the race of the candidate would influence their vote for mayor. However, differences in issue priorities and policy preferences among the various groups in the racial and ethnic mosaic of the city's politics may also have had a significant bearing. We begin to examine this possibility by turning to how votes for Dinkins and Giuliani were distributed across the racial, ethnic, and religious groups of the city (see Figure 5.2).

Each white segment gave Giuliani strong support. While he was least successful among Jews, it was notable that even they gave him 65 percent, despite being the only white group to have a large majority

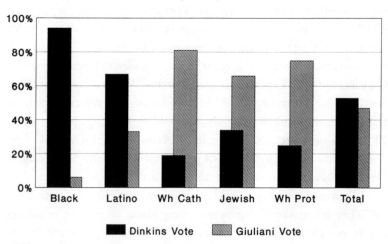

FIGURE 5.2
VOTE FOR MAYOR 1989
by Group

Source: *New York Times*/CBS exit poll
N = 2,109

of Democratic identifiers. While the pattern in Figure 5.2 leads one to see race as the simple explanation for the vote division, that explanation is too simple for reasons already noted. We must look beyond race to explore how the following five dimensions influenced voters in each demographic group:

- What issues voters reported "most important" in deciding how to vote
- Which candidate attributes they regarded as "most important" in deciding how to vote
- Voters' preference for dealing with the city's budget deficit
- Which political leaders' campaign activities were reported by voters as likely to affect their votes
- Whether voters perceived Dinkins and Giuliani as likely to engage in race-based favoritism if elected

A sixth dimension, that of the strength and nature of party identification, will be addressed in the next chapter.[4]

ISSUES

In the exit poll, respondents were asked to indicate which, if any, of a list of nine issues "mattered most in deciding how you voted." Respondents were instructed to check up to two issues. The issues listed were:

- Homeless people
- Education
- Drug abuse
- Affordable housing
- Race relations
- Corruption in city government
- City taxes
- Crime
- AIDS

Table 5.1 shows the proportion of each demographic group that identified each issue as having been most important for their vote

Table 5.1

Issues Cited as Most Important in
Respondent's Vote Decision by Group
(Cell entries are percents citing the issue as first or second most important.)

				Group		
	TOTAL	Blacks	Latinos	White Catholics	White Jews	White Protestants
(Percent of Voters)	(100%)	(28%)	(17%)	(22%)	(15%)	(7%)
Issue						
Homeless	19	34	20	11	12	8
Education	18	21	27	12	18	13
Drugs	25	21	37	26	20	21
Affordable housing	11	20	16	5	6	6
Race relations	11	14	8	8	14	10
Corruption	19	8	14	30	24	27
Taxes	5	3	3	6	6	5
Crime	20	16	15	28	27	18
AIDS	2	2	2	1	1	4

Source: *New York Times*/CBS exit poll, 1989 mayoral election; N = 2,109; weighted data

decision. Among the full set of voters, the dominant issues were drugs, 25 percent; crime, 20 percent; corruption, 19 percent; homelessness, 19 percent; and education, 18 percent. Table 5.2 also shows that the stated importance of a given issue varied markedly from group to group. Several differences stand out. For blacks and Latinos, homelessness had a high priority, while it rated much lower in the white segments. A similar pattern obtains regarding education and affordable housing, except that Jews were distinctly more concerned about education than the other two white segments. The situation was reversed for corruption and crime. These carry a high priority for whites but a relatively low one for blacks and Latinos. The issues of drugs carried a relatively high priority across all the groups, and especially so for Latinos.[5]

This pattern suggests that a social class dimension is relevant. Those who have most contact with the homeless and are in most imminent danger of becoming homeless gave homelessness a much higher priority than those who are more removed from the problem. Those whose children have the least access to private schools and whose children most direly need an effective educational system gave education a higher priority than did those with other options. By contrast, those who see themselves as funding the system and as plausible targets for theft and assault gave those matters a high priority. For this latter group, an accomplished prosecutor might have substantial appeal.

Table 5.2 shows the degree (Pearson's r) and direction of association between regarding a given issue as important to one's vote decision and the probability of voting for Dinkins. The sign of the correlation indicates whether regarding a given issue as important increased the probability of having voted for Dinkins (positive sign) or decreased that probability (negative sign). Only r's with a probability of occurrence by chance less than 5 percent are reported.

The coefficients in Table 5.2 afford some insight into the closeness of the Dinkins victory. On homelessness, education, affordable housing, race relations, and AIDS, those who saw the issue as "most important" to their vote decision in every group preferred Dinkins. Few whites, however, saw these issues as among the most important (see Table 5.1). Consider the case, for example, of white Protestants and the issue of AIDS. Among those concerned with the issue, there was a .28 correlation with a preference for Dinkins (the highest in this table), but only 4 percent of white Protestants mentioned the issue as "most important" to their vote.

By contrast, in almost every group, those who regard drugs, corruption, and crime as "most important" preferred Giuliani. For the white groups, these were high-priority issues. Only among Latinos, for whom drugs had the highest priority, was Dinkins the net preferred candidate. Conceivably, Latinos who were concerned with the drug problem had a net preference for treatment centers as against prisons or thought Dinkins would attack the problem in a way that would be more sensitive to their neighborhoods.

Table 5.2 shows that there were few statistically significant coefficients among blacks and that they were small when they did occur.

Table 5.2

Issues[a] as Correlates of Candidate Preference by Group
(Cell entries are Pearson's r's.)[b]

			Group		
	TOTAL	Blacks	Latinos	White Catholics	White Jews	White Protestants
(Percent of Voters)	(100%)	(28%)	(17%)	(22%)	(15%)	(7%)
Issues						
Homelessness	.22	c	.12	.17	.24	.15
Education	.10	c	.11	.09	c	c
Drugs	c	c	.12	−.13	−.16	−.17
Affordable housing	.16	−.09	.15	.17	.20	.15
Race relations	.13	c	.11	.22	c	.15
Corruption	−.21	−.08	c	−.16	−.20	−.24
Taxes	−.07	−.11	c	−.07	c	−.14
Crime	−.17	−.08	−.11	−.16	−.15	−.21
AIDS	.08	c	,10	.09	c	.28

Source: *New York Times*/CBS exit poll, 1989 mayoral election; $N = 2,109$; unweighted data
[a]Issues cited as first or second most important.
[b]A positive sign indicates an increased probability of voting for Dinkins, and a negative sign indicates a decreased probability of voting for Dinkins.
[c]$p \geq .05$.

Since blacks favored Dinkins 91:9, this is not surprising. Yet issue preferences did afford insight into the 9 percent who did *not* vote for Dinkins. Apparently, for that small subgroup, affordable housing, corruption, taxes, and crime were dominant issues, and on those they tended marginally to prefer Giuliani.

CANDIDATE ATTRIBUTES

In addition to asking which issues mattered most to the respondent in choosing among the candidates, the exit poll also asked which of a number of "factors" mattered most. These were essentially candidate attributes:

- His (the candidate's) political party
- Competence
- Honesty and integrity
- Debating skill
- Race of the candidate
- Cares about people like me
- Will reduce racial divisions
- Tough on criminals
- I don't like the other candidates

As can be seen in Table 5.3, the voters mentioned the following candidate attributes most frequently as "most important:" Honesty and integrity (36 percent); competence (27 percent); and tough on criminals (21 percent). These three also tended to hold the top positions for each segment. In the black and Latino groups, however, two additional candidate attributes emerged with much higher frequency than they did in any of the white segments. One was "Cares about people like me," which was mentioned as "most important" by 22 percent of the black and Latino respondents but by only 5–7 percent of the respondents in the white segments. This is evidence of an emphatic basis of support for Dinkins among blacks and Latinos. It produced a net vote in the direction of the nonwhite candidate (Table 5.4). But is this race-based voting, racist voting, or simply voting for someone who seems more likely to appreciate and respond to one's needs?

"Will reduce racial divisions" was also mentioned two to three times more frequently among blacks and Latinos than among whites. Note that while the media made much of race relations and racial tensions as the defining context of the election, they ranked only in the middle of the black and Latino priorities and near the bottom of the white priorities, as indicated in both Tables 5.1 and 5.3.

In Table 5.4, one can examine the extent to which placing a high value on each of these attributes is associated with an increased probability of voting for Dinkins (positive sign) or a decreased probability (negative sign). As in Table 5.2, those valuing a candidate who is "tough on criminals" were less likely to be Dinkins voters in every group than were those who did not so highly value this attribute.

Table 5.3

**Candidate Attributes Cited as Most Important in
Respondent's Vote Decision by Group**
(Cell entries are percents citing the attribute as first or second most important.)

			Group		
	TOTAL	Blacks	Latinos	White Catholics	White Jews	White Protestants
(Percent of Voters)	(100%)	(28%)	(17%)	(22%)	(15%)	(7%)
Candidate Attribute						
Candidate's political party	11	14	8	7	11	11
Competence	27	36	20	22	28	31
Honesty/integrity	36	26	35	47	37	47
Debating skill	6	10	9	3	3	2
Candidate's race	3	3	7	2	2	3
Cares	3	22	22	5	7	5
Reduce racial divisions	10	14	16	6	9	5
Tough on criminals	21	11	21	33	23	21
Dislike other candidates	10	9	10	11	13	3

Source: *New York Times*/CBS exit poll, 1989 mayoral election; *N* = 2,109; weighted data

Again, whites were more likely to value being tough on criminals than were blacks. The honesty and integrity attribute also worked to Giuliani's advantage, displaying a statistically significant relationships with candidate choice in each of the groups. These had the greatest force for whites, particularly the white Protestants and white Catholics, who mentioned it more frequently (47 percent) than did blacks (26 percent). (Because of the 91–9 split in candidate choice, few of the coefficients in the "Black" column were statistically significant.)

One coefficient in this column that looks sufficiently anomalous to be regarded as a possible misprint is *not* a misprint. Specifically, among blacks who cited the candidate's race as "most important," there is a −.16 correlation with voting for Dinkins. The basis for this correlation can be explained by the cross-tabulation presented in Table

Table 5.4

**Candidate Attributes[a] As Correlates of
Candidate Preference by Group**
(Cell entries are Pearson's r's.)[b]

				Group		
	TOTAL	**Blacks**	**Latinos**	**White Catholics**	**White Jews**	**White Protestants**
(Percent of Voters)	(100%)	(28%)	(17%)	(22%)	(15%)	(7%)
Candidate Attribute						
Candidate's political party	.10	c	c	.16	.19	c
Competence	c	c	c	c	c	c
Honesty/integrity	−.15	c	c	−.19	−.23	−.18
Debating skill	.07	c	c	.14	c	c
Candidate's race	.07	−.16	c	.14	c	.21
Cares	.20	.10	.27	.17	c	.18
Reduce racial divisions	.21	c	.11	.27	.28	.28
Tough on criminals	−.26	−.12	−.14	−.27	−.29	−.24
Dislike other candidates	.07	c	c	c	.18	c

Source: *New York Times*/CBS exit poll, 1989 mayoral election; $N = 2,109$; unweighted data
[a]Attributes cites as first or second most important.
[b]A positive sign indicates an increased probability of voting for Dinkins, and a negative sign indicates a decreased probability of voting for Dinkins.
[c]$p \geq .05$.

5.5. It indicates that (1) few blacks in the sample (only 2.9 percent) selected the race of the candidate as an important attribute; (2) of those who did, a smaller proportion (12 of 17, or 70.6 percent) voted for Dinkins than was the case with those who did *not* do so (where 544 or 576, or 94.4 percent, voted for Dinkins).

Two additional points are worth noting in Table 5.4. First, among those white Protestants and white Catholics who identified the race of the candidates as an important factor in the vote decision, the probability of voting for Dinkins increased. For some whites, even among so-called "white ethnics," there seemed to be value in voting *for* a black

Table 5.5

Respondent Chose Race of Candidate as Important—Blacks Only
(Cell entries are frequencies.)

		Yes	No	Total
Respondent Voted for	Dinkins	12	544	556
	Giuliani	5	32	37
	Total	17	576	593

Source: *New York Times*/CBS Exit Poll—1989 Mayoral Election; N = 593 (Blacks only)

candidate. Second, in virtually every group, valuing a candidate's ability to reduce racial divisions was associated with an increased probability of voting for Dinkins. However, few respondents in any of the groups, especially the white segments, so valued that ability (see Table 5.3).

During the final weeks of the campaign, much was made of the looming budget deficit facing the city for the next fiscal year, then estimated at about $500 million. Given the eight years of the Reagan administration's inveighing against increases in taxation and President Bush's campaign promise of "Read my lips—no new taxes," New Yorkers' responses to the deficit situation were instructive. In their general election exit poll, *New York Times*/CBS asked whether the budget deficit should be dealt with by:

- Increasing city taxes, or
- Cutting city programs, including those for housing, education, and fighting drugs.

The exist poll responses indicated that 69 percent of the voters preferred to increase taxes rather than to reduce the city's programs (see Figure 5.3). This finding illuminates the discussion of the city's preference for increased taxation at the national level to program reduction (see chapter 8). National analysts might well interpret this as New Yorkers' seeking to transfer income from the rest of the nation to New

York City. But the exit poll asked about self-taxation. A substantial majority of every group favored increased taxes over program reductions (see Figure 5.3). Moreover, this was also true in every category of household income, although the size of that majority does diminish as household income rises (see Figure 5.4).

Given these substantial levels of support for increasing taxes to solve the city's budget problems, one might well ask why the candidates walked so gingerly around this issue. The answer is likely to lie in their fear of what is sometimes called the "intense minority" principle. Those who feel strongly about an issue are apt to base much or all of their vote decision on that issue. Those who hold the opposite position may not feel strongly enough about it to let it govern their vote decision. The *New York Times*/CBS exit poll data suggest that of those who selected city taxes as an issue that "mattered most" in deciding their vote for mayor (only 5 percent of the weighted sample), 63

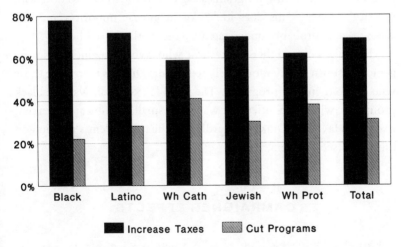

FIGURE 5.3
DEALING WITH CITY'S DEFICIT
by Group

Source: *New York Times*/CBS exit poll
$N = 2,109$

FIGURE 5.4
DEALING WITH CITY'S DEFICIT
by Household Income

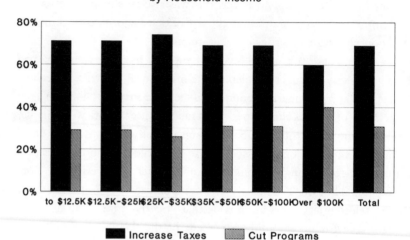

Source: *New York Times*/CBS exit poll
N = 2,109

percent favored cutting programs as against raising taxes to deal with the city's deficit. This does look like an intense minority, and one whose size is probably understated by the method used here.

Finally, as one might expect, those who favored tax increases were generally substantially more likely to support Dinkins than were those who favored cutting programs. The notable exception was the black group, for which the difference was quite small, with near 90 percent majorities favoring Dinkins regardless of the respondent's position on this issue (see Figure 5.5.)

CAMPAIGNER EFFECTS

If policy preferences about how to deal with the deficit did not divide the city along racial or ethnic lines, the same cannot be said about the campaign efforts of several of the candidates' supporters. On the

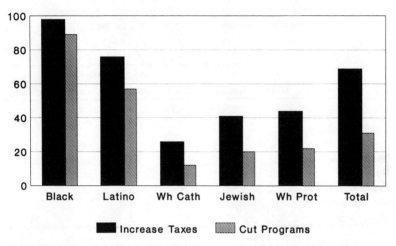

FIGURE 5.5
DEALING WITH CITY'S DEFICIT
% voting Dinkins

Source: *New York Times*/CBS exit poll
N = 2,109

Democratic side, the campaigners sought to rally the faithful and keep old supporters from wandering into the ranks of the other side. Thus, black leaders and elected officials mobilized the black vote, while Ed Koch, Mario Cuomo, the county party leaders, and the white regular political clubs were charged with retaining the votes of their supporters for Dinkins. Similarly, President Bush sought to legitimize the Republican candidate after a brutal primary battle.

However, lesser players also had considerable impact. Two in particular were Jackie Mason and Sonny Carson. Mason, a Jewish comedian with a show on Broadway, was a member of the Giuliani campaign until he made a flippantly derogatory remark about David Dinkins. Sonny Carson was a long time black nationalist who was part of the Dinkins campaign until he made anti-Semitic remarks, which he clarified by explaining that he was not anti-Semitic but was, instead, antiwhite.

As one can see in Table 5.6, Jesse Jackson was most frequently

Table 5.6

Political Campaigners Report to Have Affected Respondent's Votes by Demographic Group
(Cell entries are percents of respondents reporting the named campaigners as have affected their vote for mayor.)

	TOTAL	Blacks	Latinos	White Catholics	White Jews	White Protestants
				Group		
(Percent of Voters)	(100%)	(28%)	(17%)	(22%)	(15%)	(7%)
Political Campaigner						
George Bush	13	12	18	17	6	21
Jesse Jackson	22	25	18	22	32	23
Ed Koch	13	18	18	10	11	10
Jackie Mason	6	8	8	5	6	5
Sonny Carson	11	3	8	18	25	10
Mario Cuomo	11	16	12	9	6	16

Source: *New York Times*/CBS exit poll, 1989 mayoral election; N = 2109; weighted data
[a]Total population; those who did not answer account for the additional percentages.

reported as having affected the respondent's vote. This was true both of the whole electorate and each of the demographic groups, save for the Latino segment, where Bush and Koch matched Jackson's importance. At the other extreme, almost no one mentioned Mason.

Table 5.7 perhaps reveals more by speaking to the degree of association between having been affected by a named campaigner, and candidate choice. It gives clear evidence of white, and particularly Jewish, concern about Dinkins's association with Jesse Jackson. (For a fuller discussion of this point, see chapter 3.) This is more confirmatory of anecdotal evidence than it is surprising. The substantial and universally negative impact of Sonny Carson's comment is somewhat more surprising. Finally, in this vein, one can observe in Table 5.7 that while Jackie Mason's impact was not statistically significant in any one group, those who mentioned his comment had a slightly increased probability of having voted for Dinkins. Thus it would appear that campaigners with a strong racial thrust seemed to produce a net backlash, particu-

Table 5.7

Campaigner Effects as Correlates of
Candidate Preference by Group
(Cell entries are Pearson's r's.)[a]

				Group		
	TOTAL	Blacks	Latinos	White Catholics	White Jews	White Protestants
(Percent of Voters)	(100%)	(28%)	(17%)	(22%)	(15%)	(7%)
Political Campaigner						
George Bush	[b]	[b]	[b]	[b]	[b]	[b]
Jesse Jackson	−.06	[b]	[b]	−.18	−.28	[b]
Ed Koch	.13	.07	[b]	.15	.13	[b]
Jackie Mason	.06	[b]	[b]	[b]	[b]	[b]
Sonny Carson	−.26	−.08	−.23	−.17	−.27	−.18
Mario Cuomo	.15	[b]	.14	.15	.17	.17

Source: *New York Times*/CBS exit poll, 1989 mayoral election; N = 2,109; unweighted data
[a]A positive sign indicates an increased probability of voting for Dinkins, and a negative sign indicates a decreased probability of voting for Dinkins.
[b]$p \geq .05$.

larly so for Carson. This was *not* an electorate seeking to be racially divided.

RACIAL MISTRUST

When members of one racial group *do not* expect fair treatment from members of other racial groups, "color-blind" voting will be hard to find. The *New York Times*/CBS exit poll addressed this matter quite directly. For each of the two major candidates, it asked:

If (candidate) is elected mayor, will he favor whites over blacks?
Favor blacks over whites? Be fair to both?

Each candidate could boast that 70 percent of the electorate believed that he would be fair to both blacks and whites. However, the composition of that 70 percent is different for each candidate, showing the extent to which the underlying racial anxiety and mistrust in this election can be seen (see Figure 5.6). Eighty-five percent or more of each of the white groups saw Giuliani as likely to be "fair to both," but only 41 percent of the blacks and 67 percent of the Latinos felt this way. Conversely, no more than 65 percent of each of the white groups saw Dinkins as likely to be "fair to both," but 91 percent of the blacks and 74 percent of the Latinos did feel this way about Dinkins. The extent of this race-based mistrust is apparent in the fact that 55 percent of blacks believed Giuliani would favor whites, while 36 percent of whites believed Dinkins would favor blacks.[6]

Of the Latinos, 30 percent believed Giuliani would favor whites and 21 percent believed Dinkins would favor blacks. Thus, among the black and white populations, 39 percent mistrusted the candidate of the other race to treat people of their race fairly and blacks were less

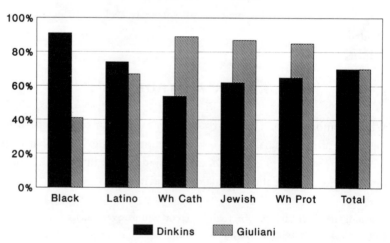

FIGURE 5.6
CANDIDATE WOULD BE FAIR
to Blacks and Whites

Source: *New York Times*/CBS exit poll
$N = 2,109$

likely to be trusting than were whites. This is a substantial amount of race-based mistrust. Tables 5.8 and 5.9 show that such mistrust was strongly associated with voting *against* the mistrusted candidate and that this effect is about the same among whites and blacks. Tables 5.10 and 5.11 show that Latinos' vote choices were also substantially affected by whether they perceived the candidate as likely to be fair to both races.

Table 5.8

**Vote and Belief on the Part of Whites
That Dinkins, if Elected Mayor, Would Favor Blacks**
(Cell entries are percents voting for named candidate)

	Whites who believe Dinkins would favor Blacks	Whites who believe Dinkins would be fair to both	Total
N	(318)	(528)	(846)
Candidate Voted For			
Dinkins	7	41	28
Giuliani	93	59	72

Source: *New York Times*/CBS exit poll, 1989 mayoral election; unweighted data

Table 5.9

**Vote and Belief on the Part of Blacks That
Giuliani, if Elected Mayor, Would Favor Whites**
(Cell entries are percents voting for named candidate)

	Whites who believe Giuliani would favor Blacks	Whites who believe Giuliani would be fair to both	Total
N	(299)	(196)	(495)
Candidate Voted For			
Dinkins	98	91	95
Giuliani	2	9	8

Source: *New York Times*/CBS exit poll, 1989 mayoral election; unweighted data

Table 5.10

Vote and Belief on the Part of Latinos That
Dinkins, if Elected Mayor, Would Show Racial Favoritism
(cell entries are percents voting for named candidate)

Latinos Who Believe

	Dinkins Would Favor Blacks	Dinkins Would Favor Whites	Dinkins Would Be Fair to Both	Total
N	(49)	(17)	(209)	(275)
Candidate Voted For				
Dinkins	22	53	84	71
Giuliani	78	47	16	29

Source: *New York Times*/CBS exit poll, 1989 mayoral election; unweighted data

Table 5.11

Vote and Belief on the Part of Latinos That
Giuliani, if Elected Mayor, Would Show Racial Favoritism
(cell entries are percents voting for named candidate)

Latinos Who Believe

	Giuliani Would Favor Blacks	Giuliani Would Favor Whites	Giuliani Would Be Fair to Both	Total
N	(11)	(94)	(167)	(272)
Candidate Voted For				
Dinkins	—	92	56	70
Giuliani	—	8	44	30

Source: *New York Times*/CBS exit poll, 1989 mayoral election; unweighted data

CONCLUSIONS

While it would be inappropriate to say that the basis of the vote decision for mayor in this election was "race pure and simple," there clearly were two strong racial components. The first was what might be called racially correlated agenda items and issue preferences. For blacks and

Latinos, homelessness, affordable housing, and education were high on the agenda. Whites, by contrast, gave the issues of corruption and crime high priority. Groups tended to vote for the candidate seen as stronger on the agenda items that were important to them. Those seeking help for the have-nots supported Dinkins, while those seeking to protect what the "haves" have supported Giuliani. While the tendency for such issues to influence vote choices existed, it was not powerful. For white groups, the correlations between issues and vote choices seldom exceeded 0.2 and never exceeded 0.3 (Tables 5.2 and 5.4).

The element of racial anxiety—mistrust of what the other fellow will do—produced a second, much greater impact in this election. Some 39 percent of the black and white population manifested such mistrust regarding the candidates, and it was powerfully associated with their voting behavior (Tables 5.8 and 5.9). This distrust may well prove more malleable than the racial differences in policy agendas. Dinkins's behavior as mayor may well be able to reduce white mistrust substantially; certainly, his history suggests that that is his forte. On the other hand, racially correlated agenda priorities and policy preferences (e.g., fighting crime vs. building housing for the homeless) may prove less tractable. Certainly, the evidence presented here is that such differences are deeply rooted in the city's social mosaic, even though they did not have a large impact on the election.

Race, then, was an important factor in determining the outcome of the election, but not in the way racial polarization is popularly construed. The great majority of voters rejected the idea that race *per se* motivated their vote, and the evidence presented here gives credence to that view. Race was, in effect, a cloak around the pattern of issue salience across the different groups and how the two candidates projected their qualities and stands. Even more, "race" simplified the deep and complex feelings about the tensions within the city and whether or not candidates would treat whites, blacks, and Latinos fairly in responding to these tensions.

Where white voters thought Dinkins would not favor blacks over whites, they were much more likely to vote for him. Thus Dinkins *was* able to construct a multiracial alliance. He not only succeeded in getting a large fraction of Latinos to back his cause, but he also retained a substantial minority of white votes, especially among non-Catholic whites. The white liberal districts gave him half their vote, the Jewish outer-borough ADs 30 percent, and even the white Catholic ADs contributed a quarter. While substantial numbers of white Democrats did defect to Giuliani, including most Koch voters, enough voted for their party's candidate to make him mayor. It is to this question of defection versus loyalty that we now turn.

6

SHIFTING ALLEGIANCES

Any campaign for elected office presents a twofold challenge: the campaign organization must mobilize the committed while also persuading the uncommitted to vote for the candidate. In an environment that is not sharply polarized and where the candidate can avoid evoking underlying cleavages, these two objectives may not conflict. But in the environment of increasing racial and class tension evident in New York at the end of the Koch era, succeeding at one of these two objectives might well mean failing at the other. Should Dinkins seek to mobilize his core African American constituency by strongly emphasizing issues important to blacks, he would perhaps be remembered as a courageous man, but not as the first black mayor of New York City. Conversely, should he base his appeal totally on swinging the white vote, he might fail to mobilize his core support. Giuliani too needed to pull a high turnout from his white, Catholic base while also swinging more liberal, Democratic votes in his direction; though these two groups were alike in many ways, the divisions between them were real, albeit far less sharp than the white-black cleavage Dinkins faced.

The Dinkins camp faced the clash of two powerful symbolic forces: the candidate's race and the importance of party identification. He was likely to benefit where these two dimensions were in tandem, as among black Democrats. But where they were conflicted—among usually Democratic voters who were not anxious to vote for a black mayoral nominee—he would have to strengthen party as a basis of identification relative to race. The extent to which he could achieve this end would determine the outcome of the election.

Three concentric circles made up the voting population in 1989. The inner circle coincided with Dinkins's natural base. In contrast to 1985, New York City's black voters eagerly supported David Dinkins, a black candidate. A second circle was comprised of white and Latino Democrats; given the Democratic party's numerical advantage over the Republicans, this group coupled with the black Democrats could ensure victory, if they all voted in accordance with their party identification. If they perceived no dissonance in voting for the Democrat candidate, even if he were black, then Dinkins's election was assured. The distant outer circle was comprised of white and Latino Republicans and Independents; this group might well be difficult to attract.

The previous chapter showed that when a candidate's race was different from the respondent's race, the voter was not likely to vote for that candidate if the respondent believed that the candidate would, if elected, favor members of the candidate's race. As can be seen in Table 6.1, Dinkins faced substantial amounts of racially based mistrust in the white segments of the electorate once he got beyond those white voters who had supported him in the Democratic primary. This would prove to be a formidable obstacle.

Dinkins adopted a moderate campaign strategy in keeping with the demands of a two-party system where candidates must appeal to

Table 6.1

**Race-Based Mistrust[a] among Whites
Who Had Not Voted for Dinkins in the Democratic Primary**

	White Democrats Who Voted For Koch in Primary	White Democrats Who Did Not Vote in Primary	White Independents	White Republicans
N	(406)	(75)	(112)	(252)
Percent believing Dinkins would favor blacks	41%	33%	33%	40%

Source: *New York Times*/CBS exit poll, 1989 mayoral election; unweighted data
[a]Measured by belief that Dinkins would, if elected, favor blacks.

the "extreme middle." Dinkins kept Jesse Jackson far from his campaign (in sharp contrast to Jackson's prominent role at Dickins's victory celebration over Mayor Koch in the primary) and actively courted the Jewish vote.

Giuliani's strategy had to be the mirror-image of Dinkins's. He could count on many white Catholics, fewer of whom were Democrats and more of whom did not trust Dinkins to be fair to whites. He could also write off the blacks and focus on courting Jews and Latinos. By focusing only on the potential white vote, his campaign erred in seeming to equate Latinos with blacks. This strategic failing probably cost Giuliani the election.

Latinos differed from blacks in a number of relevant ways. They were twice as likely to be Republicans as blacks, although the majorities of both groups were Democrats (see Figure 6.1). Latinos also differed significantly from blacks in ways that favored Giuliani on other dimensions. While 56 percent of blacks believed that Giuliani would favor whites, only a third of Latinos thought so. Less than a fourth of the black respondents had a favorable opinion of Giuliani, but half the Latinos did. Latinos had been twice as likely as blacks to have voted for Koch in the Democratic primary, with a Koch primary vote rate

FIGURE 6.1
PARTY IDENTIFICATION 1989
Blacks and Latinos

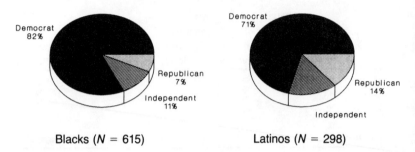

Blacks (N = 615)   Latinos (N = 298)

Source: *New York Times*/CBS survey, mayoral election

of 28 percent for Latinos compared to 15 percent for blacks. And they were open to persuasion: 27 percent of the Latinos said that they decided their vote within two weeks of the election, compared with 15 percent of the blacks. Thus his failure to court the Latinos was costly indeed for Giuliani.

THE KOCH VOTERS: TARGET OF
BOTH CANDIDATES

The candidates translated the tension between party identification and racial anxiety into an imperative to attract those who had voted for Ed Koch in the primary. Having beaten the incumbent Mayor Koch, Dinkins especially had to retain the Koch vote. Giuliani had beaten Lauder handily, and since registration in the Republican party was small and participation in its primary limited, it was clear that Giuliani would have to add a significant number of votes to his primary total for him to win the general election. The Koch primary vote was a plausible target. Giuliani's goal was to broaden his appeal to attract that vote and the votes of Independents as well.

If Dinkins barely won the election, Giuliani overwhelmingly won the campaign for the Koch vote. Of those general election voters who also participated in the Democratic primary, 47 percent reported that they voted for Dinkins in both. Of those who voted for Koch or one of the others in the primary, only one in three reported that they voted for Dinkins (see the right-hand column in Figure 6.2). The remaining two-thirds defected to Giuliani.

White Democratic primary voters largely refused to support Dinkins, the winner of that primary. Almost three-quarters of the white Catholics, two-thirds of white Protestants, and more than 60 percent of the Jews who voted for Koch in the primary voted for Giuliani in the mayoral election (see Figure 6.2). These three white groups made up 45 percent of the electorate. Had a few thousand more members of these obviously crucial groups defected, the election would have turned out differently.

On the other hand, blacks, Latinos, and whites without religious preferences not only supported Dinkins solidly in the primary, but

FIGURE 6.2
PRIMARY AND MAYORAL VOTES
1989 by Group

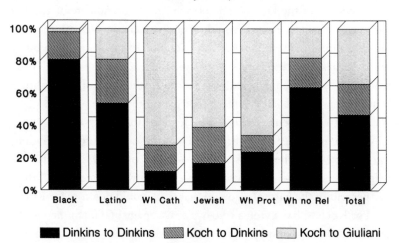

Source: *New York Times*/CBS exit poll—1989 mayoral election
Only those who voted in Democratic Primary. N = 1,950

majorities of those who initially supported Koch shifted to Dinkins in the general election. Four of five blacks voted for Dinkins in the primary. Almost all the blacks voted for Koch were in the Dinkins list by election day. More than half the Latinos supported Dinkins in the primary; Latino Koch supporters split three to two for Dinkins in the general election. Whites who reported that they had no religion heavily favored Dinkins in both elections (64 percent); the third that voted for Koch in the primary split equally between Dinkins and Giuliani on election day.

This division of Koch voters raised the intriguing question of what would have happened if Koch had run? Inevitably, some speculated that voters who were unhappy with the campaigns run by both Dinkins and Giuliani would have been relieved to vote for Koch were he on the ballot. Could Koch have won the election? We have no satisfactory measure in the survey data to declare a hypothetical winner, but we can make estimates based on indirect evidence.

The *New York Times*/CBS exit poll asked whether respondents would have voted for Koch if he were on the ballot. The question was problematic because its wording did not indicate whether it was simply a popularity question regarding Mayor Koch or applied to a particular political context. It did not specify whether Koch would be running as the winner of the Democratic primary or as a candidate of another party, or whether Dinkins would be on the ballot as well. But it does provide a minimal test. Those who said "no" to such an ambiguously worded question were not likely to vote for Koch in any event. Those who said "yes" would be subject to the further test of the political context in which Koch's name would be on the ballot.

Fifty-two percent of the respondents of the exit poll said "no," they would not vote for Koch. Thus a majority of the voters, including three-quarters of the blacks and two-thirds of the whites with no religion, were not willing to consider a further Koch candidacy. Fifty-five percent of the Latinos also said that they would not vote for Koch.

For Koch to have won a two-way race against Giuliani, he would have needed massive support from the black community, which overwhelmingly opposed him. Had Koch run as a Democrat with Dinkins not on the ballot, we conclude that Giuliani would have won the election. First, the honesty issue which Giuliani used so effectively against Dinkins would probably have been even more powerful against Koch; Giuliani could have made his charges of corrupt Democrats stick more directly to the man who had allied himself with them. Second, although the race issue would not have emerged as directly as it did in the Dinkins-Giuliani race, racial anxiety among blacks about Giuliani and their antipathy toward Koch would probably have depressed the black voting rate and split the black vote. Judging by their answer to the question, blacks, Latinos, and white liberals could not be counted in the Koch camp and were indeed available were Giuliani to make a Lindsay-style fusion appeal. If Koch had entered the race on an independent line and Dinkins were also in the race, the outcome would have depended on how white and Latino Democrats split, assuming that blacks would go to Dinkins and Republicans to Giuliani. Forty-one percent of white and Latino Democrats reported that they had voted for Koch in the primary, while 19 percent said they had voted for Dinkins. (The rest had not voted in the primary.) Only 21 percent of the white and Latino Democrats who voted for Koch shifted to Dinkins in the mayoral election. (Dinkins retained the support of two-thirds of the white and Latino Democrats who had voted for him in the primary.) Viewed the other way, white and Latino Democrats who ended up voting for Giuliani were eight times more likely to have voted for Koch in the Democratic primary than for Dinkins (67 percent to 8 percent). In a three-way election, Koch would have retained much of this group and Dinkins would have taken less than 21 percent, but a considerable fraction would still have gravitated toward Giuliani.

The longing for Koch was clearest among Democrats who had voted for Koch in the primary and then voted for Giuliani in the general election. Two-thirds of them said that they would have voted for Koch. But two-thirds of the Democrats who voted for Dinkins said that they would not have voted for Koch. It is clear that a Koch race against Giuliani and Dinkins would not have been easy. The Dinkins primary campaign had demonstrated the vulnerability of Koch's plan to run on his twelve-year record as mayor and the effectiveness of the corruption issue. These would have continued to plague the mayor. Moreover, Giuliani and Dinkins would both break away key components of the old Koch coalition: Giuliani would remove white Catholic Democrats, while Dinkins would deprive him of the majority of Latinos and minority of blacks who had voted for him in 1985. Both might have attracted white liberals who had voted for Koch in 1985. That left only the Jews, three-quarters of whom said that would vote for him. But they constituted only 15 percent of the general electorate. Although the exercise is hypothetical, we conclude that Koch probably would have lost a three-way election as well as a two-way election.

PARTY IDENTIFICATION

Party identification is a useful but imprecise measure of vote intention. As we observed in chapter 4, two-thirds of New York City voters registered as Democrats and were thereby eligible to participate in the Democratic party primary. Subjectively, about half of those voting in New York City elections during in the 1980s called themselves Democrats. Republican identifiers were in the high teens and Independents in the low twenties (see Figure 6.3). If we knew nothing else about New York City politics but that information, we would surmise that the action would take place within the confines of the Democratic party.

In 1989, based only on those who gave an answer to the party identification question in the exit poll, 60 percent of those who voted in the mayoral election identified as Democrats, 22 percent as Independents, and 18 percent as Republicans (see Table 6.2). Yet party identification was an imperfect predictor of the vote in 1989: only 53 percent of those self-identified Democrats supported Dinkins, while 47 percent of them supported Giuliani (see Figure 6.4).

The groups that comprise this enormous city generated different rates of consistency in how they translated their party identification into voting support for the candidate of the party of their choice. Among blacks in New York City in 1989, the consistency rate was highest, with over 80 percent of those who identified themselves as Democrats voting for Dinkins (see Figure 6.4). In total, 94 percent of the blacks voted for Dinkins, a rate higher than would be anticipated

FIGURE 6.3
PARTY IDENTIFICATION, 1981–89
New York City

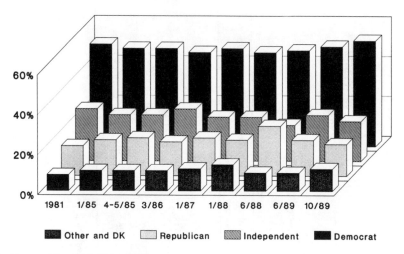

Source: *New York Times*/CBS surveys

by simply knowing that 83 percent of the blacks identified themselves as Democrats. The explanation of the increase is among the black independents, who went for Dinkins by a nine-to-one ratio. Even the black Republicans (only 7 percent of all black identifiers) tended to support Dinkins over Giuliani, by four to three (see Figure 6.5 and Table 6.2).

As Table 6.2 makes evident, Latinos also supported Dinkins strongly, if less so than the blacks. Two out of three Latinos called themselves Democrats, and of those, about four out of five voted for Dinkins. The sixteen percent of Latinos who identified themselves as Independents split almost evenly between the two candidates. Giuliani could have exploited this important battleground but seemed to ignore it. Latino Republicans (an additional 16 percent) went two-to-one for Giuliani. Thus two-thirds of voting Latinos chose Dinkins, a considerably higher proportion than in the primary election. This shift was an important ingredient in the Dinkins victory.

If blacks oversubscribed for Dinkins compared with their rate of

Table 6.2

Party Identification and Vote for Mayor by Group[a]

Party ID	Vote for Mayor	Blacks	Latinos	White Catholics	White Jews	White Protestants	White No Religion	TOTAL
Republican	Dinkins	4%	5%	3%	1%	4%	4%	3%
Republican	Giuliani	3	11	30	9	37	11	15
Independent	Dinkins	9	9	4	8	5	27	8
Independent	Giuliani	1	7	27	16	19	21	14
Democrat	Dinkins	81	53	12	25	16	34	42
Democrat	Giuliani	2	14	26	41	19	3	18

Source: *New York Times*/CBS exit poll, 1989 mayoral election; N = 2,109; unweighted data

[a]Totals may not equal 100 due to rounding.

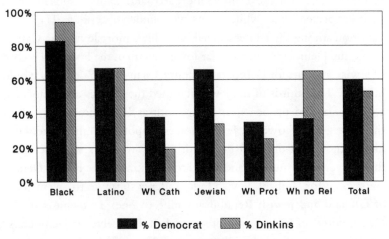

FIGURE 6.4
DEMOCRATIC PARTY ID AND VOTE
1989 by Group

Source: *New York Times*/CBS exit poll, 1989 mayoral election
N = 2,109

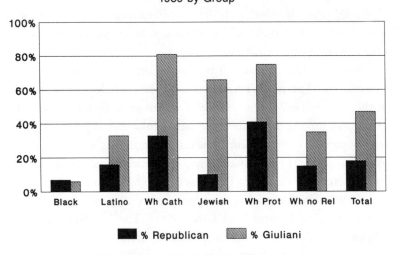

FIGURE 6.5
REPUBLICAN PARTY ID AND VOTE
1989 by Group

Source: *New York Times*/CBS exit poll, 1989 mayoral election
N = 2,109

identification with the Democratic party and Latinos subscribed at their "expected" rate, white voters were undersubscribed. There was variation among the whites as well, with Jews more loyal than Catholics to the Democrats, but at a far lower rate than the historical record of Jewish support for Democratic candidates in New York City would indicate. Two-thirds of the Jews identified themselves as Democrats, a quarter as Independents, and one-tenth as Republicans. In *each* of these categories, however, Jewish voters supported Giuliani over Dinkins, although at different rates. For every two Jews who identified themselves as Democrats and voted for Dinkins, three Jewish Democrats voted for Giuliani. Jewish Independents split two to one in favor of Giuliani and Jewish Republicans nine to one. Two-thirds of the Jewish voters of New York City identified themselves as Democrats, yet two-thirds of the Jewish voters of New York City voted for Giuliani.

The behavior of the white Catholics was less inconsistent with party identification, mostly because they were more evenly distributed among the Democratic, Independent, and Republican categories. Just over a third of the white Catholics identified with the Democrats, with their vote going more than two to one to the Republican Giuliani, a slightly higher rate than among Jewish voters. Most of the white Catholics who identified with the Republicans (a third of their total) voted for Giuliani, as did the Independents. In all, 81 percent of white Catholics supported Giuliani.

White Protestants (only 8 percent of the total) were 41 percent Republican, 35 percent Democrat, and 24 percent Independent. In each of these categories, they supported Giuliani more than Dinkins. The Democrats among the white Protestants broke only slightly for Giuliani (19 percent to 16 percent), but the Independents were about four to one in favor of Giuliani and the Republicans about ten to one. In all, 75 percent of the white Protestants voted for Giuliani.

Whites who identify with no religion are a small (3 percent) but important group in New York City politics. They are probably more influential in the city's cultural and social circles than their number alone would indicate. Hence their pattern of party and candidate support is especially interesting. This group behaved differently from

much of the rest of the white population. Whereas most whites identified with the Democrats but did not vote for the Democratic candidate
Dinkins, this group had the reverse pattern: only a little more than a
third of this white-no-religion group identified themselves as Democrats (and almost half as Independents), yet two-thirds of them voted
for Dinkins.

LOYALISTS AND DEFECTORS

The 1989 mayoral election featured near-unanimous black support for
the Democratic candidate and the defection of a sizable proportion of
white voters in a heavily Democratic city to the Republican candidate.
We shall investigate the implications of these shifts by studying both
the Democrats who strayed and those who stayed.

The issues reported by white Democrats who defected to Giuliani
as influencing their vote closely resembled those reported by white
Republicans who voted for Giuliani: drug abuse and corruption (see
Table 6.3). By way of contrast, white Democrats who stuck by Din-
kins appeared to have had issue priorities quite similar to those of white
Republicans who defected to Dinkins: homelessness and education.

A similar pattern exists when candidate characteristics are examined (see Table 6.3). The Democratic defectors fixed on the same
candidate attributes that Giuliani Republicans found important, honesty and the likelihood that the candidate would be tough on crime.
The small number of Republicans who defected to Dinkins, on the
other hand, had distinctly different candidate attributes in mind than
did their Republican loyalist counterparts, being far more concerned
with the candidates' ability to reduce racial divisions and to care about
people like the respondent.

This suggests that Giuliani benefited greatly from the white population's concerns about drug abuse, corruption, and crime. His campaign played to those issues and to candidate attributes relevant to
those issues, and it was effective. This underlying anxiety is reflected
in the fact that within each set of party identifiers, Giuliani voters were

Table 6.3

**Opinions of Whites by Vote for
Mayor and Party Identification**
(cell entries are percents)[a]

Party Identification Vote for Mayor	Democrat		Republican		Total
	Dinkins	Giuliani	Dinkins	Giuliani	Sample
Percent Mentioning:					
Issues					
Drug abuse	11	26	9	23	23
Homelessness	15	7	32	5	20
Education	15	12	14	8	20
Corruption	6	19	6	21	17
Candidate Attributes					
Honesty	16	37	0	38	27
Tough on Criminals	2	31	6	33	20
Competence	17	22	17	22	19
Cares about people like me	7	6	15	1	7
Reduce racial divisions	12	1	20	0	7
Party of candidate	12	5	4	8	6
Race of candidate	2	1	9	1	3
Optimistic about city's future	56	46	47	36	49

Source: *New York Times*/CBS election day poll (*N* = 1,008)
[a]Percentages may add up to more than 100% as respondents were allowed to give up
to two responses.

substantially less likely to be optimistic about the city's future than were those who voted for Dinkins (see Table 6.3).

To the extent that Dinkins was able to retain the loyalty of white Democrats and cause white Republicans to defect (in the latter case, only to a small degree), Dinkins appears to have projected successfully the desire of his supporters to identify with a caring and compassionate candidate who could identify with the downtrodden and conciliate racial conflicts. While these appeals were not sufficient to win a majority of the white vote, or even of the white Democratic vote, they were sufficient (given Dinkins's effective mobilization of his core constituency and Latinos) to win the election. And that after all is the goal of electoral politics.

ANATOMY OF THE SHIFT

Historically, except for moments of internal dissension and challenge from a fusion opponent, the Democratic nominee for mayor of New York City has been able to count on the overwhelming support of Democratic identifiers and on a substantial Independent vote as well. Clearly, this did not happen among white voters in the 1989 mayoral election. What then was the relative importance of various factors in determining this shift?

Two elements are quite clear: racial mistrust and party identification. For whites, as noted in chapter 5, it was almost a necessity, although by no means sufficient, condition that Dinkins be perceived as likely to be fair to whites as well as blacks for the respondent to vote for Dinkins. The lack of race-based mistrust was a primary, though not the complete, explanation for white support of Dinkins. While party identification was a far less effective basis for predicting the vote in the 1989 election than in most New York City mayoral elections, white Democratic identifiers still voted for Dinkins at 1.6 times the rate that white Independents did.

We assessed the relative weights of factors bearing on this shift using linear regression analysis. However, we excluded the dominant elements of racial mistrust and party identification from the equations in order to reveal the effect of other variables. We have therefore treated racial mistrust and partisanship as exogenous variables. We analyzed white Democrats and white Independents separately. (Because 93 percent of whites who did not trust Dinkins to treat both blacks and whites fairly voted for Giuliani, we restricted the analyses to those whites who believed that Dinkins would treat both blacks and whites fairly.)

White Democrats who believed that Dinkins would treat both blacks and whites fairly (56 percent of all white Democrats) and white

Independents with the same belief about Dinkins (55 percent of all white Independents) thus constituted the crucial group that might tip the balance between the two candidates. In each instance, the dependent variable was the respondent's vote for Dinkins or Giuliani. The independent variables were:

- Issues mentioned as most important
  Homelessness
  Education
  Drugs
  Corruption
- Candidate attributes mentioned as most important
  Honesty
  Cares about people like me
  Has the ability to reduce racial divisions
  Would be tough on crime
- Campaigner impacts
  George Bush
  Jesse Jackson
  Edward Koch
  Jackie Mason
  Sonny Carson
  Mario Cuomo
- Demographics

The relative impacts (betas) of each statistically significant variable are presented in Table 6.4. For each of the populations studied, the variables account for a substantial amount of variance beyond what racial mistrust and party identification explain (32 percent in the case of white Democrats and 35 percent in the case of the white Independents). Moreover, based on the stepwise regression used, no single variable accounted for the bulk of the explained variance.

With racial mistrust and party identification treated as exogenous variables, the most powerful of the remaining variables for both white Democrats (Section A of Table 6.4) and for white Independents (Section B of Table 6.4) was whether the respondent wanted a candidate who would be tough on crime. In both groups, that worked to the advantage of Giuliani. Dinkins's strength in these categories derived

Table 6.4

Impacts of the Variables[a] (betas) for Those Believing Dinkins Would Treat Both Blacks and Whites Fairly

A. White Democrats

Variable	beta	Level of Significance
Tough on crime	.35	.0000
Corruption	.17	.0013
Reduce racial divisions	−.13	.0130
Drugs	.13	.0138
Honesty	.12	.0267
Education	.12	.0283
Homelessness	−.11	.0351
Adjusted R^2 = .32		

B. White Independents

Variable	beta	Level of Significance
Tough on crime	.29	.0000
Reduce racial divisions	−.27	.0001
Corruption	.24	.0006
Homelessness	−.17	.0097
Honesty	.12	.0267
Adjusted R^2 = .35		

[a]A negative sign (−) means that the variable worked against voting for Giuliani.

from his perceived ability to reduce racial divisions. At much weaker levels, Dinkins also had respondents' concerns about homelessness working for him. Countering that at much stronger levels in both groups, however, was the corruption issue working for Giuliani.

Only one demographic variable, education, showed at any level of significance above .05, and that worked to Giuliani's advantage only among white Democrats. One may speculate that the more powerful issue and candidate attribute variables masked the impact of the demographic variables or were their antecedents. However, Table 6.5 indicates that these speculations are not well founded, since the correlations (Pearson's r) between the variables are small. In no case did the demographic variables correlate strongly with the dependent variable, the

Table 6.5

Correlations of Demographic Variables
with Vote and Major Independent Variables

A. White Democrats[a]

Regression Variables	Demographic Variables[b]			
	Sex	Age	Education	Family Income
Vote	−.079	−.037	.221	.067
Tough on Crime	−.038	.065	.168	.149
Corruption	−.017	.046	.104	.067
Reduce racial				
divisions	.018	−.020	−.127	.006
Drugs	−.006	−.007	.031	−.046
Honesty	−.059	−.067	.088	.029
Homelessness	−.026	.050	−.030	.076

B. White Independents[a]

Regression Variables	Demographic Variables[b]			
	Sex	Age	Education	Family Income
Vote	.032	−.085	.181	.117
Tough on crime	−.041	.007	.164	.191
Corruption	−.012	.029	−.012	.012
Reduce racial				
divisions	−.009	−.020	.008	−.087
Honesty	−.074	−.105	.011	.111
Homelessness	.051	.302	−.102	−.117

[a]Those believing that Dinkins would treat both blacks and whites fairly.
[b]Education and family income dichotomized as close as possible to the median. Age dichotomized for maximum impact in two categories: 18–59 and above 60.

vote. Nor, with one notable exception, were demographic variables strongly correlated with any of the issue or candidate attributes that proved to be drivers in the regressions. (Among white Independents, being over sixty years of age was associated with concern about homelessness.)

Demographics were not absolutely unrelated to candidate preference, but the relations between them were weak, nonlinear, and inconsistent across the racial and ethnic groups we considered. For example, though support for Dinkins among nonblacks dropped as the level of

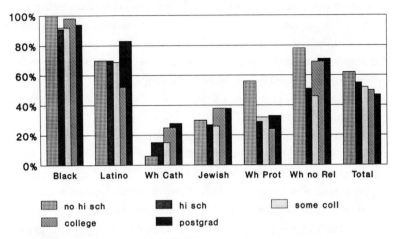

FIGURE 6.6
VOTE FOR DINKINS
by Education and Group

Source: *New York Times*/CBS exit poll, 1989 mayoral election
N = 2,109

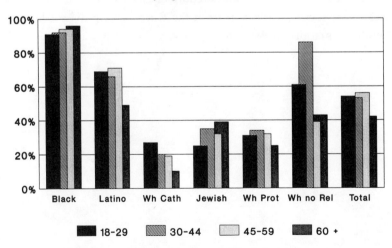

FIGURE 6.7
VOTE FOR DINKINS
by Age and Group

Source: *New York Times*/CBS exit poll, 1989 mayoral election
N = 2,109

education increased, the pattern of decline was reversed among Jews with a college education (see Figure 6.6). Similarly, with regard to age, Dinkins's share of the vote tended to decline with the age of the respondents (with occasional reversals and discontinuities), except among Jews over sixty, who gave Dinkins 39 percent of their support compared with 25 percent for Jews between the ages of eighteen and twenty-nine (see Figure 6.7).

There are two problems with attempting to discern and interpret such anomalies. First, they are based on quite small cell sizes. Second, one runs the risk of losing sight of the forest for the trees. Focusing on the forest, it is clear that ethnic divisions overwhelmed social class variables in the 1989 New York City mayoral elections.

In sum, defections from traditional Democratic voting patterns in 1989 had strong roots in race-based mistrust. However, fear about crime and a weariness with corruption also worked heavily against Dinkins as a black Democrat. Working for him among whites was Democratic party identification, concern for reducing racial divisions, and concern about homelessness. In conjunction with Dinkins's strong turnout in the black community and the Latino shift in his favor, the fact that a substantial minority of white Democrats and Independents trusted Dinkins, wanted him to reduce racial tensions, and address the legacy of social polarization from the Koch years provided Dinkins with the margin necessary for victory.

7

THE POLITICAL ECOLOGY OF NEIGHBORHOODS

As Tip O'Neill, the former Speaker of the House of Representatives, was fond of observing, "all politics is local politics." This is certainly true for New York City. Although media attention focuses on citywide trends, politicians must build their electoral majorities on the basis of highly varied local neighborhoods. Certain traits, such as race, religion, ancestry, and life-style, cut across the city and create bonds among similar neighborhoods. But while shorthand concepts like "Italians" or "outer-borough Jews" capture certain realities, they also mask differences within these groups as they are expressed in specific places.

Every area of New York City has its unique aspects and combines the ingredients of New York City's rich cultural heritage in a somewhat different way. As recently as 1989, large areas of Brooklyn, Queens, and the Bronx were independent villages. Neighborhoods have kept their distinctness as different clusters of ethnic groups, or even factions of ethnic groups with distinct political cultures, have settled in different areas. As waves of demographic change wash over the city, neighborhoods continually take on new cultural identities. New York is, as Mayor Dinkins is fond of saying, "a gorgeous mosaic."

The organization of New York's political system reinforces this fragmentation. To begin with, New York City has five political systems rather than one, since each county (or borough) has its own county party organization, leadership, and rules. "Tammany Hall" actually applies only to Manhattan; Democratic bosses in other boroughs, such as Ed Flynn and Charles Buckley in the Bronx or John H. McCooey in Brooklyn, have sometimes been just as important to New York's political development as Tammany's William Marcy Tweed or Richard Croker.

The smallest unit of political party organization within the city's five boroughs are its sixty New York State Assembly Districts (ADs), which perform the function of wards. Each AD, which had 1980 populations of about 118,000, in turn had roughly 100 election districts (EDs), or precincts, with an average of about 500 voters. (There were 5,300 EDs in New York City in the mid-1980s.) Each AD elects one male and one female party district leader, or more if the AD has been broken into several parts (as in Manhattan and Queens). The district leaders in turn elect the county leader, the modern equivalent of the old-fashioned "boss." In most ADs, including black and Latino ADs, the district leaders do not face challenges for reelection and serve as the political captains of the county organization. Many are legislators or relatives of legislators.

In the West Side and Greenwich Village in Manhattan and the brownstone neighborhoods of Brooklyn, however, white reformers have challenged and displaced the regulars for either district leaderships or the assembly nomination. In Bedford-Stuyvesant and Crown

Heights, black insurgent reformers have taken over district leaderships or assembly positions. In other cases, two "regular" factions have competed for power, as in the jockeying between the Howard Golden and the Tony Genovesi factions of the Brooklyn organization. In general, as chapter 1 noted, these organizations are weaker and less central to the political system than their counterpart organizations a generation ago.

Nevertheless, to a degree that might surprise those who classify New York as a "reformed" city, regular Democratic political clubs still hold the district leaderships and produce the candidates who hold state assembly and city council seats. These basic building blocks of politics, along with the reform clubs, both reflect and shape the political cultures of their neighborhoods. A fully developed study of New York City politics must, therefore, not only look at citywide trends but analyze how they are rooted in the political cultures of specific places.

At the time of the 1982 reapportionment, the Democrats held the assembly and the governor's office and drew the AD boundaries to maximize the electoral chances of incumbent assembly Democrats while carving out some districts to satisfy the gradually growing electoral numbers of blacks and Puerto Ricans. In return for this right, the Republicans, who controlled the state senate, were allowed to redistrict the senate seats. Republican Bay Ridge in Brooklyn thus had one senate district but was divided among several ADs.

Our research on the 1989 mayoral primary campaign focused on seven ADs selected by two basic criteria, race/ethnicity and political organization. We selected three white ADs, two black ADs, and two Latino ADs for intensive scrutiny. The white ADs included the liberal, cosmopolitan, upper-middle-class 67th AD on Manhattan's Upper West side; the more conservative, lower-middle-class, Jewish 45th AD stretching from the southern boundary of Flatbush to Manhattan Beach in Brooklyn; and the 31st AD in the Queens neighborhoods of Richmond Hill and Ozone Park, which was heavily Italian American and conservative. These ADs encompassed the spectrum of white voters and varied from the reform-oriented 67th to the more regular Democratic 45th and 31st.

The black ADs included the 70th in Harlem, home to the city's black Democratic establishment, and the 43rd in Crown Heights, Brooklyn, a heavily West Indian area represented by a member of the coalition of Brooklyn black insurgents.[1] The Latino ADs (the 53rd and the 73rd) had the two highest percentages of Puerto Ricans in New York City. The 73rd AD in the South Bronx was represented by an assemblyman who had been at odds with the Bronx County Democratic Organization early in his career, while the 53rd AD in Bushwick was a solid part of the Brooklyn regular organization. Table 7.1 shows the racial and ethnic makeup of these ADs according to the 1980 census. By the 1989 elections, the details had changed, but the general patterns were similar.

While each AD and the neighborhoods which comprise it have distinctive characteristics, each shares certain qualities with other ADs

Table 7.1

Demography of Population in Selected ADs, 1980
(percents)

AD	Total Population	non-Latino White	Jewish[a]	Italian	non-Latino Black	Asian	Latino
31	118,210	80	10	23	2	3	15
43	117,416	9	2	1	79	1	9
45	117,408	92	29	16	1	3	4
53	117,421	19	3	10	18	1	61
67	118,949	75	23	3	9	2	13
70	118,963	2	0	0	77	1	19
73	116,902	4	1	1	36	1	58
(Study ADs)							
Av.	117,720	34	10	8	36	2	28
(60 ADs)							
Av.	117,853	51	10	11	24	1	21
St Dev	761	32	8	11	26	.5	17

Source: New York State Legislative Task Force on Reapportionment
[a]The census does not ask about religion. Percent of Eastern European extraction was used as a surrogate for Jews. Comparison with the survey results and other estimates indicate that this surrogate measure provided a reasonable estimate of the number of Jews.

in the city. For example, the Upper West Side of Manhattan (AD 67) is quite distinctively upper-middle-class, well-educated, liberal, and reform-oriented—classic Woody Allen territory. In this regard, it resembles the 61st and 64th ADs in Manhattan and parts of the 51st and 52nd in Brooklyn, like Brooklyn Heights and Park Slope. Similarly, our other ADs resemble other outer-borough Jewish, outer-borough white Catholic, Latino, and black ADs. For example, eleven other outer-borough Italian ADs resembled the 31st; a net of eight ADs resembled the predominantly native-born black 70th AD. In other words, the seven ADs in our study represented much of the city.

THE STUDY ADS

The study ADs (see Table 7.1) contained more blacks and Latinos and fewer whites than the citywide average for all ADs, but close to the average of two crucial white voting blocs, Jews and Italians. The higher the ratio of the standard deviation to the average, the more concentrated a given group is in a few ADs. Table 7.1 shows that blacks were most concentrated, Latinos less so but still clustered, and whites were more evenly spread. Interestingly, among whites, both Jews and Italians were relatively concentrated, and Italians were more concentrated than any other group but blacks.

These raw population figures do not translate directly into the voting population in Democratic primaries. This fact is central to understanding New York City's politics. As the previous chapters have described, many factors mediate between population and voting. Because blacks and Latinos are substantially younger and less likely to be citizens than whites, fewer blacks and Latinos are eligible to vote. Since they are more likely to be working-class or poor, and to have less education, even eligible blacks and Latinos may be less likely to register. But those who do register are more likely to be Democrats. Figure 7.1 shows the racial breakdown in the seven study ADs of the 1980 voting age population, and Figure 7.2 presents the counterpart distribution of the "prime voters" in these ADs (those who regularly

FIGURE 7.1
VOTING AGE POPULATION
by AD and Group

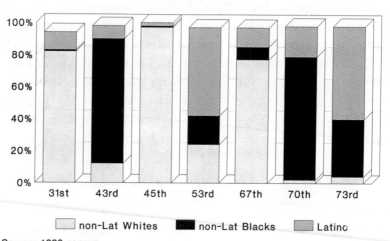

Source: 1980 census
Asians and others excluded.

vote in Democratic primaries), whom we surveyed at the time of the 1989 Democratic primary.[2]

Figures 7.1 and 7.2 reveal that considerably fewer Latinos appeared among Democratic prime voters compared to their voting age population and that the Democratic prime voters contained more whites and blacks than the general voting age population. The South Bronx (AD 73) was, according to the 1980 census, the most heavily Latino area of New York City, yet blacks actually outnumbered Latinos among the prime voters in this district. Latinos were also heavily underrepresented in heavily Latino Bushwick (AD 53) as well as Harlem (AD 70). Latinos made up 55 percent of the voting age population in Bushwick and 19 percent in Harlem, but only 45 percent of Bushwick's prime voters and 7 percent of Harlem's.

In the black and Latinos districts, women made up almost two-thirds of the Democratic voters in the black and Latino districts, yet male assembly members still represented those ADs.[3] In black areas,

FIGURE 7.2
PRIME VOTERS BY AD AND GROUP

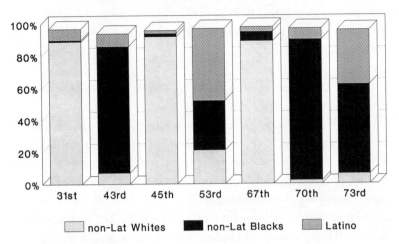

Source: Wagner Institute 1989 Democratic prime voter survey
Asians and others not reported
$N = 2,107$

blacks generally made up more of the electorate than they had of the 1980 population, reflecting, among other things, continued racial change in these ADs.

The seven assembly districts in our study typified the critical voting groups in New York City politics: white Manhattan liberals, outer-borough Jews and Italians, native-born and West Indian blacks, and Puerto Ricans. In the Democratic mayoral primary of 1989, two of the ADs could be counted as stalwart supporters of Mayor Edward I. Koch, namely Midwood/Kings Highway (AD 45) and Richmond Hill (AD 31). Both had middle-class, white ethnic populations: the 45th had the highest percentage of East European ancestries that characterize most Jews in New York City, and the 31st was predominantly Italian. Two of the ADs could be assumed to be solidly behind the black challenger, David N. Dinkins, namely Harlem (AD 70) and Crown Heights (AD 43).

The three others represented potentially decisive swing groups:

white liberals on Manhattan's Upper West Side (AD 67) and the Latino districts (ADs 53 and 73) that had gone strongly for Koch in 1985 but had swung toward Jesse Jackson in the 1988 presidential primary. The political battles of 1989 would be fought on this terrain.

THE BLACK ADS: HARLEM (70TH), CROWN HEIGHTS (43RD)

Harlem (70th AD). The 70th Assembly District stretches north from the top end of Central Park and extends west to the Hudson above the Upper West Side and east to the East River above East Harlem. It is separated from the upper Manhattan districts of Inwood and Washington Heights along 143rd Street, roughly the boundary between Harlem's black and Inwood's predominantly Dominican populations. Though much of Harlem was a white ethnic working-class area with many Jewish and Italian residents through the 1920s, it had emerged as New York's largest African American community by the 1930s. By the 1950s it was solidly black; 125th Street served as the black community's main commercial artery (though most businesses were still owned by whites), and it remains the site of the recently rehabilitated Apollo Theater and a New York State office building.

New York's first black officials were elected from Harlem in the mid-1930s. The first blacks elected to the city council, the Reverend Adam Clayton Powell and Benjamin Davis, a member of the Communist party, were insurgents, but Harlem also had a strong regular Democratic political organization headed by J. Raymond Jones, "the Harlem Fox."[4] (His home club, the Carver Democratic Club, elected the late Daniel L. Burrows to become the second black state assemblyman in 1938; Burrows later introduced his future son-in-law, David N. Dinkins, to politics through the club.)

The Carver Club's connection to the Manhattan county organization, together with the growing importance of black votes, enabled many of Harlem's regular black politicians to achieve upward mobility. Dinkins became an assemblyman, board of elections member, and county clerk through Jones's auspices; the Carver Club's other alumni include federal judge Constance Baker Motley, former borough president and mayoral candidate Percy Sutton, and U.S. Congressman Charles Rangel.

In recent decades, however, Harlem entered a period of severe decline. Between 1970 and 1980, it lost a large fraction of its population and experienced extensive housing abandonment. At the same time, boosted by heavy immigration from the West Indies, the black population of Brooklyn (as well as Southeastern Queens and the Northern Bronx) grew rapidly and displaced Harlem as the center of the black population in New York City. Despite the continued political successes and citywide influence of the "Harlem Establishment," emerging leaders from Brooklyn and Queens have gradually begun to challenge Harlem's leaders as political spokespersons for New York's African Americans.

Crown Heights (43d AD). Brooklyn's counterpart to Harlem as the center of black settlement has been Bedford-Stuyvesant in north-central Brooklyn. Bed-Stuy developed somewhat later than Harlem, becoming a majority black neighborhood during World War II. As Brooklyn's black population grew during the 1950s and 1960s, the black community pushed southward into Crown Heights, formerly a middle-class Jewish area with large and impressive homes on the side streets off Eastern Parkway, which ran east-west along the ridge that gave the area its name. Crown Heights had originally been a center for the growth of Jewish political leadership on the borough, city, and state level. Illustrious alumni of its own formidable Madison Democratic Club include former assembly speaker Stanley Steingut, former state comptroller Arthur Levitt, and former mayor Abraham Beame.

With the increased pace of West Indian immigration and racial change in the 1960s and 1970s, however, Crown Heights increasingly became a neighborhood for black immigrants from Jamaica, Barbados, and Trinidad; the Jewish population gravitated toward the southern periphery of the borough. While the Afro-Caribbeans of Crown Heights were poorer than the previous white residents, they separated themselves somewhat from the native-born blacks to the north in Bed-Stuy and created a vibrant immigrant community striving for upward mobility and, for some, achieving the status of middle-class home owners. North-south streets like Nostrand Avenue became major immigrant commercial districts. As better-off blacks moved steadily southward, the northern part of the neighborhood became relatively less well off. Yet even the northern part of Crown Heights did not experience the wholesale property abandonment and depopulation that occurred in central Harlem or parts of Bedford-Stuyvesant.

In the middle of Crown Heights south of Eastern Parkway could be found the world headquarters and home colony of the Lubavitcher sect of Hasidic Jews, existing somewhat uneasily side-by-side with Crown Heights' West Indian population. No less incongruous, an exact replication of the red-brick home of the spiritual leader of the group (the Rebbe) towers over the gray stucco structures in Kfar Habad, outside of Tel Aviv, Israel. The Rebbe has never been to Israel, but his followers there evidently feel closer to him because of this structure replicated from Crown Heights.

Like Harlem and Bed-Stuy, Crown Heights was the scene of an early attempt by blacks to take power in the local Democratic party. A biracial, left-leaning insurgent group, the Unity Democratic Club, launched this attempt in the late 1950s. Its candidate, Thomas Jones (unrelated to Harlem's J. Raymond Jones) went on to be assemblyman and later a superior and appellate court judge. Though the Unity Club died out after its leader, Jones, left politics for the bench in the early 1960s, Crown Heights is currently represented by a black assemblyman associated with Brooklyn's black insurgent coalition whose father is a well-known minister. He has, however, also made overtures to the county Democratic organization. Compared to Harlem, therefore, Crown Heights is more middle-class, much more West Indian, yet less aligned with the regular Democratic party.

THE LATINO ADS: THE SOUTH BRONX (73RD) AND BUSHWICK (53RD)

The South Bronx (73rd AD). Movies like *Fort Apache* and books like *The Bonfire of the Vanities* have made the South Bronx a national symbol of urban decline. Indeed, both Presidents Carter and Reagan used the South Bronx as a setting in their campaigns. The area began life quite differently, however. In the 1920s, it had been a major expansion zone for upwardly mobile Jews seeking a way out of the crowded districts of the Lower East Side. But as the more affluent populations moved northward along the elegant Grand Concourse, the South Bronx developed as a solidly lower-middle-class apartment house district.

All this changed beginning in the 1950s, however. The construction of the Cross Bronx Expressway connecting the George Washington Bridge to the west with the New England Thruway to the east displaced five thousand households and demolished the heart of the neighborhood. A number of large public housing projects were also constructed in the neighborhood. Simultaneously, the racial composition of the South Bronx changed dramatically as the white population departed, the Puerto Rican population increased rapidly, and blacks were moved into the public housing projects. The 1970s saw a spiral of arson for profit, disinvestment, and abandonment of the South Bronx housing stock, causing the area's population to decline rapidly, leaving behind perhaps the poorest constituency bases of any assembly district in New York City. Outside the relatively stable housing projects, the decimated private housing is predominantly Puerto Rican.

The powerful Bronx County Democratic organization has long held sway over almost every assembly district. Political opposition occasionally arises, as in former assemblyman Jose Serrano's initial attempt to stake out an independent political position in the 73rd AD. More recently, however, Serrano made a deal with the regulars to get their endorsement to succeed Robert Garcia as the U.S. congressman representing the southern portion of the Bronx. The district leaders in the 73rd have always been allied with the country organization. This pattern of a successful insurgent making peace with the regular county party organization has been repeated many times, despite the overall weakening of the regular county party organizations over time. The fact that its assemblyman has been at all independent differentiates the South Bronx from another Puerto Rican neighborhood, Bushwick.

Bushwick (43rd AD). Bushwick lies on the northern edge of Brooklyn adjacent to Queens. It was originally settled in the late nineteenth century by Germans, who provided both the workers in and part of the market for Brooklyn's previously extensive brewing industry. By the 1930s, as Italians succeeded the Germans, Bushwick entered a half-century of decline. After World War II, the neighborhood became increasingly Puerto Rican, although traces of the previous Italian population, including the mafia, persist. Today, like the South Bronx, Bushwick is one of the poorest parts of New York City. It remains an expanse of dense, old tenement houses, often of wood frame construction. It shows no signs of political independence; instead, it is dominated by one of the most regular of Brooklyn's political clubs.

THE WHITE ADS: THE UPPER WEST SIDE (67TH), MIDWOOD/KINGS HIGHWAY (45TH), AND RICHMOND HILL (31ST).

The Upper West Side (67th AD). The Upper West Side is Manhattan's classic cosmopolitan intellectual neighborhood. Stretching from Central Park West to the Hudson River from 54th Street to 95th Street, the 67th AD contains large apartment buildings along the avenues and row houses along the streets. The former were built largely for and by the upwardly mobile Russian Jewish managerial and professional stratum that prospered in New York from the 1920s into the 1950s. After some relative loss of prestige, the area once more attracted a broad range of younger professionals in the 1970s and experienced an explosive gentrification in such areas as Columbus Avenue during the 1980s. The impressive buildings along Central Park West house some of the most affluent people in New York, though they are more likely to be lawyers, artists, writers, or movie stars rather than the bankers and corporate titans who inhabit the Upper East Side across the park.

The Upper West Side has traditionally been one of the major concentrations of reform Democrats in New York City, the sort of activists analyzed by James Q. Wilson in *The Amateur Democrat.*[5] Its district leaders include some of the most hard-line reformers in New York; they have been in office so long that they now constitute an entrenched local establishment.

Midwood/Kings Highway (45th AD). This area on the southern reaches of Brooklyn contrasts with the Upper West Side. Although it too has apartment buildings along its major avenues, most of the district is far less dense than Manhattan, and some parts have impressive single family homes. For the most part, however, the Midwood/ Kings Highway area was settled by upwardly mobile lower-middle-class Jews escaping from congested neighborhoods in Manhattan and the northern part of Brooklyn. In the 1930s Sheepshead Bay, at the southern end of the district, was a sleepy fishing village and resort; by the 1950s construction of the Belt Parkway had opened the area to more intense development. By the late 1960s it had become a receiving area for households moving south from Flatbush, which was becoming increasingly black and West Indian. As a result, the district's population tends to be much older than that of either the black and Latino districts or the gentrifying Upper West Side. It is also the most heavily Jewish district in New York as measured by Russian and Polish ancestry in the 1980 census. Culturally and politically, the district is thus more conservative than the more cosmopolitan Jews of the Upper West Side.[6]

The 45th AD has tended to align itself with the county regulars in Brooklyn. It was, for example, an electoral stronghold for Mayor Abraham Beame in the 1977 Democratic primary. Though its current assemblyman, Daniel Feldman, was first elected as a reformer, he now works with the regulars. The membership of the club is mixed, however, and some prominent reformers do live in the district. Most important, this area represents the heart of the Koch constituency, older outer-borough middle- or lower-middle-class Jews living in apartment buildings.

Richmond Hill (31st AD). Richmond Hill in Queens is even less densely settled than the Midwood/Kings Highway part of Brooklyn; it is made up of detached or semidetached single family or small multifamily houses, many of which are of frame construction built up after the turn of the century. Its residents have a similar social class to that of the 45th, but Italian Americans constitute the majority of Richmond Hill. As a result, it is even more conservative. Indeed, the 31st AD was one of the few in New York City to vote for George

Bush in 1988. However, during the 1980s the area has felt some of the influx of Latino immigrants that has changed other parts of Queens. It remains Catholic and conservative, though less monolithic than in the past.

The district is represented by an Italian American who won office on both the Democratic and the Conservative party lines. Its two political clubs are associated with the county Democratic organizations, though they are sometimes at odds with each other. Politically, it thus resembles such other Italian American enclaves as Bensonhurst, Staten Island, or the eastern sections of the Bronx.

THE COMPOSITION OF THE STUDY ADS

These ADs illustrate the striking variety of neighborhoods in New York City and, in some areas, the great variation within neighborhoods. One half of a block may differ demographically from the other half, and of course the individuals in any given block may differ from one another. Politicians and their advisers, however, think in terms of larger units of analysis and classify neighborhoods in terms of their dominant ethnic groups. In that sense, intraneighborhood variety is eclipsed by shorthand description. New York's neighborhoods are discussed as if they were ethnically homogeneous, containing one, and at most two, dominant groups. For the purposes of economy and coherence, we shall mirror that usage.

Figure 7.3 portrays the ethnicity and religion that our sample of prime Democratic voters declared before the 1989 mayoral primary. AD 31 was predominantly white Catholic, ADs 43 and 70 black, and AD 45 Jewish. Three ADs in our sample were more "mixed," that is, made up of groups of different background. "Mixed" in New York City at the beginning of the 1990s must not be confused with "integrated."

The 53rd and 73rd ADs each had lower-class black and Latino populations, while the 67th AD was composed primarily of upper-middle-class Jews and whites with no religious affiliation. These individuals gave the 67th AD a reputation for progressive liberal politics.

FIGURE 7.3
GROUPS IN STUDY ADS

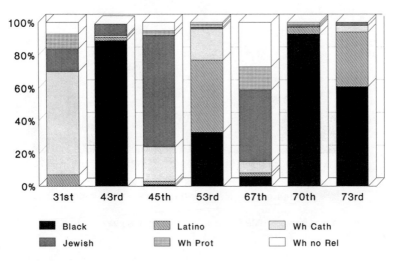

Source: Wagner Institute 1989 Democratic prime voter survey
N = 2,107

Ethnic differences were related to social differences. The samples in the seven ADs varied greatly from one another by educational background: only 9 percent of the Bushwick respondents (53rd AD) were college graduates, compared with three out of four respondents in Manhattan's upper West Side 67th AD (see Figure 7.4).

The variation of social class identification was also pronounced. A third of the black and Latino 53rd, 70th, and 73rd ADs declared themselves middle-class, compared to two-thirds in the white Catholic 31st and the Jewish 45th. More than half the respondents in the affluent 67th AD also identified themselves as members of the middle class. In the black and Latino ADs, about a third of the respondents reported membership in the working class.

The age structure also varied greatly (see Figure 7.5): in the 45th AD of Midwood/Kings Highway in Brooklyn, the majority of respondents were above sixty-five years old; in the 67th AD of West Side Manhattan, the thirtysomething and fortysomething ages predomi-

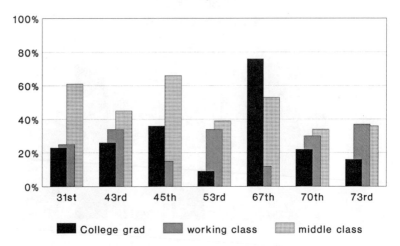

FIGURE 7.4
EDUCATION AND SOCIAL CLASS
in Study ADs

Source: Wagner Institute 1989 Democratic prime voter survey
N = 2,107

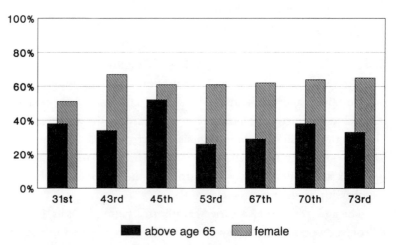

FIGURE 7.5
GENDER AND AGE
in Study ADs

Source: Wagner Institute 1989 Democratic prime voter survey
N = 2,107

nated among our respondents. Females accounted for almost two-thirds of the sample in every AD except the 31st AD of Richmond Hill in Queens, in which the gender ratio was about even, consistent with the gender composition of their registered voters.

VOTING IN THE ADS

Democratic political clubs in New York City's assembly districts, whether regular or insurgent, seek to maximize votes for their candidates while discouraging primary challenges and swamping their Republican opponents, if any. In the past, the regular clubs wielded great influence, if not outright control, over vote-getting and the policy influence and patronage that flow from putting elected officials in office. Over time, insurgent clubs have also built power bases in some ADs. Our survey data allow us to trace the effects of these basic patterns of political cohesion and organization. Specifically, we can explore how the dominance of a given demographic group relates to the vote decisions of respondents who are members of that group or outside it. We can also explore the relevance of local-level political organization.

Generally, people choose to live in a neighborhood that reinforces their political attitudes and preferences and may indeed help shape and develop them. Not incidentally, these neighborhoods also reflect the economic, religious, and social circumstances of their inhabitants. Given this background, one is not surprised by the mayoral candidates that each of the study ADs favored. Figure 7.6 illustrates the vivid differences in support for George Bush in 1988 across the seven ADs. Bush won 29.7 percent of the vote in New York City, but our study ADs ranged from a high 53.7 percent in the 31st to a low of 5.6 percent in Harlem (the 70th).[7]

On the eve of the Democratic primary, the ADs also varied greatly in their support for Koch or Dinkins. Dinkins did exceedingly well in black majority ADs, and Koch did well in outer-borough white ADs. The contest was much closer in the swing ADs. The ADs supported Dinkins in roughly the same rank order as their percentage of black

FIGURE 7.6
BUSH VOTE, 1988
by AD

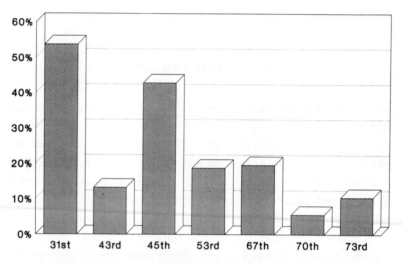

Source: New York City Board of Elections

voters (see Table 7.2A and B). The 70th AD in Harlem was most supportive, with 80 percent declaring for Dinkins, followed by 70 percent in the 43rd in Brooklyn's Crown Heights and 62 percent in the South Bronx 73rd AD. Conversely, the white outer-borough ADs supported Koch, just as they had Bush. Respondents in the heavily Jewish 45th AD supported Koch by 63 percent, while he got 58 percent of the prime voters in the predominantly white Catholic 31st.

The race was more competitive in the Latino ADs and the Upper West Side. Bushwick (the 53rd) favored Dinkins over Koch by the narrow margin of 41 to 36. This AD also generated the most "undecided" answers, at 22 percent. In the liberal 67th AD, where Jews and whites who said they had no religion made up two-thirds of the sample, 56 percent said that they would vote for Dinkins and 32 percent for Koch; it had the fewest "undecided" voters.

The election results closely followed these dispositions, spelling defeat for Mayor Koch. Dinkins's share of the two-candidate vote in the study assembly districts by the four largest ethnic and religious groups is portrayed graphically in Figure 7.7. (Groups with fewer than ten respondents in an AD were excluded.)

Did a more homogeneous environment increase the likelihood that out-group voters would support the candidate favored by the larger group? Did members of the nondominant groups feel free to express their political independence by preferring a different candidate? Did nondominant group members respond by expressing more indecision about their choice than did members of the dominant group?

Much of the variation across ADs can be explained by the ethnic composition of the AD: Jews and white Catholics gave Koch the strongest support, while Latinos and blacks supported Dinkins. But interesting deviations from this pattern also emerged. As the percentage of blacks in an AD decreased, the likelihood of blacks favoring

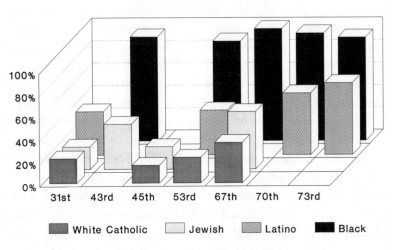

FIGURE 7.7
DINKINS VOTE IN PRIMARY
by Group and AD

Source: Wagner Institute 1989 Democratic prime voter survey
N = 2,107

Dinkins also decreased. For example, in the 93 percent black 70th AD, blacks chose Dinkins (rather than Koch, one of the other Democratic candidates, or no answer) by 83 percent; in the 89 percent black 43rd AD, only 83 percent of the black voters chose Dinkins (see Table 7.2D). (This may also suggest a slight difference between native-born and West Indian blacks.)

Of particular comparative interest are the 73rd and 53rd ADs. Blacks were a minority of the population in both, but formed a majority of the Democratic prime voters in the 73rd, but not in the 53rd. In the 53rd, Bushwick, blacks supported Dinkins by only 65 percent. This suggests that the concentration of blacks fostered uniformity of support for Dinkins and that being a minority within an AD where the majority favored Koch may have undermined support for Dinkins. Black support for Dinkins was also relatively low in the predominantly white ADs, though the sample of blacks was too small to be statistically reliable.

The contrast between the two Latino districts, the 73rd and the 53rd, suggests that differences in local political leadership across ADs of a given racial type may have a significant impact. Latinos were a majority of both the population and the prime voters of the 53rd, but they were less likely to support Dinkins than in the 73rd, where they were a minority of prime voters. Note, however, that the assembly district leadership strongly supported Dinkins in the 73rd but was more lukewarm in the 53rd.

For these two cases, then, Latino concentration among prime voters did not foster support for the black candidate. To the contrary, the 53rd's "machine" Democratic orientation appears to have bolstered support for Koch more than was true in Harlem or the South Bronx.

The pattern among whites also supports the notion that differences of AD political culture or political ecology helped to shape the overall vote. White Protestants were a minority everywhere, but they were much more favorably disposed to David Dinkins on the Upper West Side than anyone else. Similarly, whites reporting no religion were clustered in this area and strongly supported Dinkins.

Jews on the Upper West Side were also far more likely to support Dinkins than were Jews in any of the other neighborhoods where

Table 7.2

Dominant and Nondominant Group Voting by AD[a]

(percents; each AD has about 300 respondents; total 2,107)

	AD 31	AD 43	AD 45	AD 53	AD 67	AD 70	AD 73
A. Vote Intention for All Respondents							
Dinkins	21	70	18	41	56	80	62
Koch	58	13	63	36	32	6	17
undecided	21	18	19	22	13	14	21
B. Percent Black	1	85	2	35	6	91	61
C. Dominant Group							
dominant group	WCath	Blacks	Jews	Lat / Bl	Jew / WNR	Black	Bl / Lat
% dominant group in survey	63	89	68	44 / 33	44 / 27	93	61 / 33
D. Vote Intention in the Dominant Group							
Dinkins	17	76	16	33 / 65	44 / 70	83	74 / 49
Koch	60	6	64	49 / 8	43 / 22	4	7 / 28
E. Vote Intention for Respondents not from Dominant Group							
Dinkins	30	59	20	20	39	53	24
Koch	55	26	62	54	47	35	58
F. Undecided in the Dominant and Nondominant Groups							
dominant group	23	18	20	19	9	14	20
non-dominant group	15	15	18	26	14	12	18

Source: Wagner Institute 1989 Democratic prime voter survey

[a]Totals may not equal 100 due to rounding.

they were numerous. Given how strongly outer-borough Jews had previously supported Koch, it did not make much difference whether they were a minority in a white Catholic neighborhood (the 31st) or a majority in a neighborhood that also included white Catholics (the 45th); they remained staunch Koch supporters. (Unlike the difference between Harlem blacks and Crown Heights blacks, there did not seem to be a concentration effect among outer-borough Jews.) Among white Catholics, only those living in the Jewish AD seemed to favor Koch as much as the Jews did; elsewhere their support for him was more uniform and guarded.

These patterns show qualitative differences among the local political cultures of the ADs. Ethnic concentration of an AD promoted voting homogeneity, including those who were not in the majority group, even though they provided lower levels of support than did majority group members. The political orientation of the dominant group was also important. In the case of the 53rd AD, Bushwich, this worked against Dinkins and for Koch; in the Upper West Side, the reverse was true.

There is an interesting relationship between neighborhood ecology and the tendency of nonmajority group respondents to have made up their minds about how to vote. In six out of the seven ADs, the nonmajority group members were less likely to report that they were undecided about how they would vote compared to their dominant-group neighbors (see Table 7.2.E). While the numbers are small (the undecided rate was about 20 percent), the pattern is consistent. Perhaps where nonmajority group members felt isolated, they responded by making a firmer voting choice.

In sum, three important patterns have emerged:

1. A high degree of ethnic concentration usually produced a high level of support for the candidate identified with the group (Dinkins with blacks; Koch with conservative Jews and white Catholics).

2. The local political culture of the AD appears to have influenced how Democratic prime voters cast their ballots, whether or not they were in the dominant group.

3. Those not in the dominant group in their AD reported more certainty about their vote than those in the dominant group.

FROM PRIMARY TO GENERAL ELECTION: HOW THE ETHNIC GROUPS SHIFTED

In chapter 6, we devoted considerable attention to the bases upon which normally Democratic voters opted for Giuliani, a Republican, in the general election. Our AD-level data set permits us to revisit this question from a slightly different perspective. Here, we are less interested in "why did they switch" than in "how did they switch." Specifically, we find that the pattern of transition from the primary to the general election gives some evidence of strategic voting, that is, of voting for one's enemy at one stage in order to clear the way for one's friend.

We reinterviewed more than a third of the original sample of Democratic prime voters just before the November general election to explore how the racial factor and the campaign would affect their final vote decision. Figure 7.8 shows that 54 percent of the reinterviewed voters reported that they chose Dinkins in both the primary and the general election.[8] An additional 26 percent shifted from Koch to Giuliani, while 16 percent went from Koch to Dinkins and 5 percent moved from Dinkins to Giuliani. Put another way, almost two-thirds of the Koch voters defected to Giuliani. This is quite consistent with our discussion in chapter 6 based on the citywide CBS/*New York Times* exit poll data. Interestingly, however, we find that 10 percent of the Dinkins primary voters also defected to Giuliani, suggesting that at least some Democratic voters, primarily white Catholics, wanted badly to defeat Koch but not to replace him with Dinkins.

On the other hand, nine out of ten Dinkins voters and two out of five Koch voters did stand by the party's nominee. As with white Catholics, about 6 percent of Latino prime Democrats voted for Dinkins but ended up with Giuliani in the general election. But among Latino Koch voters, a substantial majority shifted to Dinkins. Among Jews, a substantial minority shifted to Dinkins as well, while a small fraction of white Catholics stuck with their party's candidate. Together, these enabled Dinkins to win the general election, if barely.

After some early problems, especially in the primary, the Giuliani campaign picked up steam as election day approached. The Dinkins

FIGURE 7.8
PRIMARY AND MAYORAL VOTES
1989 by Group

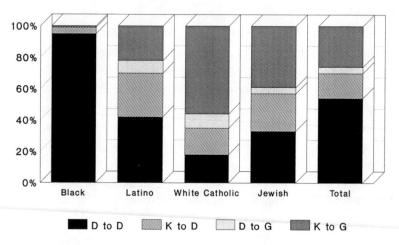

Source: Wagner Institute 1989 Prime voter reinterview survey
N = 815

campaign had mobilized its natural base before primary day in September and now had to exert itself to win over Democrats who had voted for Koch. One way to measure the relative success of the Giuliani campaign and Dinkins's relatively weak appeal within the former Koch constituency is to compare what voters stated just before the primary that they would do in a hypothetical Dinkins/Giuliani contest with what the same people reported two months later that they would actually do shortly before the mayoral election (see Figure 7.9).

Sixty-four percent of the total sample of prime Democrats chose Dinkins over Giuliani both in the hypothetical question at the primary and for their actual November vote choice. Remarkably, 19 percent of these prime Democrats also chose Giuliani twice (see Total column). Even more interesting were the other two numbers: the move from Giuliani to Dinkins and from Dinkins to Giuliani. Although in both cases the numbers were small, Giuliani won twice as many of those changing their minds (12 percent to 6 percent) than Dinkins.

FIGURE 7.9
CHOICE FOR MAYOR BY GROUP
Interview and Reinterview

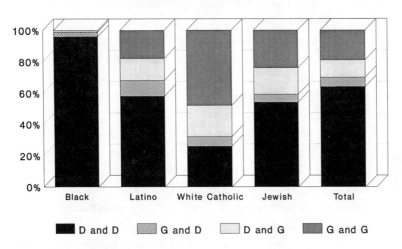

■ D and D ▨ G and D ☐ D and G ▨ G and G

Source: Wagner Institute 1989 Democratic Prime voter reinterview survey
$N = 815$

The data on which Figures 7.8 and 7.9 are based lead to some important conclusions about the relationship between ethnicity and political behavior in the 1989 mayoral elections:

1. Blacks bonded with Dinkins early on and stayed with him. Nineteen out of twenty black prime Democrats reported choosing Dinkins for both the primary and the mayoral vote, and almost all stuck by their initial decision.

2. Almost half the white Catholic prime Democrats began in Giuliani's column, while a quarter began in the Dinkins camp. During the campaign, almost half of the latter defected from Dinkins to Giuliani, while only 6 percent went in the other direction. Almost two-thirds of the white Catholic Democrats, including three-quarters of those who had supported Koch in the Democratic primary, went on to vote for Republican Giuliani in the general election. Only one-third ended up in the Dinkins camp.

3. Jewish prime Democrats provided an interesting amalgam. A

third were loyal Dinkins voters, and a quarter of the Koch voters chose Dinkins, giving him a majority of these Jewish prime Democratic voters.[9] But 40 percent also crossed party lines, shifting from Koch to Giuliani between the primary and the mayoral election. Moreover, 17 percent of all the Jews initially favored Dinkins but then defected to Giuliani, while only 6 percent initially favored Giuliani but ultimately moved to Dinkins.

4. The split of the Latinos may have saved the election for Dinkins. First, 42 percent were loyal to Dinkins in both elections. More than half of those who supported Koch in the primary, or 28 percent of the Latino prime Democratic vote, also moved to Dinkins in the general election. Only 30 percent of the Latino Democratic vote ultimately went to Giuliani. Of those who initially favored Dinkins over Giuliani at the time of the primary, only 20 percent later defected to Giuliani, while 36 percent of those who initially favored Giuliani defected to Dinkins. Since far more initially favored Dinkins, Giuliani still got half again as many defectors as Dinkins. Given that Dinkins won by only 47,080 votes, the disproportionate shift of Latinos toward Dinkins clearly made a difference of that critical magnitude.

These figures show that Dinkins's momentum eroded and Giuliani's surged as the election campaign progressed, except among Latinos. Dinkins had already attracted the bulk of his natural electorate and had to scramble to win over a substantial share of his primary opponent's base. As the campaign came to its conclusion, Giuliani successfully raided white Democratic strongholds. Had Giuliani paid more attention to and been more effective in the Latino districts, the final result might well have been different.

DEMOCRATIC DEFECTORS TO GIULIANI

As we might surmise from chapter 6, the Democratic defectors to Giuliani described above were concentrated in the two white outer-borough ADs, the 31st and the 45th (see Figure 7.10). He won 69 percent of the votes in the white Catholic 31st and 58 percent of the Jewish 45th. In ADs that gave most of their primary votes to Ed Koch, the Republican

FIGURE 7.10
PRIMARY AND MAYORAL VOTE
by AD

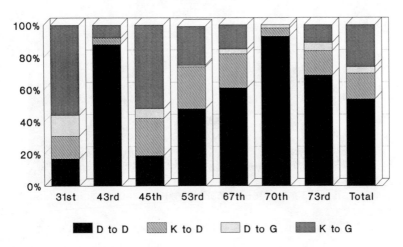

Source: Wagner Institute 1989 Democratic Prime voter reinterview survey
$N = 815$

candidate won an impressive majority of the Democratic voters. More-over, a significant number of anti-Koch voters cast "strategic" ballots for Dinkins in the primary and Giuliani in the general election in these ADs. Although present in every AD except the 43rd, strategic voting was strongest in the 31st, amounting to 17 percent of its total vote. Al-though Dinkins won the 53rd AD, Giuliani did better there than in any other minority AD, winning more than a quarter of the votes of our panel. This may reflect both the lingering Italian influence in this AD and the "machine" orientation of its political culture.

Dinkins excelled in and kept defections to a minimum in the two black ADs, the 43rd and the 70th. He also won in the 60-percent range in the 73rd, the Latino district in which blacks make up two-thirds of the Democratic prime voters. As would be expected from the Latino shift toward Dinkins, he also kept defections to a minimum in the Latino 53rd, although they were larger there than in other minority ADs. Dinkins also did extremely well among the cosmopolitan liberal

FIGURE 7.11
CHOICE FOR MAYOR BY AD
Interview and Reinterview

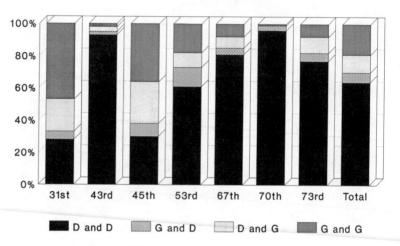

Source: Wagner Institute 1989 Democratic Prime voter reinterview survey
$N = 815$

white Democratic voters of the 67th AD. Giuliani made no great inroads among Democratic prime voters in these districts.

Figure 7.11 measures the shift from initial intentions by AD (analogous to that provided for groups in Figure 7.9). It shows that Dinkins retained overwhelming support in the black 43rd and 70th ADs and also did well in the white liberal 67th and the Latino/black 73rd. Moreover, even in the Latino 53rd AD in Bushwick, Dinkins succeeded in bringing more initial Giuliani supporters to his side than shifted from him to Giuliani. In the white ADs, however, a consistently large majority of those who changed their minds ended up with Giuliani, although the size of this group varied, being largest in the 45th and smallest in the 67th.

Both Democrats initially favoring Giuliani and those who defected from Dinkins as an initial choice to Giuliani as the ultimate choice were heavily concentrated in the 31st and 45th. He had solid support at the time of the primary and capitalized on it; the trade-off in defectors was heavily in his favor. Almost half the voters in the 45th who reported at the time of the primary that they would favor Dinkins in the general election ultimately shifted to Giuliani. Even in the liberal 67th AD, more of those who initially favored Dinkins shifted to Giuliani during the course of the campaign than the reverse, although the absolute level of change was low.

Turning to Figure 7.12, we see the net effect of the two campaigners on the groups across the study ADs. It shows the extent to which each group that had a significant presence in the AD voted for Dinkins. Blacks were extremely loyal to Dinkins across the board, regardless of neighborhood. (The one black respondent in the white Catholic 31st AD voted for Giuliani.) White Catholic support for Giuliani also varied little by AD, at about two-thirds of the Democratic prime voters. (Three out of the four white Catholics interviewed in the Upper

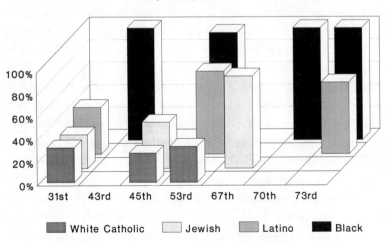

FIGURE 7.12
DINKINS VOTE IN MAYORAL ELECTION
by Group and AD

Source: Wagner Institute 1989 Democratic Prime voter reinterview survey
$N = 815$

West Side 67th AD did support Dinkins. It is reasonable to suppose that they, like the black in Richmond Hill, were self-selected residents of a cosmopolitan area. Their vote-choice was consistent with other values they held, values that differed from those of most white Catholics in other parts of the city.)

It is worth remembering, however, that a third of the white Catholic Democrats outside Manhattan did remain loyal to their party's nominee even though he was black. As with the Latino shift towards Dinkins, he could not have won the election without the support of this liberal minority of the white population.

Jewish support for Dinkins or Giuliani was highly sensitive to geographical setting. Jews in the 31st and 45th ADs supported Giuliani more heavily than they did the candidate of their own party, Dinkins, though less so in the 45th than in the 31st. In the black Crown Heights 43rd AD, six of the eight Jews from the area of the Lubavitcher Rebbe supported Giuliani. By contrast, Jews in the Upper West Side 67th AD supported Dinkins strongly, as did the handful of Jews in the black 70th and the Latino 53rd.

Latinos also proved to be highly sensitive to geographic location and political ecology. In the white Catholic 31st AD, the small Latino population gave Dinkins only 42 percent support. In the two districts where they made up a substantial portion of the population (a third of the respondents in the 53rd AD and 44 percent of the 73rd AD), they gave Dinkins 74 and 64 percent of their support, respectively. The differential rate was significant because the 53rd AD was dominated by a regular Democratic club, while the 73rd was represented by a sometime insurgent. In the primary, these respondents split the other way, with only 33 percent of the Latino vote in the 53rd going to Dinkins, compared with half of the Latino vote in the 73rd (compare Figure 7.7). That Dinkins was able to mobilize Latino votes in the 53rd was an important element of his victory; Giuliani's campaign, by contrast, was absent from ADs like the 53rd, and this absence may have been a factor in his defeat. The permanent minority status of the Republican party as an organizational entity and its token presence in most of the city handicapped its candidate.

NETWORKS, PARTICIPATION, AND INTEREST

NETWORKS

Only about one in five respondents indicated that a family member, religious leader, political leader, or community leader had made an effort to sway them.[10] While the rate was low, it did vary slightly along what appear to be the social and political contours of the city. In the Koch ADs (31 and 45), only 13 percent of the sample indicated that anyone had urged support for a candidate, compared with 20 percent in the swing ADs (53, 67, and 73) and 22 percent in the ADs considered loyal to Dinkins. The Koch campaign's lack of a field operation and Dinkins's substantial field effort may have contributed to these differences.

Personal attempts to influence voters were greatest in the black ADs, where they came largely from political and community leaders, and such efforts were least evident in the white Catholic AD. Using a summary measure of those who said that two or more agents had urged support for a candidate (see Table 7.3), this happened to 12 percent of the respondents in Harlem (70th AD) compared to only 1 percent in white Catholic Richmond Hill (31st AD). This finding makes sense in light of the fact that the Dinkins candidacy was a point of great pride and hope for the residents of Harlem. At the same time, Giuliani was running in the Republican primary and had not yet sought to mobilize networks of influence into the white Catholic Democratic prime voters of Queens.

Another indicator of the impact of a political network lies in whether the respondent thought that most of his or her friends and family supported the same candidate that the respondent did (see Figure 7.13). Affirmative answers to this question coincided with level of interest in the primary campaign: the black ADs (70 and 43) had the highest levels, while the white Catholic 31st and the conservative Jewish 45th had the lowest. Though the white ADs were only slightly less unanimous in supporting Koch than the black ADs were for Dinkins, the black ADs appear to have communicated this sentiment

Table 7.3

Networks in the Primary Campaign
(percents; each AD had about 300 respondents; total 2,107)

	AD 31	AD 43	AD 45	AD 53	AD 67	AD 70	AD 73
Said that two or more of the following had urged support for a candidate							
	1	8	4	7	6	12	9
1. % who said that a family member had urged support for a candidate							
	7	6	8	7	7	8	9
2. % who said that a religious leader had urged support for a candidate							
	1	6	3	3	1	7	6
3. % who said that a political leader had urged support for a candidate							
	4	10	7	11	9	12	10
4. % who said that a community leader had urged support for a candidate							
	2	10	3	9	9	12	9

Source: Wagner Institute 1989 Democratic prime voter survey

through networks of family and friendship more than was true in the white ADs.

At the same time, the data suggest that the mass media were a much more pervasive influence than social and political networks within a given AD. Television reaches the broadest spectrum of the population, and it had an overriding impact. But one consequence of relying on this medium is that campaigns can no longer target narrow segments of the electorate. This was especially problematic for Mayor Koch, many of whose white Catholic potential supporters were not strongly interested in the Democratic primary.

The primary campaign began in earnest during the heat of summer; the election itself took place on September 12, 1989. Interest in the race was slow to build since many were preoccupied with the concerns of summer. Our survey was conducted in the first ten days of September, and in every AD the undecided voters had disproportionately little or no interest in the campaign. A rational campaign would thus have concentrated its expenditures on those whose interest was lower, on the whole, than on those who had already made up their minds.

In our survey of the seven ADs, interest was lowest among the Democratic voters of the white Catholic pro-Koch 31st AD. To have

FIGURE 7.13
NETWORKS AND CAMPAIGN INTEREST
in Study ADs

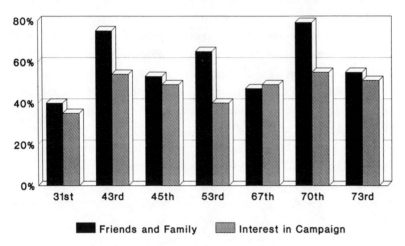

■ Friends and Family   ▨ Interest in Campaign

Source: Wagner Institute 1989 Democratic prime voter survey
N = 2,107

a chance of winning the election, the Koch campaign would have to increase the interest of this constituency and secure its vote. But its nearly exclusive commitment to television made it impossible for the Koch campaign to target a narrow segment of voters such as those in the 31st AD.

PARTICIPATION

On the eve of the primary election, the ADs clearly varied considerably in terms of how much campaign activity had taken place. For those ADs considered solid Dinkins districts (AD 70 and AD 43), one in three respondents answered "yes" to six or more of the items in our participation scale (see Figure 7.14). The rate was only one in five in the Koch ADs (31 and 45). The participation rate was high among the three swing ADs as well, although Bushwick was lower than the other two. Conversely, 32 percent of the respondents in Koch ADs reported that they participated in three or fewer activities, compared with only 23 percent in the Dinkins ADs and 25 percent in the swing ADs.

The summary participation score upon which Figure 7.14 is based provides a way to rank ADs in terms of political party activity. The 67th AD on the Upper West Side of Manhattan scored highest: this district has many reform Democratic clubs, and its residents tend to be tuned in. They are the prototypical "amateur Democrats" motivated by civic duty.[11] Using our summary participation measure, 39 percent of the respondents of the 67th AD participated in six or more political activities. The black ADs also ranked well on this summary measure, while the Latino ADs trailed the black ADs but still did notably better than the white ADs. If we decompose the summary index into the measures that reflect grassroots club activity and those that reflect citywide campaign activity through the mass media, the differences across ADs become even clearer (see Table 7.4).

FIGURE 7.14
PARTICIPATION IN STUDY ADS
in 6 or more of 9 activities

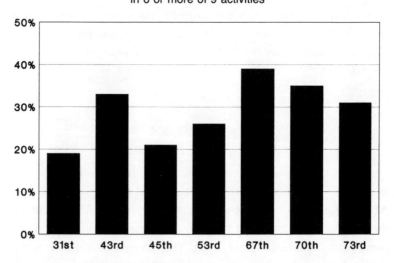

Source: Wagner Institute 1989 Democratic prime voter survey
N = 2,107

Table 7.4

Participation in the Primary Campaign by AD
(percents; each AD had about 300 respondents; total 2,107)

	AD 31	AD 43	AD 45	AD 53	AD 67	AD 70	AD 73
Elements of the participation score							
1. % who were asked to sign a nominating petition for a candidate							
	15	26	17	26	50	31	24
2. % who received campaign literature under the door							
	20	39	25	35	32	41	35
3. % who attended a meeting at which a candidate spoke							
	9	16	16	15	22	25	15
4. % who received campaign literature in the mail							
	80	88	82	86	90	89	79
5. % who received a phone call asking to support a candidate							
	29	46	29	23	40	27	30
6. % who saw or heard campaign commercials on radio or TV							
	93	96	94	89	90	95	96
7. % who saw or heard any news stores about candidates							
	78	78	80	73	92	81	82
8. % who paid a lot of attention to this campaign							
	77	79	81	70	86	78	76
9. % who listened or watched the candidates debate							
	56	64	68	52	57	63	65

Source: Wagner Institute 1989 Democratic prime voter survey

At one time, regular Democratic clubs dominated politics in the neighborhoods, providing patronage to political workers and services to the white ethnic laborers who populated them.[12] Their leaders thrived on voters who needed jobs, favors from government, or help with the police, courts, or welfare agencies. Over time, however, the ability of these clubs to control access to political careers and political benefits weakened, while the people of these districts grew less in need of their intervention. Party functions shifted directly to legislators. Since the Democratic party was less likely to be the necessary intermediary between the citizen and the government, the clubhouses lost some of their functions and much of their vitality.[13]

The decay of regular Democratic organizations in white, ethnic, outer-borough districts is reflected in the level of party activity our survey found in the 31st and 45th ADs. Only 20 percent of the respondents in the 31st AD and only 25 percent in the 45th AD received campaign literature drops; only 15 percent and 17 percent were asked to sign petitions; finally, only 9 and 16 percent attended a meeting at which a candidate spoke. As might seem logical, the Dinkins campaign had no presence during the primary in the 31st and 45th ADs, Koch strongholds. But, surprisingly, neither did Koch's. By contrast, grassroots campaign activities were considerably more prevalent in the black and Latino ADs and the upper West Side (67th).

Petitioning is particularly important. By law, a mayoral candidate must file ten thousand valid signatures in technically proper form. Regular clubs still use petitioning to control access to the ballot. In 1985 the black mayoral candidate was initially ruled off the ballot for technical violations in his petition forms. Whether one was asked to sign a nominating petition for any candidate for office is thus an excellent measure of the differences in the political life of the ADs. The 67th was alive with political ferment, given that half the respondents claimed to have been asked to sign a petition. In the 70th, which had produced a black candidate with citywide potential, about a third of the respondents reported having been asked to sign. But in the 31st and 45th, activity was minimal, though it was enough to get the candidates supported by the clubs in these ADs qualified for the ballot.

Mass media was a different story. The proposition that the political climate varies greatly from neighborhood to neighborhood is well known to every local politician, yet it confounds the practice of politics in the age of electronic media. In the past, campaigns attempted to reach the voter on a personal basis; today, the most "personal" appeals to which voters are exposed are commercials that are broadcast simultaneously to millions of other equally anonymous voters in front of their television sets. The voter has little personal contact with the party activists, let alone with the leaders or the candidates. Politics remains, however, even in this age of homogenized messages, closely linked to one's group affiliation and neighborhood experience.

The mayoral campaign was no exception: in all ADs, roughly eight out of ten respondents said they paid a high degree of attention to the campaign and saw or heard news stories about the candidates, although only roughly six out of ten saw the candidates debate. Given that all candidates must buy time in the New York City media market to be credible, the Koch, Dinkins, Giuliani, and Lauder campaigns spent a great deal of money mounting electronic warfare. It is not surprising, then, that more than nine out of ten respondents did see or hear campaign commercials on TV or radio.

In New York City, as in other large jurisdictions, campaigns have a citywide focus. District clubs may distribute campaign literature, for example, but the mayoral candidate's campaign headquarters generally prepares it and pays for it. The clubs may mobilize volunteers for campaign purposes, but the central campaign headquarters solicits the volunteers and organizes them into a coherent effort. Two of the most important centralized campaign functions are organizing telephone banks and mounting a direct mail campaign. The receipt of mailed literature and telephone calls is thus a good index of how much penetration the central campaigns achieved.

While the receipt of campaign mail did not vary much, the Koch ADs had rates of penetration that were eight to ten points lower than in the black ADs and the Upper West Side. The South Bronx lagged the other areas. Phone bank activity showed greater variation. The highest level was again achieved in a black AD, the 43rd in Crown Heights, while the Upper West Side was also high, reflecting its overall level of political mobilization. But, while lower than the 43rd or 67th, phone bank penetration in the Koch ADs was comparable to or better than in Harlem, the South Bronx, and Bushwick.

As with levels of grassroots activism at the AD level, the Koch campaign thus was at some disadvantage in field activities. Instead, it invested its resources in media activities, while the Dinkins campaign had both a media campaign and extensive field operations. Whether this difference was decisive to the electoral outcomes cannot be known from the available data, but it obviously worked in Dinkins's favor.

NEIGHBORHOOD CONCERNS

In many ways, the primary was a referendum on the record of Mayor Koch. In office since 1978, he had managed to antagonize many in the city, even those who were formerly in his electoral coalition. Most notable among them were blacks and white liberal reformers, many of whom had voted for Koch in 1977, 1981, and 1985.

In each of the study ADs, prime Democrats reported that they had generally been Koch supporters in the past, ranging from 62 percent in Harlem's 70th AD to 91 percent in the Midwood/Kings Highway 45th AD (see Figure 7.15). But by the summer of 1989 their evaluation of Mayor Koch had taken on a dual quality. They saw him as having made a major contribution to the city, but many also saw him as one who had caused harm to the city and especially to some of its neighborhoods.

Evidence of this ambivalent opinion is provided in Figures 7.16 and 7.17. Two points are clear: the Mayor had polarized opinion about his citywide role in all the ADs, and his policies were also perceived to have had a net negative impact on certain neighborhoods. On the one hand, reasonably large proportions of respondents felt that the

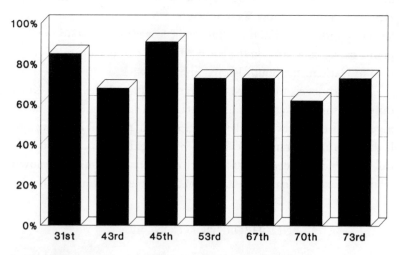

FIGURE 7.15
PREVIOUS SUPPORT FOR KOCH
by AD

Source: Wagner Institute 1989 Democratic prime voter survey
$N = 2,107$

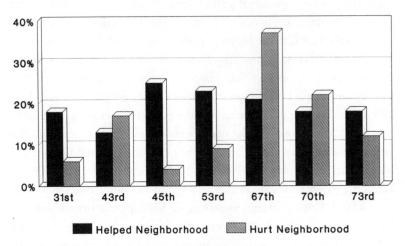

FIGURE 7.16
KOCH'S EFFORTS: NEIGHBORHOOD
by AD

Source: Wagner Institute 1989 Democratic prime voter survey
$N = 2,107$

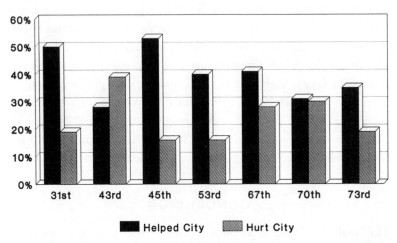

FIGURE 7.17
KOCH'S EFFORTS: CITY
by AD

Source: Wagner Institute 1989 Democratic prime voter survey
$N = 2,107$

mayor's policies had helped the city in all the ADs, even Harlem and the South Bronx. In every AD, respondents assessed Koch's impact on the city more favorably than his impact on their neighborhoods. Yet at the same time there was also sentiment among sizable proportions of each of the ADs that the mayor's policy had hurt the city. Except for the Upper West Side, this negative view was directed more at the Mayor's citywide impact than his effect on their neighborhood.

The net impact of the mayor's activity on the neighborhood and the city was determined by subtracting the percentage in an AD reported that Koch had helped (1) the neighborhood and (2) the city from the percentage that said he had hurt (1) the neighborhood and (2) the city. The results are displayed in Figure 7.18. Predictable patterns and some interesting departures are evident. Respondents in the two black ADs gave Mayor Koch a net negative rating for his impact both on the neighborhood and on the city. Conversely, the two white outer-borough ADs, the 45th and the 31st, gave him net positive assessments, though more strongly for his citywide impact than for his effect on their neighborhoods. Mayor Koch's candidacy thus polarized the population.

Figure 7.18 also reveals two anomalies that reinforce some of the differences in political orientation already noted. The Upper West Side 67th AD gave the mayor a substantially less positive net rating of his impact on the city compared to the other white ADs and gave him a strong net negative rating of his impact on their neighborhood. While many factors may have contributed to this perception, the Koch administration's support for numerous controversial development projects on the Upper West Side was quite probably the primary stimulus. Similarly, the South Bronx (73rd) had a much less positive net rating of the mayor's impact on the city and neighborhood than did Bushwick (53rd), though this may partly be due to the larger number of black respondents in the 73rd as opposed to the 53rd.

CONCLUSION

This analysis of politics at the assembly district level has confirmed many of the conclusions drawn in the previous chapters, but it also has substantiated the case that, even in an era of candidate-oriented,

FIGURE 7.18
KOCH'S NET IMPACT BY AD
Neighborhood and City

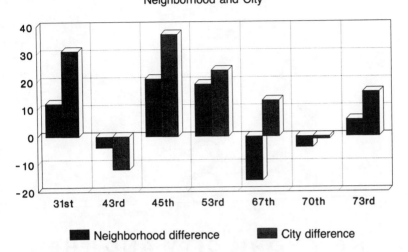

■ Neighborhood difference   **■ City difference**

Source: Wagner Institute 1989 Democratic prime voter survey
$N = 2,107$

media-driven politics, the local political ecology and grassroots campaigning still count. The larger stereotypes that practitioners often use as a shorthand for the city's complex political fabric hide important nuances across specific places. Moreover, people gravitate to specific neighborhoods because of their particular character and tend to absorb some of that character. Thus Catholics and Jews in the liberal, cosmopolitan Upper West Side present a different political profile than these groups do in Richmond Hill or Midwood. Moreover, Catholics in the Jewish 45th AD behaved a little differently than in the Catholic 31st, just as there were more Jewish Democrats prepared to vote for Giuliani in the 31st than in the 45th.

Although they may be less important than the uniformities of race and ethnicity that cut across neighborhoods in determining political outcomes, these nuances in the detail of neighborhood political ecologies had a real impact. Sometimes, as in an extremely close race such as the 1989 mayoral election, these details can be decisive.

8

NEW YORK CITY AND THE NATION—A COMPARISON

Having examined the issues and cleavages that informed voting behavior in New York City through the lens of the 1989 mayoral election, we now turn to the question of whether these patterns resemble or differ from those in other urban centers and the nation as a whole.

There is general agreement that contemporary American cities continue to face major difficulties and may well be approaching, if not already engulfed in, the latest stage of the urban crisis in the form of increased social polarization and the emergence of more concentrated forms of poverty.[1] Using data collected just before the 1988 presidential election, this chapter considers political and attitudinal patterns of consensus and cleavage that have emerged as metropolitan areas live through their ordeal.

The urban-nonurban tension is an important feature of American politics and political culture. The unresponsiveness and rejection that urban dwellers often feel from exurbanites and the national government were vividly captured by the infamous *New York Daily News* (October 30, 1975) headline during the city's fiscal crisis of the mid-1970s: "Ford to City: DROP DEAD!"

Since cities (certainly New York City) concentrate minority groups and attract large numbers of immigrants, their populations differ from that of the nation as a whole. Are differences in attitudes and values "merely" a function of demographics, or does living in a city like New York shape attitudes and values over and above what is common for a given ethnic group?

The empirical bases for analyzing this question are two 1988 presidential election surveys: (1) the National Election Studies (NES) survey entailing face-to-face interviews with a national cross-section of 2,040 adults and (2) the New York City Presidential Election Survey (NYCES), a random-digit-dial telephone survey of 1,280 adult residents of New York City.[2]

ATTITUDINAL CLEAVAGES

Four issue-related attitude items in the NES questionnaire were used:

- Attitude toward government services and spending
- Attitude toward level of defense spending
- Attitude toward government's having responsibility for jobs and a good standard of living
- Attitude toward government aid to minorities

Our initial analysis entailed comparing New York City with the U.S. on each of these four items. It afforded, as well, some perspective on the United States over time. The results are presented in Table 8.1 as ratios of opposed responses. Thus, for example, in 1980 for every adult in the nation who favored more government services even at the cost of more government spending, 1.4 adults favored fewer government services in order to reduce government spending. By 1988 national sentiment on this issue had swung around so that 1.2 adults favored more government services for every adult who favored fewer. As for New Yorkers' views on this matter, in 1988 they rejected the proposition that one should reduce government services in order to save money by a ratio of 4.7:1.[3]

A national candidate who had chosen to make the role of government in ensuring jobs and a good standard of living a central issue in the 1988 campaign, and who stressed that government has a primary responsibility for these matters, would (if votes hinged solely on this issue) have thus gained two votes for each vote lost in New York City in 1988. At the same time, that candidate, nationwide, would have lost 1.8 votes for each vote gained.

Table 8.1 suggests three points: (1) public opinion on these issues in New York City clearly differs from that of the nation as a whole; (2) the difference is not solely a function of the higher incidence of minority groups in New York City; white New Yorkers also differ substantially from the U.S. as a whole on these matters; (3) while the nation as a whole moved in New York's direction on the issues of reducing government services and increasing or decreasing defense expenditures, that has not happened with the two issues that most polarize New York City and the U.S.

People in New York and the U.S. are at polar opposites in the distribution of their opinions with regard to governmental responsibility for ensuring that each person has a job and a good standard of living and with regard to governmental aid for minorities. Moreover, national public opinion has not changed much over the eighteen-year period observed. While Table 8.1 clearly indicates that New Yorkers think differently about the issues in question than the U.S. as a whole, can one infer from this that urban America is similarly distinct from the nonurban United States? Figure 8.1 suggests an answer.

In Figure 8.1, the left-hand column in each set (the black column)

Table 8.1

Ratios of Opposed Responses on Selected Items: U.S.A. and New York City Compared

	U.S.A.							New York City '88			
	'72	'74	'76	'80	'82	'84	'88	Total	Whites	Blacks	Latinos
A. Government Services								**Reduce Government Services**			
Reduce / Agree	1					1	1	1	1	1	1
Not Reduce / Disagree				1.4		1.0	1.2	4.7	4.1	5.0	5.0
B. Defense Spending								**Defense Spending**			
Decrease / Decrease			1		1	1	1	3.2	4.5	3.7	1.8
Increase / Increase			6.0		6.0	1.1	1.0	1	1	1	1
C. Responsibility for Jobs & Standard of Living								**Government Responsible Jobs & Standard of Living**			
Government / Agree	1	1	1	1	1	1	1	2.0	1.4	3.9	3.7
Individual / Disagree	1.4	1.5	1.6	1.6	1.6	1.3	1.8	1	1	1	1
D. Government Help for Minorities								**Government Help for Minorities**			
Government Help / Agree	1	1	1	1	1	1	1	2.6	1.5	5.6	6.3
Help Themselves / Disagree	1.2	1.3	1.3	2.2	1.9	1.2	1.5	1	1	1	1

Note: The national data for 1972–1984 are based upon the analysis of NES data by J. Merrill Shanks and Warren E. Miller in their paper "Policy Direction and Performance Evaluation," presented at the 1985 meeting of the APSA in New Orleans. See especially their Tables 9, 10, 15, and 17. The 1988 national data are from the NES data and the 1988 New York City data are from the NYCES.

FIGURE 8.1
RESPONSES AND URBANIZATION

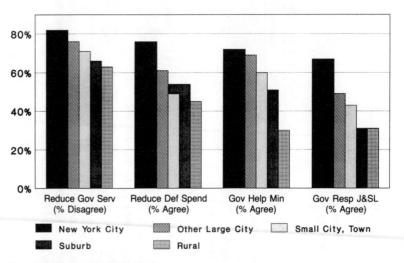

Source: NES and NYCES, 1988

presents the preferences of the New York City respondents as drawn from the NYCES data. The remaining columns, reflecting the preferences of the rest of the nation, are drawn from the 1988 NES data set with the fifty-five cases from New York City removed. (Henceforth the NES data set without these fifty-five cases will be referred to as "U.S.") The U.S. data set has been divided into four segments relevant to urbanization, ranging from large cities other than New York City, to small cities and small towns, to suburbs, and finally to rural areas.[4]

Examination of Figure 8.1 suggests that New York City is at one end of a continuum regarding the issues in question, rather than being unique. That New York is archetypical rather than atypical can also be seen in Figure 8.2, which scales the percentage agreeing with the particular issue category by type of place along a horizontal axis of the average size of that place category. New York City proves to be a nearly linear extrapolation from the data from "Small City/Small Town" and "Other Large Cities."

FIGURE 8.2
ISSUE PREFERENCES AS A FUNTION OF MEAN POPULATION SIZE

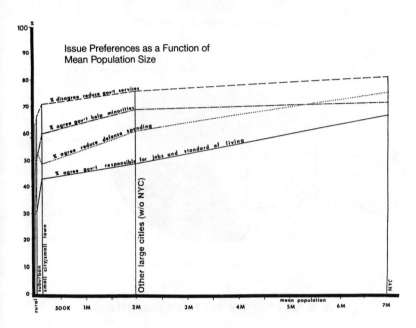

Thus, while New York City is unique in terms of its size, the distinctiveness of its attitudes on the issues in question seems consistent with an extrapolation based upon its size. However, that size is a major factor. With size come complexity and a diminution of a community's ability to reinforce its mores through face-to-face interaction. This may cause people to develop a greater penchant for expanding the role of government.

To place these data in proper political perspective, note that the top eleven central cities contain approximately 8.6 percent of the voting age population of the United States (see Figure 8.3). If these central cities have values and policy preferences distinct from those of the rest of the country (as, for example, in regard to the proper role of government in assuring jobs and standard of living, or in regard to government aid for minorities), their feeling of isolation may not be entirely illusory.

FIGURE 8.3
VOTING AGE POPULATION
USA, 1988
(based on NES respondents)

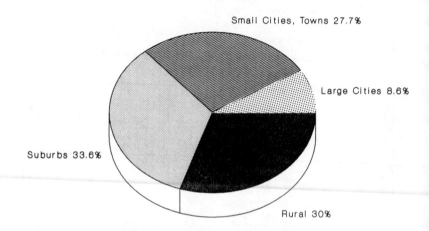

Small Cities, Towns 27.7%

Large Cities 8.6%

Suburbs 33.6%

Rural 30%

A MATTER OF DEMOGRAPHICS?

Using New York City as an archetype of the major American central cities might be inappropriate if the demography of New York City is substantially different from that of other major U.S. cities, and if aggregate differences in policy preferences are purely a function of demographic mix. The data reveal that New York City is indeed substantially distinct in certain aspects of its demography. On the other hand, aggregate policy preferences do not appear to be a pure function of demography.

Figures 8.4, 8.5, and 8.6 show how New York City differs demographically from other large cities in the NES data set. New York City is much less black, much more Latino, much less Protestant, much more Catholic, and much more Jewish. Can inferences on the New York City experience still be considered a basis for inference about other less large cities? Might the differences in policy preferences between New York City and the rest of the nation simply be a function of demographic mix? Would one still observe substantial differences

FIGURE 8.4
GROUPS AND URBANIZATION

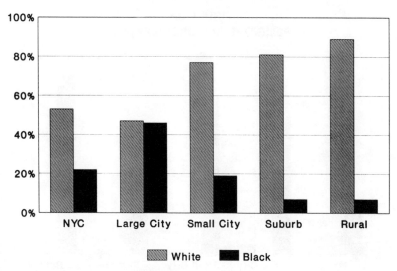

Source: NES and NYCES, 1988
Others and no answer not reported

FIGURE 8.5
LATINOS AND URBANIZATION

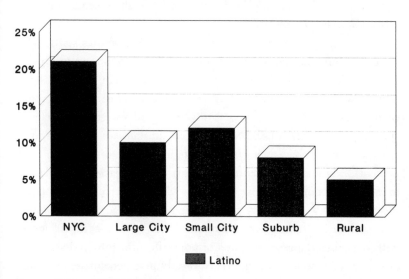

Source: NES and NYCES, 1988

FIGURE 8.6
RELIGIONS AND URBANIZATION

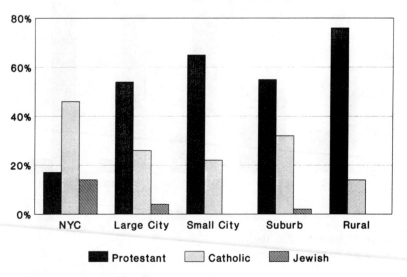

Source: NES and NYCES, 1988

in policy preferences *within demographic categories* when comparing New York City and the rest of the nation?

The relevant data are arrayed in Table 8.2. It shows statistically significant and substantively important differences among groups of New Yorkers and between them and respondents in the rest of the nation. White Catholics seem least affected on these issues by whether or not they are New Yorkers. Only in regard to reducing defense spending are white Catholic New Yorkers substantially more supportive (71 percent) than their counterparts in the rest of the nation (48 percent). A similarly substantial difference among blacks is found only in regard to reducing defense spending, which 19 percent more blacks support in New York City than in the rest of the country. Among blacks, there is also a statistically significant difference (at the .05 level) with regard to the government's responsibility for jobs and standard of living, but the level of difference is only nine percentage points in this case.

Table 8.2

**Policy Preferences on Selected Items within Demographic Groups
New York City and U.S. Compared[a]**

	Basic Demographic Category			
	White Protestant	White Catholic	Black	Latinos
Item				
Reduce government services				
% disagree				
New York City	78%	80%	83%	83%
U.S.	61%	73%	84%	75%
Reduce defense spending				
% agree				
New York City	81%	71%	79%	65%
U.S.	44%	48%	60%	63%
Government help minorities				
% agree				
New York City	59%	54%	85%	86%
U.S.	45%	45%	79%	44%
Government responsible for jobs and standard of living (JSL)				
% agree				
New York City	40%	58%	80%	79%
U.S.	40%	52%	71%	57%
% prefer Dukakis				
New York City	74%	43%	85%	67%
U.S.	36%	44%	84%	63%

Key: Solid line box means $p < .001$
    Dashed line box means $p < .01$
    Dotted line box means $p < .05$

[a]In this table and in all subsequent tables in this chapter, the term "U.S." refers to the national population *minus* the population of New York City. That, in turn, is based on the NES data set with New York City respondents deleted.

New York City Latinos, by contrast, differed substantially from those in the rest of the country on three out of the four issues. Interestingly, the sole issue on which New York City Latinos manifested no difference was the one issue on which all the other demographic groups did manifest such a difference—reducing defense spending. Their 65/63 percent support for a reduction makes them the most conservative of the New York City groups on this issue and the most liberal of the U.S. groups on that issue.

Perhaps the most remarkable differences are between the white Protestants of New York City and their counterparts nationwide. On three of the four issues under consideration, the New York City group is more "liberal." The differences range from a low of fourteen percentage points regarding the government's role in helping minorities to a high of thirty-seven percentage points in regard to reducing defense spending. Only on the government's role regarding jobs and standard of living do New York City's white Protestants resemble the U.S. sample. On this item, white Protestant New Yorkers are also least similar to nonwhite New Yorkers.

Thus the data support the hypothesis that New Yorkers have substantial policy differences with respondents in the rest of the nation even when compared within a given racial or ethnoreligious group. This raises the prospect that other large cities are similarly distinctive from the nonurban United States, but since the NES data set has only 121 cases of respondents from other large cities, we cannot explore that possibility.

ASSESSING THE ROLE OF THE DIVISIVE ISSUES

To what extent, if any, did these policy preference differences inform the respondents' candidate preferences? The method used to answer that question follows the approach taken in chapter 3, which used the voter decision model developed by Campbell, Converse, Miller, and Stokes, as modified in subsequent studies in conjunction with Downs's spatial model.[5] The former essentially entails explaining the dependent variable of the voter's candidate preference using three types of independent variables seen to impinge immediately upon the vote, namely, issue variables, respondent's party identification, and candidate personality characteristics.[6]

For this chapter we built matched regression models—one utilizing the NYCES data set and one utilizing the NES data set—consisting of eight similar independent variables (four issue items, party identification, and three personality items) and a dependent variable that was a surrogate for candidate preference. The issue items were reduction or increase of government services, reduction or increase in defense spending, government help for minorities, and governmental responsibility for jobs and standard of living. The party identification question was similar to that used in the NES, and the personality characteristics selected were leadership strength, knowledgeability, and honesty of the candidates.

As in chapter 3, we sought a method that would allow us to compare the impacts of the several issues both within and between populations and population segments. Accordingly, we chose linear regression, with its relatively accessible b's, betas and R^2s. Having selected that option, we could no longer use a dichotomous dependent variable, so we use the "feeling thermometer" (and the NYCES variant thereof) for the dependent variable.

To avoid an attitude "pulling" a candidate liked on some other basis "toward" the respondent's preferred issue position, we excluded two variables from the matched models. These were the issue item concerning drugs and the personality item concerning "caring about" people like the respondent. Each had such a high correlation with candidate preference that it would mask other relationships; the wording of both was also prone to the unwanted "pulling." For example, the NES item on drugs asked "Which candidate do you think will do a better job of solving this problem, Bush or Dukakis?"

When we regressed our dependent variables on the eight independent variables selected for the matched models, they explained 55 percent and 68 percent of the variance in the New York City and U.S. samples. When segmented by demographic categories, the difference in variance explained disappears for many categories. For example, among white Catholics these eight variables explain 72 percent of the

New York City variance and 70 percent of the U.S. variance. These are sufficient amounts of variance explained to warrant attention.

Analysis based on data from a single point in time makes it difficult to know the direction of the arrow of causality. Within this constraint, however, two questions may help illuminate, if not completely resolve, what is causing what. First, how consistent were respondents' positions on the independent variables, on the one hand, with their evaluations of the candidates, on the other? The R^2 is a measure of this consistency, that is, how much information independent variables contain about the dependent variable.

Second, what relative "impact" does each independent variable have on the dependent variable? Rank orderings of these impacts within a population or population segment may be inferred from the rank ordering of the betas associated with the independent variables within that population or population segment. We have seen that there are substantial differences in preferred policies between urban and nonurban America. To what extent do those differences inform electoral behavior? For this, we turn to a comparison of the R^2s.

By comparing the upper-left cells of Table 8.3 and 8.4, one may readily conclude that issue differentials contain substantially more information about candidate evaluation differentials in the U.S. than in New York City (46 percent of variance explained vs. 31 percent). However, looking down the left-hand columns and comparing them, one finds that this difference either shrinks considerably or disappears. The one notable exception is the startling contrast between New York City Latinos and U.S. Latinos. Most of the difference between the two upper-left-hand cells seems traceable to these two groups of Latinos.

While it is possible that the difference is due to poor interviewing in the NYCES, that seems highly improbable on three grounds. First, respondents who indicated even the faintest desire to be interviewed in Spanish were interviewed by one of a select group of Spanish-speaking interviewers with proven records, even if it meant a call-back appointment. Second, a Spanish-speaking supervisor monitored these interviews and commented frequently on their richness. Finally, the refusal rate among Latino respondents was half that of non-Latinos.

Differences in education account for some of the differences in the

Table 8.3

Variance in Candidate Evaluation Differential Explained by the Four Issues in the New York City Sample[a]

		Subgroup				
	Base	Very Likely to Vote[b]	Male	Female	Educ.—H.S. Grad or less	Educ.— >H.S. Grad
Overall	31%	38%	33%	29%	18%	40%
Group						
Black	21%	21%	13%	27%	14%	25%
Latino	9%	15%	27%	4%	4%	19%
White Catholic	41%	46%	41%	42%	34%	45%
White Jewish	45%	47%	42%	51%	34%[c]	46%
White Protestant	34%	33%	46%	20%	47%	40%

[a]Except as noted below, all entries are significant with $p < .0001$.
[b]Respondent's self-report of likelihood of voting: "likely" for NES, "very likely" for NYCES.
[c]$p = .0012$.

Table 8.4

Variance in Candidate Evaluation Differential Explained by the Four Issues in the U.S. Sample[a]

		Subgroup				
	Base	Very Likely to Vote[b]	Male	Female	Educ.—H.S. Grad or less	Educ.— >H.S. Grad
Overall	46%	49%	53%	41%	39%	56%
Group[c]						
Black	29%	28%	30%	26%	32%	25%
Latino	52%	54%	62%	42%	44%	67%
White Catholic	48%	51%	52%	45%	45%	50%
White Protestant	44%	47%	49%	41%	39%	51%

[a]All entries are significant with $p < .0001$.
[b]Respondent's self-report of likelihood of voting: "likely" for NES, "very likely" for NYCES.
[c]White Jewish deleted because of too few cases.

ability of these issues to predict candidate evaluation, but a substantial gap remains.[7] For New York's black and Latino populations and the national black population, these issues work significantly less well than they do for the other demographic segments. However, it is worth noting within both Tables 8.3 and 8.4 that the issue model works much better for Latino men than for Latino women. Perhaps, more than in other groups, Latino women turn to males for direction in these matters.

These issues do account for moderate to substantial amounts of variance in most of the basic demographic segments; but what is the relative impact of each of the issues in question? For purposes of economy, we shall look at only those respondents who said that there were "likely to vote" in the case of the NES data (80 percent of respondents for U.S.) or "very likely to vote" in the case of the New York City data (80 percent of respondents). The betas are presented in Table 8.5.

In both New York City and the U.S., the defense spending issue had the largest impact on the average likely voter in 1988 (at least in terms of the four issues examined to this point). While this issue showed a substantial and polarizing relationship to the degree of urbanization (see Figure 8.1), the nation has been moving in the direction of

Table 8.5

**Standardized Regression Coefficients (betas) of the
Four Issues in the New York City and U.S. Samples
—Likely Voters Only[a]—**

	Population	
	New York City	U.S.
Issue		
Defense spending	.37	.32
Reduction of government services	.19	.26
Government responsibility for jobs and standard of living	.16	.21
Government help for minorities	.15	.10

[a]"Very likely" in NYCES.

Table 8.6

**Standardized Regression Coefficients (betas) of the
Four Issues in the Basic Demographic Segments in the
New York City and U.S. Samples
—Likely Voters Only[a]—**

			Group		
	Black	Latino	White Catholic	White Jewish	White Protestant
New York City					
Issue					
Defense spending	.22	.44	.47	.36	.43
Reduction of government services	[b]	[b]	.24	.34	[b]
Government responsible for jobs and standard of living	.15	[b]	.25	[b]	[b]
Government help for minorities	.29	[b]	[b]	.20	.32
U.S.					
Issue					
Defense spending	.23	.28	.30	[b]	.32
Reduction of government services	.28	.37	.21	[c]	.26
Government responsible for jobs and standard of living	[b]	.21	.15	[c]	.18
Government help for minorities	.18	.14	.26	[c]	.20

[a]"Very likely" in NYCES.
[b]Not significantly different from zero.
[c]Too few to analyze.

its urban component over time (see Table 8.1). By contrast, government aid to minorities, on which there is also substantial urban/nonurban polarization and on which there has been relatively little movement over time, had relatively little impact in both populations.

Considering patterns within groups (see Table 8.6), the relationships seen in Table 8.5 tend to hold, with notable exceptions. Specifically, defense spending had the greatest impact in every group except blacks. For them, government help for minorities or nonreduction of government services topped the list. Government help for minorities or governmental responsibility for jobs and standard of living tended to have a substantial impact among white Catholics, blacks, and Lat-

Table 8.7

Standardized Regression Coefficients (betas[a]) of the
Eight "Matched" Items in the New York City and U.S. Samples
—Likely Voters Only[b]—

	Population	
	New York City	U.S.
Item		
Strong leader	.33	.37
Honest	.25	.08
Party identification	.19	.31
Defense spending	.13	.15
Government responsibility for jobs and standard of living	.08[c]	.09
Reduction of government services	.06[c]	.11
Knowledgeable	[d]	.06[c]
Government help for minorities	[d]	[d]

[a]All coefficients significant at $p < .0001$ unless otherwise noted.
[b]"Very likely" in NYCES.
[c]$p < .001$.
[d]Not significantly different from zero.

inos. In this regard, it may be worth recalling that preferences on these issues are quite polarized between white Catholics on the one hand, and blacks and Latinos on the other, and that this is true in both New York City and U.S. samples (see Table 8.2).

For the most part then, though with some exceptions, the most divisive issues did *not* "drive" the 1988 Presidential election either in New York City or in U.S. However, they did have substantial impact within the groups, when viewed solely in the context of issues. What, then, happens when issues are placed in the context of party identification and candidate personality characteristics? The overall effect may be observed in Table 8.7

In this larger context, the impact of issues drops markedly, which is consistent with chapter 3 as well as earlier studies.[8] In New York City and in the U.S., the extent to which likely voters perceived the candidates unequally as strong leaders was the major factor in their vote decisions. In New York, the next strongest influence was the perception of honesty, followed by party identification. On the issues, only defense spending had any substantial impact in New York City, and that well below party identification. In the rest of the United States, party identification was the second most powerful variable, followed by defense; the beta for defense was half that of party identification, and the other issue items fell below that. While the differential on honesty had considerable impact in New York City, it had almost no impact in the rest of the United States.

Repetition of this analysis within demographic groups indicates that the pattern of "strong leader" and party identification being the two strongest variables in the U.S. and comprising two of the top three in New York City ("honesty" being the third) holds up in every group in the U.S. and in every non-Latino white segment in New York City (see Tables 8.8 and 8.9). However, party identification proved to have virtually no consequence among New York City blacks and Latinos. Among New York City blacks, this may be a statistical artifact, since less than 4 percent of the group identified as Republicans. But with 20 percent of New York Latinos identifying Republican, party identification's lack of impact is not artifactual. For this group, party bonding simply is not strong. For both blacks and Latinos in New York City, the perception of honesty as a characteristic of a candidate had a relatively large impact, as it did for New York City Jews. Conceivably, these three groups tend to be more victimized by the corruption in New York City than the other groups, and thus are more sensitized to the issue.

CONCLUSION

This chapter has sought to ascertain how much the adult populations of New York City (and perhaps other large cities) diverge from the rest of the nation on a number of central policy issues, to discover whether these differences go beyond what can be explained by differ-

Table 8.8

Standardized Regression Coefficients (betas[a]) of the
Eight "Matched" Items in the U.S. Samples
—Likely Voters Only[b]—

			Group		
	Total	Black	Latino	White Catholic	White Protestant
Item					
Strong leader	.37	.35	.23[d]	.29	.44
Honest	.08	[f]	[f]	[f]	.09
Party identification	.31	.22	.51	.33	.29
Defense spending	.15	.18[d]	.13[e]	.10[e]	.15
Jobs and standard of living	.09	.17[d]	[f]	.12[d]	.10
Reduce government spending	.11	[f]	.15[e]	.14[d]	.08[d]
Knowledgeable	.06	[f]	[f]	.10[e]	[f]
Government help minorities	[f]	[f]	[f]	[f]	[f]

[a]All coefficients are significant at $p < .001$ unless otherwise noted.
[b]In the U.S. sample, "likely" voters comprised 81 percent of the respondents.
[c]The Jews in the sample were too few to analyze.
[d]$p < .01$.
[e]$p < .05$.
[f]Coefficient not significantly different from zero.

ences in demographic composition (whether there is an "urban" component), and to assess how much these issues and differences on them informed the vote decision in 1988.

It was shown that New York City and other big cities have substantially different policy preferences from those of nonurban America. While these differences have clear demographic components, they also appear to have an urban component. Moreover, these issues appear to inform the vote decision (as manifested in candidate evaluation) in the sense that policy preferences can be used to predict candidate evaluation. However, party identification and candidate personality characteristics had a larger impact than issues on the vote decision in 1988.

It should not be inferred that the issue cleavages identified are of no account. Rather, they should be viewed as "fault lines" in our political substructure. To the extent that campaigns make them salient,

Table 8.9

Standardized Regression Coefficients (betas[a]) of the
Eight "Matched" Items in the New York City Samples
—Likely Voters Only[b]—

				Group		
				White	White	White
	Total	Black	Latino	Catholic	Jewish	Protestant
Item						
Strong leader	.33	.34	e	.32	.21[c]	.46
Honest	.25	.22[c]	.32	.15[c]	.26	e
Party identification	.19	e	e	.19	.21	.45
Defense spending	.13	.12[d]	.19	.17	e	e
Jobs and standard of living	.08	e	e	.11[c]	e	e
Reduce government spending	.06	e	e	.09[d]	.12[d]	e
Knowledgeable	e	.18	e	.17	.19[c]	e
Government help minorities	e	e	e	e	e	e

[a]All coefficients are significant at $p < .001$ unless otherwise noted.
[b]In the New York City sample, "very likely" voters comprised 80 percent of the respondents.
[c]$p < .01$.
[d]$p < .05$.
[e]Coefficient not significantly different from zero.

they have the potential to evoke a major cleavage along urban, racial, and ethnic lines, to the likely disadvantage of the urban areas and the racial and ethnic minorities involved.

New York City emerges as a logical extension of how attitudes change as one moves from rural areas through suburbs and small cities to large cities. But its intensity and complexity have also shaped the attitudes of some of its component groups in ways that cause them to differ from their counterparts nationwide. The election of David Dinkins in 1989—made possible by the minority of support he got from white Catholics and Jews and the shift toward him of Latinos, combined with extraordinary mobilization of his natural base in the African American community—was not a fluke. New York City's white Catholics, for example, were substantially more willing in 1988 to cut the defense budget than were those of a similar background nationally. Similarly, Latinos in New York City were much more supportive of an expanded economic role for government than were their counterparts nationwide (Table 8.7). These "urban attitudes" well served David Dinkins and the cause of a liberal, multiracial, insurgent coalition in 1989.

9

LESSONS

Despite his narrow margin of forty-seven-thousand votes, and despite the fact that as the Democratic nominee he could have been considered the odds-on favorite, David N. Dinkins's victory over Rudolph Giuliani in November 1989 was a major political achievement and a turning point in New York City's political development. Seen from the perspective of Mayor Edward I. Koch's electoral triumph in 1985, there was every reason to think that a Dinkins victory would be highly improbable. To begin with, the incumbent mayor still enjoyed extensive powers and considerable electoral strength. Moreover, Koch had benefited from and helped to prolong the pattern of racial and ethnic polarization in the city's voting patterns dating at least from the 1966 referendum on the police review board. He had assembled a Jewish/ white-Catholic alliance that constituted a majority of both the Democratic primary and the general electorate. To this core he had wedded extensive support in the Latino community, and, though he had alienated their leadership, he gained the votes of substantial fractions of white liberals and blacks as well.

Compared to how racial transition in the mayoralties of other large cities took place, Dinkins was also in an especially weak position. If highly mobilized, blacks might constitute perhaps as much as 33 percent of the Democratic primary electorate, but only 28 percent of the general electorate. This was far less than was true of such cities as Chicago, Philadelphia, and Atlanta; only Los Angeles was comparable (indeed, blacks constituted less than 16 percent of L.A.'s population when Bradley was first elected in 1973).[1]

Moreover, as the aftermath of Mayor Washington's death in Chicago illustrated, divisions between black factions could reverse racial succession even in majority black cities.[2] The 1985 mayoral campaign had been fraught with division within the black community along gender, ideological, and geographic lines; the potential coalition among white liberals, Latinos, blacks, and public sector labor unions was also in disarray. While the 1988 Jackson campaign addressed some of these divisions and the Dinkins candidacy gave all parts of the black community and the potential insurgent coalition someone to rally around, these divisions remained for Dinkins's opponents, Koch and Giuliani, to seek to mobilize. How, then, did Dinkins prevail?

RACE AND NEW YORK CITY ELECTORAL POLITICS

The first way to answer this question is to rely on the classic patterns of ethnic alignment in New York City politics: if you know an area's racial and ethnic makeup, you know its vote. In both the primary and the general election, there can be little doubt that the voting was highly racially polarized. Most blacks voted for the black candidate and most whites for the white candidate. In this view, the inexorable turn of the demographic wheel finally caught up with New York City politics: a new majority of minority groups cast Edward Koch out of office and enabled David Dinkins to defeat Rudolph Giuliani.

However plausible at a superficial level, this explanation does not bear up well under closer scrutiny. What is interesting about the 1989 mayoral elections in New York City was not their degree of racial polarization, which was to be expected, but the degree to which they were *not* governed by race alone. Indeed, if this were the only factor at work, David Dinkins might well have lost the primary and certainly would have lost the general election, for non-Latino whites constituted 56 percent of the voters. To the contrary, Dinkins had a great incentive to prevent whites from becoming racially polarized and to construct a biracial alliance.

Dinkins's major difficulty was how to do this while simultaneously mobilizing his core African American constituency. His strategy was to conduct a two-level campaign: one public, citywide, and directed at swing constituencies among Jews, white liberals, and Latinos, and a second relying on the networks extending around the major organizational players in the black community, especially black elected officials, black ministers, and black public sector trade unionists. The first campaign was highly visible to whites, the second much less so, but no less effective. His ability to conduct such a bifurcated dialogue was facilitated by racial segmentation in New York City's mass media, the importance of radio station WLIB, owned by one of Dinkins' closest allies, in the black community.[3] He could speak to the black community through channels to which whites did not listen.

To a considerable extent, this strategy worked: the Dinkins campaign successfully mobilized black voters to unprecedented levels of turnout and uniform vote for Dinkins while simultaneously attracting large numbers of Latinos and white liberals to his cause. Of Dinkins's 540,000 primary votes, blacks cast almost two-thirds. To yield this amount, black ADs turned out at historically unprecedented rates, almost twice as frequently as in white Catholic ADs. They also backed Dinkins by nine to one. It was in this sense that the election was most obviously racially polarized, but black solidarity for Dinkins was merely in line with the similar ethnic solidarity that Jews had shown for Koch, or indeed that the Irish or Italians have shown when candidates of their ancestry compete against those of others.

The massive mobilization of black voters left Dinkins over a third of the way short of victory in the primary, however. In that election, Latinos gave Dinkins about 70,000 votes, enabling him to cover a bit less than a third of his remaining ground. The remainder, clearly, would have to come from non-Latino whites: the secular young white liberals of the Upper West Side or brownstone Brooklyn, the older Jewish residents of outer Brooklyn who identified with Dinkins's liberal, labor base, and the minority of liberals among middle-class white Catholics. In the event, these groups all produced for David Dinkins despite having heavily backed Mayor Koch in 1985. Dinkins got about 95,000 votes from white liberal ADs, 65,000 from outer-borough Jewish ADs, and 53,000 from non-Latino Catholic ADs. Combined with Latino support, this put him over the top.

Winning the primary was only the first part of the battle, as chapters 5 and 6 observed. For many reasons, winning the general election would be even harder: the underlying electoral terrain was less favorable, the opposing candidate had not been sullied by twelve years of incumbency but was strong on the issues most dear to white voters, and, unlike Mayor Koch, the opponent was free to take off the gloves and fight a bare-fisted battle. A far lesser candidate, Bernard Epton, had nearly beaten the Democratic nominee in Chicago, Harold Washington. Rudolph Giuliani was far more formidable. Once more, racial polarization was David Dinkins's enemy.

Dinkins won 900,000 votes in the general election, barely nosing out Giuliani. This time, blacks provided just over half (512,000) of these ballots because blacks made up a smaller share of the general electorate and because, in contrast to the primary, their turnout rate more closely approximated the citywide rate while white Catholic ADs mounted the highest turnout rate. Dinkins had much farther to go in this race. Latino ADs helped by shifting strongly in Dinkins' direction, giving him three-quarters of their votes, but low turnout offset this shift. Latino ADs thus gave Dinkins about 137,000 more votes, still leaving him 263,000 short of victory. Even more than before, Dinkins had to get these votes from non-Latino whites.

Once more, sufficiently large minorities of whites supported Dinkins to put him slightly ahead of Giuliani. The white liberal ADs provided 115,000 of these votes, outer-borough Jewish ADs provided 80,000, and the non-Latino Catholic ADs gave him 68,000. Dinkins obviously could not have been elected without a solid African American base. But equally obviously he needed support from other quarters. In order of numerical importance, these came from white liberals, Latinos, outer-borough Jews, and outer-borough white Catholics. Had these latter two constituencies, both of which gave most of their votes to Rudolph Giuliani, been even 20 percent less supportive of Dinkins, he would have lost the election. The secret to Dinkins's success in the general election was not that one group, such as Latinos, shifted in his favor, but that major components of *all* the major non-black ethnic groups, including Italian American Democrats, backed their party's candidate, even though he was black, against an attractive Republican candidate. In short, the 1989 mayoral election turned out the way it did precisely because of the ways in which it was *not* racially and ethnically polarized.

THE SOCIAL, IDEOLOGICAL, AND ORGANIZATIONAL ROOTS OF A BIRACIAL COALITION

How did this happen? The previous chapters have identified a number of important elements. First, many if not most of the highly educated, cosmopolitan, secular whites who have been attracted to and help to drive New York's postindustrial economy cast their lot with Dinkins. They did so partly because they were not attracted to the values and rhetoric articulated by Edward Koch and Rudolph Giuliani and partly because they believed in the need to lessen racial tensions in the city. Above all, this group felt that David Dinkins would not favor blacks over whites but would treat the races equally. This was reinforced by the political ecology of New York City. This group was clustered in places like the Upper West Side in Manhattan or Park Slope in Brooklyn that are highly politically attuned and well mobilized. Given the evidence of the 67th AD, they felt that Mayor Koch's policies had hurt their neighborhoods. Liberal political activists in these areas were able to pull out their vote and keep most of it in Dinkins's column despite the relentless onslaught that Giuliani mounted on Dinkins's personal financial integrity in the closing days of the campaign.

Latinos also played a pivotal, if more ambivalent, role. In the primary they turned out in comparatively high numbers, but many were still attracted to Mayor Koch, who received a third of their votes. Clearly, being able to vote for a minority candidate who "cared about people like me" and who would work to reduce racial tensions counted for a great deal with this constituency, despite its greater ideological conservatism than among blacks or liberal whites and despite the history of political competition between blacks and Latinos. Latinos identified Dinkins as being effective on issues they cared deeply about, such as homelessness and the drug epidemic. What is more, Giuliani failed to pick up on the ways he might have appealed to this constituency, despite their shared Catholicism and relative conservatism. Giuliani's attacks on Dinkins seemed to have strengthened Latino identification with him.

Just as significantly, not all the traditional white ethnic base of the Democratic party defected to Dinkins. A large minority of Jews and a smaller minority of white Catholics stood by their party despite the deep racial cleavages within New York City. This is a critical part of the story: in Chicago, for example, white Catholics massively revolted from their party's black nominee in 1983. If New York's Italian and Irish American Democrats had behaved like their Irish, Italian, and Polish counterparts in Chicago, Dinkins might well have lost. They did not because, however racially divided, New York is not as racially polarized as Chicago. It is not as polarized, in part, because New York is much less black than Chicago as well as much more Jewish. Its leading black politician thus had to project a much more biracial rhetoric; the perceived threat to white political hegemony, indeed white survival, was correspondingly much smaller.

Which is not to say that a perceived racial threat was absent in New York City. In point of fact it was widespread, especially among white Catholic neighborhoods, and accounted for a considerable part of the defection from the democratic nominee. But racially based mistrust was far from universal. Where it was absent, Dinkins had a fighting chance to win over white voters. The degree of racial trust fostered by New York's heritage of left-liberal multiracial, labor-based politics constitutes a precious political resource and, under the blows of racial conflict, one that is deeply at risk.[4] Even in conservative white ethnic neighborhoods, this ethos remains embedded, if attenuated, in local political cultures and the now-tattered fabric of regular Democratic party organizational politics.

The Dinkins campaign brilliantly achieved unity among black leaders, Latino leaders, the major public sector trade unions, and white reform political clubs. The Jackson campaign had enabled many of these elements to work together, yet Dinkins transcended that campaign's other weaknesses, which would have been fatal to him. His backers carefully positioned Dinkins to be the basis for unity in the black community and the black/Puerto Rican/labor alliance. In the event, the campaign ran a strong and effective grassroots operation to turn out key constituencies.

But credit must also be given to the Democratic party establishment in effecting a Dinkins victory in the general election. Dinkins was viewed as trustworthy and nonthreatening by an important minority of whites because he was a product of the Democratic party organization. After the primary, Mayor Koch and Governor Cuomo lined up strongly behind Dinkins when the assault on him grew strongest. Chapter 5 suggested that their endorsements had a positive effect on vote choices for Dinkins among white Catholics and Jews. Moreover, the regular Democratic party organizations had their power and access on the line: a Giuliani mayoralty could hurt them badly. Thus material interest reinforced and stiffened a partly forgotten or perhaps poorly learned political ethos. There were strong organizational roots, therefore, for a Dinkins victory not only from the now-united insurgent reform coalition of blacks, Latinos, and white liberals, but also from the regulars. While Democratic regulars obviously could not, and did not, hold even close to half their constituents for their party's nominee, it is probable that they helped those who did stay loyal feel comfortable with that choice.

Dinkins of course had help from his opponents. Edward Koch had alienated himself even from many within his core constituencies of outer-borough Jews and white Catholics. This disaffection grew out of both his rhetoric on race and the scandals. In the general election, Giuliani missed a major opportunity to win over Latino voters, who started out with a high regard for him, disproportionately called themselves conservatives, and were extremely concerned about the devastating impact of the drug trade on their communities. If he could have evenly split the Latino vote between himself and Dinkins, as Koch had, rather than lose it by 25/75, the election would have been a literal dead heat.

IMPLICATIONS FOR THE FUTURE OF NEW YORK CITY POLITICS

Despite the triumph of the Dinkins victory and his remarkable ability to overcome divisions that would have defeated many another black candidate, the narrow scope of the win must be kept in mind. Rudolph Giuliani came within a hair's breadth of making his own kind of history, becoming the first Republican mayor of New York in a quarter of a century and the only Republican to have taken control of a big city Democratic stronghold. To do so, he would only have had to recreate the relatively conservative white Catholic-Jewish alignment that has, to varying degrees, constituted a potential majority in the New York City electorate since the 1966 Police Community Review Board referendum.

Giuliani came close. A more populist, less "white" appeal might have enabled him to win greater support from Latinos (who would have seen him as "caring more about people like me"). Had he been able to introduce more elements of Lindsay-style reform rhetoric into his campaign, he might have appealed more strongly to white liberals. Unfortunately for him, Giuliani was a prisoner of his origins, having had to withstand a $13 million onslaught from Ronald Lauder asserting that he was too liberal. His rootedness in conservative Republican politics kept him from making greater gains among Jews, Latinos, and white liberals.

Nonetheless, the coalition that Edward Koch assembled, and that Rudolph Giuliani came so close to reassembling, remains implicit in the New York City electorate. David Dinkins's coalition remains a fragile, if also remarkable, achievement. Two elements lie at its heart: among almost all blacks and most Latinos, a pride and excitement that a leader from outside the ranks of the white political establishment has succeeded to the highest office in the city and cares deeply about those who have been excluded from the corridor of private power and public privilege; and among a large minority of whites, the perception that a black mayor leading a biracial coalition can respond more effectively to the problems dividing the city while not favoring blacks over whites. In the best of times, these would be difficult expectations to meet; responding to them during a recession will be all the more difficult. Yet David Dinkins and his allies have been presented with an extraordinary opportunity to renew the ideals of urban liberalism in a way that genuinely incorporates all the varied elements of New York City's gorgeous social mosaic and transcends tribal commitments and attachments to any one element. Should he meet this challenge, he and his co-workers will have made a signal contribution to American political development.

APPENDIX A

QUESTIONNAIRE ITEM
WORDINGS

ISSUE ITEMS

Question regarding government services and spending
NES: Some people think the government should provide fewer
services, even in areas such as health and education, in
order to reduce spending. Suppose these people are at one
end of the scale at point 1. Other people feel it is more
important for the government to provide many more services even if it means an increase in spending. Suppose
these people are at the other end, at point 7. And of course,

some other people have opinions somewhere in between at points 2, 3, 4, 5, or 6. Where would you place yourself on this scale, or haven't you thought much about this?

NYCES: It has been argued that the government should provide fewer services, even in areas such as health care and education, in order to reduce government spending. Do you agree or disagree with that position? (Follow-on questions as appropriate.) Would you say you strongly agree or somewhat agree? Would you say you strongly disagree or somewhat disagree?

Question regarding level of defense spending

NES: Some people believe that we should spend much less for defense. Others feel that defense spending should be greatly increased. Where would you place yourself on this scale, or haven't you thought much about this?

NYCES: With regard to defense spending, would you say the U.S. should increase defense spending, leave it at the current level, or reduce defense spending? (Follow-on questions, as appropriate.) Would you say greatly increase or moderately increase defense spending? Would you say greatly reduce or moderately reduce defense spending?

Question regarding government's having responsibility for jobs and good standard of living

NES: Some people feel that the government in Washington should see to it that every person has a job and a good standard of living. Others think that the government should just let each person get ahead on their own. Where would you place yourself on this scale, or haven't you thought much about this?

NYCES: Some people believe that it is the responsibility of the government in Washington to see to it that every person has a job and a good standard of living. Do you agree or disagree with that position? (Follow-ons as appropriate.) Would you say you strongly agree or somewhat agree?

Would you say you strongly disagree or somewhat disagree?

Question regarding government aid to minorities

NES: Some people feel that the government in Washington should make every effort to improve the social and economic position of blacks and other minorities. Others feel that the government should not make any special effort to help minorities because they should help themselves. Where would you place yourself on this scale, or haven't you thought much about this?

NYCES: Some people believe that the government should make special efforts to help blacks, hispanics, and other minority groups. Do you agree or disagree with that position? (Follow-ons for strength of agreement/disagreement as appropriate.)

Party Identification (Identical in NES and NYCES)

Generally speaking, do you usually think of yourself as a Republican, a Democrat, an Independent, or what?

(If Republican/Democrat) Would you call yourself a strong Republican/Democrat or a not very strong Republican/Democrat? (If Independent or no preference) Do you think of yourself as closer to the Republican party or to the Democratic party?

Strong Democrat
Weak Democrat
Independent Leaning Democrat
Independent Independent
Independent Leaning Republican
Weak Republican
Strong Republican

Candidate Personality Characteristics (Lead-in wording identical in NES and NYCES. Specific items as indicated. "Strong leader" was first item in NYCES.)

I am going to read a list of words and phrases people may use to describe political figures. For each, tell me whether the word or phrase describes the (candidate/person) I name. Think about George Bush/Michael Dukakis. In your opinion, does the phrase "he is intelligent" (NES only) describe George Bush/Michael Dukakis *extremely well, quite well, not too well*, or *not well at all?* (How about)

Compassionate	NES only
Moral	NES only
Inspiring	NES only
Provides strong leadership	NES and NYCES
Decent	NES and NYCES
Knowledgeable	NES and NYCES
Patriotic	NYCES only
Honest	NES and NYCES

Dependent Variable Item—Candidate Evaluation

NES: I'd like to get your feelings toward some of our political leaders and other people who are in the news these days. I'll read the name of a person and I'd like you to rate that person using something we call the feeling thermometer. Ratings between 50 degrees and 100 degrees mean you feel favorable and warm toward that person.

Ratings between 0 degrees and 50 degrees mean that you don't feel favorable toward the person and that you don't care too much for that person.

You would rate the person at the 50 degree mark if you don't feel particularly warm or cold toward the person.

If we come to a person whose name you don't recognize you don't need to rate that person. Just tell me and we'll move on to the next one.

(Ratings of Bush and Dukakis used)

NYCES: Now I would like to get your feelings toward some of our political leaders. As I mention each name, please tell me whether you feel *very favorable, somewhat favorable, somewhat unfavorable*, or *very unfavorable* toward that person. If I mention a person whose name you do not recognize, just tell me and we'll move on to the next one.

[Those who responded simply "favorable" or "unfavorable" were asked whether that was "somewhat" or "very." If they insisted on simply "favorable" or "unfavorable" they were coded as "somewhat" in the designated direction. There was a neutral point for those who volunteered that they felt neither favorable nor unfavorable. Thus a five-point scale was developed.]

APPENDIX B

A VERY BRIEF INTRODUCTION TO ANTHONY DOWNS' SPATIAL THEORY OF PARTY COMPETITION

In 1957, drawing on the work of the economist Hotelling, Anthony Downs suggested a theory of political party competition rooted in a notion somewhat like the following.

Imagine two push-cart vendors selling ice cream at the same price on the boardwalk of a beach. Let us call them Mary and Alice.

Imagine further that the population is uniformly distributed along the beach in a straight line parallel to the boardwalk, which is, let us say, 1,000 yards long and runs along an east-west axis.

Assume that each person at the beach uses the following decision rule: BUY FROM THE NEAREST VENDOR

Let Mary and Alice begin the summer at opposite ends of the boardwalk, with Mary at the west end and Alice at the east end. They will thus have divided the market equally between them (Figure B.1).

Figure B1

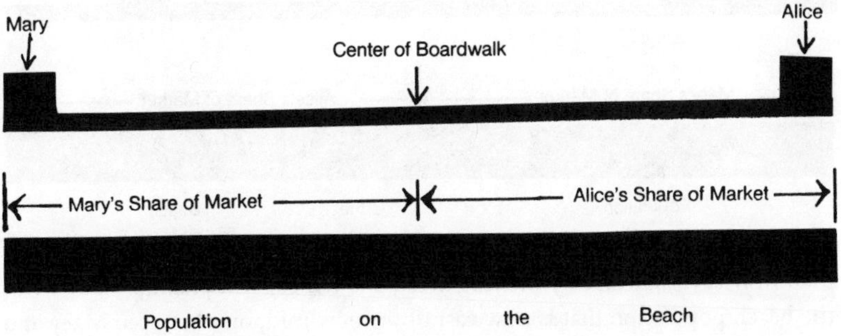

Alice, observing the behavior of those on the beach, soon guesses their decision rule (buy from the nearest vendor). She also realizes that if she moves her cart west a few dozen yards, those at the east end of the beach will still be closer to her than to Mary, but some of those west of the center of the boardwalk will now also be closer to her than to Mary, i.e., that such a move will increase Alice's share of the market (Figure B.2). So Alice moves west a bit.

Figure B2

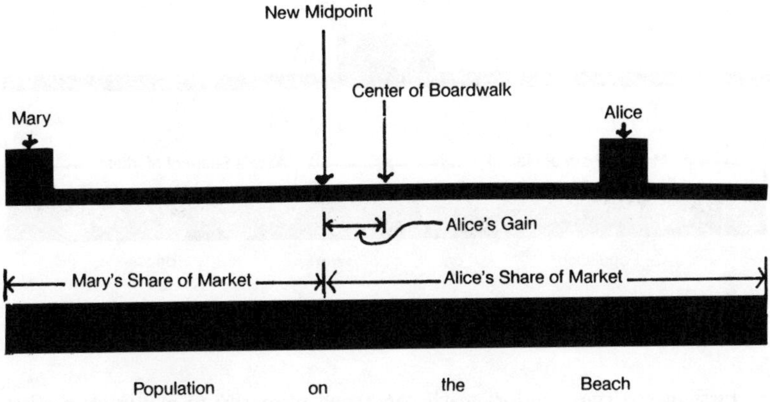

Mary, being no fool, makes a counterpart adjustment, thereby recovering her market share (Figure B.3).

Alice, recognizing that she has lost her advantage, moves west again—again recognizing that those to the east of her new position will still be closer to her

Figure B3

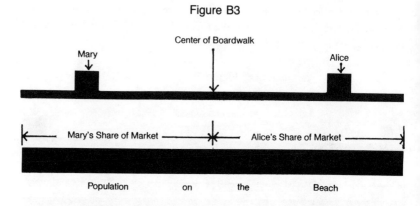

than to Mary, and that by moving west, she (Alice) will pick up that part of the beach population that is now east of the new midpoint between Mary and herself. Mary, of course, counters.

Through a series of such iterations, the two vendors inevitably converge at the center of the boardwalk, again splitting the market equally between them (Figure B.4).

Figure B4

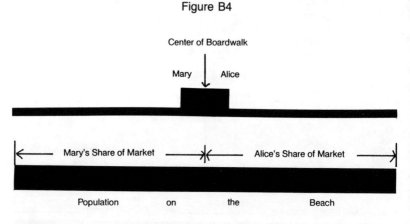

Two points are of special importance in this illustration.

- First, given two vendors, each concerned primarily to maximize market share, and given a population of potential buyers who use a proximity (i.e., distance minimization) rule, and who are distributed as described, convergence to the center is a logically inevitable outcome.
- Second, the convergence at the center is a stable equilibrium. That is to say,

there is no position on the boardwalk to which either vendor can move from the center position without *reducing* that vendor's market share, if the other vendor remains at the center.

If all of this seems sensible, then the reader may wish to consider a hypothetical political situation. Imagine two parties competing for the vote of an electorate. Imagine a single issue election, let us say the mix of "guns" and "butter," with the "all guns" position at the right end of the issue continuum, and the "all butter" position at the left end. Now imagine an electorate distributed as in Figure B.5, that is, symmetrically, with the great bulk of the electorate in the middle ground, and with the modal position being in the center (½ guns, ½ butter). (Note: In Figure E, the vertical distance from any point on the horizontal line to the curved line represents the number of potential voters in this electorate who are at that issue position.) Let each of the members of this electorate use the proximity rule and have the right to abstain if he or she wishes to do so.

Figure B5

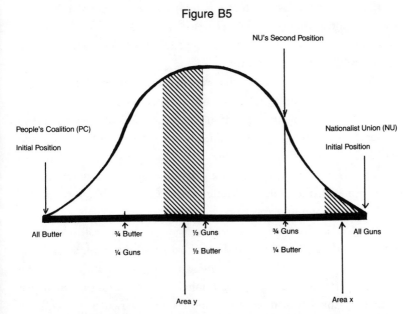

Assume that the parties begin at the extreme positions on the continuum, i.e., with the People's Coalition (PC) advocating all butter and the Nationalist Union (NU) advocating all guns. Assume further that each party would truly like to win the election. Imagine that in pursuit of that goal, the Nationalist Union moves to a ¾ guns and ¼ butter position. While those in area x might well choose to abstain, those in area y would now be closer to the NU position than they would be to the PC position. If all of these potential voters follow the proximity rule (vote for the nearer party or abstain), the NU will have a major net gain in votes—area y being considerably larger, i.e., containing many more voters, than area x. Given the logic that drove Mary and Alice, in our earlier illustration, will the PC have any choice but to move to ¾ butter and ¼ guns, and will the two not eventually converge?

Note that such convergence is *not* independent of the shape of the distribution of policy preferences within the electorate. Imagine all aspects of the situation as before—a desire to win on the part of each of the parties, the proximity decision rule, and the right to abstain on the part of the potential voters, *except* that the distribution of policy preferences within the electorate is highly polarized (U-shaped, as it were), as shown in Figure B.6. Therein, as one can see, the distribution is again symmetric, *but* in this case, the bulk of the electorate is located at the ends of the continuum.

In these circumstances, what would induce either party to move from its initial position? Consider the likely result of the NU moving from its initial "all guns" position to the position of ¾ guns and ¼ butter. It risks losing (to abstention) the very large number of votes in Area x^1 in return for gaining the much *smaller* number of voters in Area y^1. This is not a move that a party seeking to win would make. By symmetry, the same reasoning affects the PC. Therefore, in this situation, one would expect no convergence.

Logical as all of this may be, the reader may well ask what all of this has to do with real political party behavior. After all, so eminent an observer, philosopher, and politician as Edmund Burke defined a political party as a "body of men united for promoting by their just endeavors the national interest, upon some particular principle in which they are all agreed" [See B. W. Hill (ed.), *Edmund Burke on Government and Society* (Glasgow: Fontana/The Harvester Press, 1975),

Figure B6

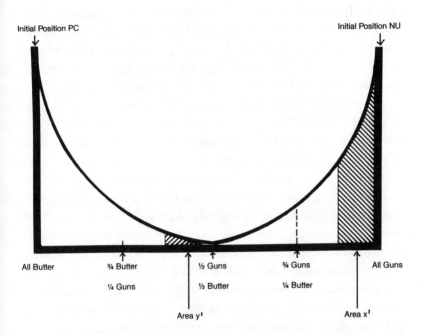

p. 113.] What has such an entity to do with politicians portrayed as vendors seeking to maximize market share? Downs would reply that while Burke's definition may well describe the origins of parties, that definition does *not* serve us well in our efforts to understand those parties that have been successful in electoral competition for office over time. He offers an alternative.

Baldly put, Downs suggests that we regard a political party as a coalition of politicians united for the purpose of winning elected office in order to enjoy the perquisites thereof. To that end, in the Downs model, parties will offer whatever policies are required to get them elected. The voter in this model votes for the party with the set of policies closest to his or her most preferred positions. Both the politician and the voter are rational utility maximizers in this model— the politician's utility being informed primarily by maximizing votes (maximizing the probability of winning, in more refined versions of the model), and the voter's by maximizing the likelihood of obtaining desired policies.

This model is clearly offensive to some—indeed, perhaps to many. Frequently these are people who, from their own experience, know that politicians very often do care about both policy and principle, and who believe that many voters know very little about policy, at least as these people would define having such knowledge. Nevertheless, the model may well warrant serious consideration by the reader.

Consider for a moment the concept of "economic man," defined in the discipline of economics as "rational profit maximizer"—one whose utility stream is essentially informed solely by the maximization of profit. A model based upon that concept has proven quite useful to economists, despite the fact that most of us would be hard pressed to name a businessperson of our acquaintance who does not put the health of his or her children, and the respect of friends and loved ones, above profit maximization. Moreover, these people tend to be genuinely interested in the product or service that they bring to market. Restauranteurs are generally quite interested in the preparation of food, and computer manufacturers are usually truly interested in information processing. However, if either indulges an interest in product to so great an extent as to exclude a concern for profit, that entrepreneur is likely soon to be gone from the marketplace. So too it may well be with political parties. Those who place specific policies so high in their priorities as to exclude a concern for winning elections are, in due course, gone from electoral contention. That constraint may well suffice to make the Downs model relevant.

As to the ostensible issue-ignorance of voters, a persuasive brief to that effect has been made by so distinguished a scholar as Philip Converse. [Cf. Philip E. Converse, "The Nature of Belief Systems in Mass Publics," in David E. Apter (ed.), *Ideology and Discontent* (New York: Free Press, 1964), pp. 206–61.] Yet, strong evidence to the contrary has been presented by such noteworthy scholars as V. O. Key, Jr., Gerald M. Pomper, and Morris P. Fiorina . [Cf. V. O. Key, Jr., *The Responsible Electorate* (Cambridge, Mass.: Harvard University Press, 1966); Gerald M. Pomper, "From Confusion to Clarity: Issues and American Voters, 1956–1968," *American Political Science Review,* 66 (1972), 415–28; Morris P. Fiorina, *Retrospective Voting in American National Elections* (New Haven: Yale University Press, 1981.]

Using a limited set of issues, and operationalizing on the basis of Downs' issue-distance model, the present analysis has explained amounts of variance as high as 65% (See, for example, the R^2 row of Table 3.4). So, there is some substantial reason to believe that enough voters behave as hypothesized to make the Downs model worth one's attention.

This brief introduction to Downs's spatial theory of party competition is just that—an introduction. The theory is rich with explanatory potential and has been the cause of lively intellectual debate within the discipline, producing over time increasingly relevant versions of the model. Again, the interested reader is urged to read the original (Downs 1957) as well as Enelow and Hinich (1984) (see notes 8 and 9 to chapter 3).

APPENDIX C

OPERATIONALIZATION OF VARIABLES

Dependent Variable: Candidate Evaluation Differential (CED)

$$CED_r = ED_r - EB_r \text{ where}$$

r = rth respondent
CED_r = Candidate Evaluation Differential for respondent r.
ED_r = Respondent r's evaluation of Dukakis (on the "feeling thermometer" or NYCES equivalent)
EB_r = Respondent r's evaluation of Bush

Independent Variables: These were of two basic types, Candidate Issue Differentials (CIDs) and Candidate Personality Characteristic Differentials (CPDs).

$$CID_{ri} = |P_{ri} - \mu P_{Bi}| - |P_{ri} - \mu P_{Di}| \text{ where}$$

r = rth respondent

i = ith issue

CID_{ri} = Candidate Issue Differential for respondent r on issue i

P_{ri} = Preferred position of rth respondent on issue i

μP_{Bi} = Mean perceived position of Bush on issue i

μP_{Di} = Mean perceived position of Dukakis on issue i

$$CPD_{rp} = CPS \text{ Dukakis}_{rp} - CPS \text{ Bush}_{rp} \text{ where}$$

r = rth respondent

p = pth personality characteristic

$CPS \text{ Dukakis}_{rp}$ = Candidate Personality Score assigned to Dukakis by respondent r on personality characteristic p

$CPS \text{ Bush}_{rp}$ = Candidate Personality Score assigned to Bush by respondent r on personality characteristic p

With three exceptions, the independent variables were either CIDs or CPDs, and treated as above. The exceptions were:

Party identification: Treated as a seven-point scale with a 0 midpoint, for Independents who did not "lean"

Drugs (NES):   A dichotomous variable

Drugs (NYCES): Treated by the same logic as a CED or CPD

NOTES

CHAPTER 1
UNDERSTANDING NEW YORK

1. The remainder voted for minor party candidates or voted for other offices but not for mayor.
2. Wallace Sayre and Herbert Kaufman, *Governing New York City* (New York: W. W. Norton, 1965), xxxvi, xlvii.
3. Nathan Glazer and Daniel P. Moynihan, *Beyond the Melting Pot: The Negroes, Puerto Ricans, Jews, Italians, and Irish of New York City* (Cambridge: MIT Press, 1970 (1963).
4. Nathan Glazer, "A New Look At The Melting Pot", *The Public Interest,* Special Issue: Focus on New York, 16 (Summer 1969): 181.

5. Martin Shefter, "New York City's Fiscal Crisis: The Politics of Inflation and Re-trenchment," *The Public Interest* 48 (Summer 1977): 98–127.

6. This section is based on John Mollenkopf, *A Phoenix in the Ashes: The Rise and Fall of the Koch Coalition in New York City* (Princeton: Princeton University Press, forthcoming), chapter 3, "The Postindustrial Transformation of New York City."

7. See, for example, Tom Bailey and Roger Waldinger, "The Changing Ethnic Division of Labor," in John Mollenkopf and Manuel Castells, eds., *The Dual City: Restructuring New York* (New York: Russell Sage Foundation, 1991).

8. Emanuel Tobier, "Estimating Population Change in the 1980's" (Urban Research Center, New York University, September 1990).

9. Elizabeth Bogen, *Immigration in New York* (New York: Praeger, 1987), 5.

10. Regina Armstrong, "New York and the Forces of Immigration," paper presented to a conference on Future Shocks to New York, Citizens Budget Commission, January 24, 1989.

11. John Mollenkopf and Manuel Castells, Introduction to Mollenkopf and Castells, eds., *Dual City.*

12. V. O. Key, Jr., *Southern Politics in State and Nation* (New York: Harper and Row, 1947).

13. Regina Reibstein, "Mayoralty Elections in New York City," *City Almanac* 4, no. 3 (October 1969).

14. Warren Moscow, "The Mayors of New York City," *City Almanac* 8, no. 1 (June 1973): 4. See also Bernie Bookbinder, *City of the World: New York and its People* (New York: Harry N. Abrams, 1989), chapter 2, "New York Politics: Bosses and Reformers."

15. James Q. Wilson, *The Amateur Democrat* (Chicago: University of Chicago Press, 1962).

16. One curiosity of this chapter in New York City's political history is that Meade Esposito won a primary election for Democratic party district leader in the Canarsie section of Brooklyn as a reformer supported by Eleanor Roosevelt. Esposito went on to become the Brooklyn Democratic county leader and one of New York City's best known political bosses.

17. This recalled his father's authorship of the National Labor Relations Board; Mark H. Maier, *City Unions: Managing Discontent in New York City* (New Brunswick: Rutgers University Press, 1987). On Wagner's new alignment of political forces, see Theodore Lowi, "Machine Politics—Old and New," *The Public Interest* (Fall 1967): 83–92.

18. Norman Adler and Blanche Blank, *Political Clubs in New York* (New York: Praeger Publishers, 1975), demonstrates the decline of political clubs in the late 1960s and early 1970s compared to the state of affairs in the 1930s described in Roy V. Peel,

Political Clubs of New York City (New York: Putnam, 1935). See also Alan Ware, *The Breakdown of Democratic Party Organization, 1940–1980* (New York: Oxford University Press, 1985).

19. Richard Wade, "The Withering Away of the Party System," in Jewel Bellush and Dick Netzer, eds., *Urban Politics New York Style* (Armonk, N.Y.: M. E. Sharpe, 1990), 280.

20. Examples of these innovations and bureaucratic resistance to them are captured in Diana R. Gordon, *City Limits: Barriers to Change in Urban Government* (New York: Charterhouse, 1973).

21. James Q. Wilson, "The Mayors vs. the Cities," *The Public Interest,* Special Issue: Focus on New York, 16 (Summer 1969): 25–37.

22. Edward T. Rogowsky, Louis H. Gold, and David W. Abbott, "Police: The Civilian Review Board Controversy," in Jewel Bellush and Stephen M. David, eds., *Race and Politics in New York City: Five Studies in Policy-Making* (New York: Praeger, 1971).

23. Introduction to David W. Abbott, Louis H. Gold, and Edward T. Rogowsky, *Police, Politics and Race* (Cambridge: Harvard-MIT Joint Center for Urban Studies, 1969), 2.

24. Rogowsky, Gold, and Abbott, "Police," 70.

25. David Eichenthal, "Changing Styles and Strategies of the Mayor," in Bellush and Netzer, *Urban Politics New York Style,* 71.

26. Quoted in Michael Kramer, "The City Politic: Racism and the Runoff," *New York Magazine* 6 (June 25, 1973): 8.

27. Richard Reeves, "Splitting the Jewish Vote," *New York Magazine* 6 (June 18, 1973): 57.

CHAPTER 2
THE EVOLUTION OF THE KOCH COALITION

1. This chapter is based on John Mollenkopf, *A Phoenix in the Ashes: The Rise and Fall of the Koch Coalition in New York City* (Princeton: Princeton University Press, forthcoming), chapter 5.

2. Jack Newfield and Wayne Barrett, *City for Sale: Ed Koch and the Betrayal of New York* (New York: Harper and Row, 1988), 134.

3. Ibid., 137.

4. *New York Times,* September 23, 1977, section 2, p. 9.

5. J. Phillip Thompson, "The Impact of the Jackson Campaigns on Black Political

Mobilization in New York, Oakland, and Atlanta" (Ph.D. dissertation, CUNY Graduate Center, 1990), chapter 1; John C. Walter, *The Harlem Fox* (Albany: SUNY Press, 1989), describes J. Raymond Jones's role in enlarging black influence within the Tammany organization. Jeffrey Gerson, "Building the Brooklyn Machine: Jewish and Black Succession in the Brooklyn Democratic Party Organization, 1919–1964," (Ph.D. dissertation, Political Science Program, CUNY Graduate Center, 1990), describes how the regular organization absorbed and prospered from black electoral challenges in Brooklyn. Adler and Blank's study of political clubs found that only 5 percent of black club members belonged to reform clubs. Norman Adler and Blanche Blank, *Political Clubs in New York* (New York: Praeger Publishers, 1975).

6. Martin Shefter, *Political Crisis/Fiscal Crisis: The Collapse and Revival of New York City* (New York: Basic Books, 1987), xiii.

7. Ibid., 177.

8. Ibid., 179.

9. NBC News poll results, New York City Democratic primary, September 10, 1985; WABC/*Daily News* exit poll.

10. WABC/*Daily News* exit poll, "Profile of the Answers" item 8.

11. Walter, *The Harlem Fox*.

12. NBC News poll results, New York City Democratic primary, September 10, 1985.

CHAPTER 3
THE 1988 PRESIDENTIAL ELECTION IN NEW YORK CITY

1. The New York City Presidential Election Survey (NYCES) was a random-digit-dial telephone survey of 1,280 adult residents of New York City carried out in the six-week period before the 1988 presidential election. NYCES was funded by the Robert F. Wagner, Sr., Institute of Urban Public Policy at the Graduate Center of the City University of New York. The telephone survey was implemented by the Survey Research Lab of the Center for Social Research at the CUNY Graduate Center.

2. The percentage of New York City's voters in 1988 estimated to fall in each category was:

Non-Latino blacks	21%
Non-black Latinos	22%
Non-Latino white Catholics	22%
Non-Latino white Jews	14%

Non-Latino white Protestants	4%
Others	17%

. For ease of reading, these categories in the text are often reduced to blacks, Latinos, white Catholics, Jews, and white Protestants. This demographic categorization approximates the conventional wisdom prevalent in political circles in New York City. Those who follow city politics tend to group New Yorkers into "white ethnics"—meaning white Catholics like the Italians and Irish, as well as outer-borough Jews (living outside of Manhattan, most likely in Brooklyn and Queens), blacks, and Latinos. Sometimes as an afterthought, they add white Protestants and all others. For a description of which white ethnic groups live near others in Queens, see William Kornblum and James Beshers, "White Ethnicity: Ecological Dimensions," in John Mollenkopf, ed., *Power, Culture, and Place: Essays on New York City* (New York: Russell Sage Foundation, 1988), pp. 201–21. Here and throughout the remainder of our analysis, we do not present figures on Chinese or other Asian voters because our samples are too small to be statistically reliable.

3. *New York Times,* April 21, 1988, p. D25.

4. As between these two possibilities (a "great deal" and "little" Jackson influence), Latinos were more likely to prefer Dukakis if they thought Jackson would have a great deal of influence. Non-Latino whites, on the other hand, took the opposite position: they were substantially more likely to favor Dukakis if they believed that Jackson would have little influence with him than if they believed that Jackson would have a great deal of influence in a Dukakis administration.

5. The National Election Studies (NES) Survey is conducted every four years by the Survey Research Center at the University of Michigan for the Interuniversity Consortium for Political and Social Research (ICPSR). We are grateful to the ICPSR for making early tabulations of the NES available to us.

6. Eighty-seven percent of the respondents placed themselves somewhere on the liberal-conservative scale as opposed to saying "don't know" or refusing to answer.

7. The NES and the NYCES used different interview formats. The NYCES used a telephone interview format that imposed serious constraints on the interview instrument. It was designed to require no more than thirty minutes, and the interviews generally stayed within that limit. By comparison, the NES employed face-to-face interviews that took about three hours. A second constraint was related to question wording; NYCES questions had to be much shorter than their NES equivalents. Question wordings for both the NES and the NYCES items are presented in Appendix A. The third concession made in the telephone survey was to forgo numerical scales such as the "feeling thermometer" and the seven-point attitude scales introduced by Benjamin E. Page and Richard A. Brody, "Policy Voting and the Electoral Process," *American Political Science Review* 66 (1972): 979–95. Many respondents would find it difficult to conceptualize such abstractions without a visual example before them. Therefore, the "feeling thermometer" was

replaced with descriptive words in two-stage questions. For example: "Increase spending, decrease spending, or leave as is?" If "increase" or "decrease," "a lot or a little?" Alternatively questions were phrased as two-stage "Agree-Disagree" items, with "strength" as the second stage. Numerical scales were not used because they could not be shown to the respondents; without showing the scales, we feared systematic measurement error.

8. The seminal work is Anthony Downs, *An Economic Theory of Democracy* (New York: Harper & Row, 1957). The model has been the basis of important studies of voting behavior, for example, Arthur S. Goldberg, "Discerning a Causal Pattern among Data on Voting Behavior" *American Political Science Review* 60 (1966): 913–22; Otto A. Davis, Melvin J. Hinich, and Peter C. Ordeshook, "An Expository Development of a Mathematical Model of the Electoral Process," *American Political Science Review* 64 (1970): 426–48; Brody and Page, "Policy Voting;" John E. Jackson, "Issues, Party Choices, and Presidential Votes," *American Journal of Political Science* 19 (1975): 161–85; Gregory B. Markus and Philip E. Converse, "A Dynamic Simultaneous Equation Model of Electoral Choice," *American Political Science Review* 73 (1979): 1055–70; Morris P. Fiorina, *Retrospective Voting in American National Elections* (New Haven: Yale University Press, 1981); Gregory B. Markus, "Political Attitudes during an Election Year," *American Political Science Review* 1982 (76): 538–60; Michael M. Grant and Norman R. Luttberg, "The Cognitive Utility of Partisanship," *Western Political Quarterly* 40 (1987): 499–517; and George Rabinowitz and Stuart Elaine Macdonald, "A Directional Theory of Issue Voting," *American Political Science Review* 83 (1989): 93–121.

9. The idea of "issue-distance" heavily informs the Downs model and lies at the heart of that model's explanation of the tendency of the policy positions of parties in two-party systems to converge. It has proven a powerful concept, giving rise to so-called "spatial" models of party and voter behavior. For the interested reader who is not conversant with the Downs model, Appendix B provides a brief introduction. For a more thorough treatment, see the quite readable original, Anthony Downs, *An Economic Theory of Democracy*. For a general treatment of spatial models, see James M. Enelow and Melvin J. Hinich, *The Spatial Theory of Voting: An Introduction* (New York: Cambridge University Press, 1984).

10. The formulae for operationalizing the variables are presented in Appendix C.

11. Gregory B. Markus, "Political Attitudes during an Election Year," *American Political Science Review* 76 (1989): 538–60.

12. In the cases of Markus and of Rabinowitz and Macdonald, this procedure is followed to be true to the premises of Downs' model, a different, but also worthy, motivation.

13. Since we wanted to compare the impacts of the several issues both within and between populations and groups, and to assess the efficacy of our analytic model in these populations and demographic groups, the relatively straightforward interpretability of b's, beta's and R^2's made linear regression, and not logit or probit, the

most attractive option. Having selected that option, the use of a dichotomous dependent variable was no longer appropriate, so a surrogate for candidate preference had to be found. For that purpose, the "feeling thermometer" (and the NYCES variant of it) was selected as the dependent variable.

14. See Markus and Converse, "A Dynamic Simultaneous Equation Model," and Mark A. Schulman and Gerald M. Pomper, "Variability in Electoral Behavior," *American Journal of Political Science* 19 (1975): 1–18.

15. As shown in the figure below:

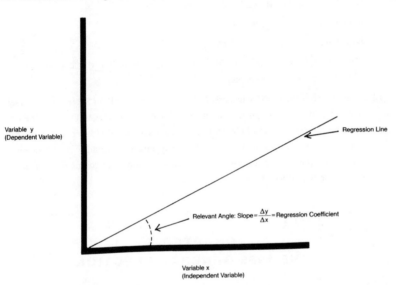

16. We use a variant of the regression coefficient, the standardized partial regression coefficient, also known as the "beta," to analyze the relative impacts of the independent variables. The standardized regression coefficient comes into play when the two variables under consideration are measured on different scales. In effect, the beta puts them on a common scale. The term "partial" indicates that the impacts of the other variables are being controlled (or "partialed out") prior to assessing the impact under consideration.

CHAPTER 4
THE 1989 MAYORAL PRIMARIES

1. January 31, 1989, p. 16.
2. *New York Newsday,* July 31, 1989, p. 4.

3. On the day of the primary election, Dinkins deployed some seven thousand volunteers, many union members, at half the 1,573 polling sites in the city.

4. For races other than the mayoral contest, the amounts were lower. *New York
Observer,* September 18, 1989.

5. *New York Newsday,* July 3, 1989, pp. 7 and 21.

6. *New York Observer,* September 18, 1989.

7. The Republican candidates held only two debates.

8. *New York Newsday,* July 27, 1989, p. 25.

9. *New York Times,* August 2, 1989, p. B1.

10. *New York Newsday,* July 31, 1989, p. 4.

11. *New York Observer,* September 18, 1989. Further analysis at the level of assembly
districts is presented in chapter 7.

12. Data are from the CBS/*New York Times* primary exit poll on September 12, 1989.
It was based on a random sample of thirty-nine polling sites throughout the city.
Pollsters interviewed 2,014 Democratic primary voters and 513 Republican primary
voters as they left the polling places. The error due to sampling was plus or minus
three percentage points for Democratic voters, and plus or minus five percentage
points for Republican voters.

CHAPTER 5
THE 1989 GENERAL ELECTION

1. See the discussion in chapter 1.

2. See William Kornblum and James Beshers, "White Ethnicity," in John Mollenkopf,
ed., *Power, Culture, and Place* (New York: Russell Sage Foundation, 1989), as
well as Jonathan Rieder, *Canarsie: Jews and Italians of Brooklyn Against Liberalism*
(Cambridge: Harvard University Press, 1985).

3. Each of these had been mentioned in numerous previous questions, so differential
awareness was not likely a major influence.

4. The data analyzed in the remainder of this chapter are from the *New York Times/
CBS* exit poll for the 1989 New York City mayoral general election.

5. Drugs are a problem in most poor black and Latino neighborhoods, but the crack
trade is particularly prevalent in certain Latino neighborhoods such as Washington
Heights. The top echelons of the cocaine trade are dominated by the Cali and
Medellin cartels based in Colombia; Dominicans have a reputation for dominating
middle-level dealing.

6. This is based upon all whites in the sample, not only those in the three white groups reported in Figure 5.6.

CHAPTER 7
THE POLITICAL ECOLOGY OF NEIGHBORHOODS

1. The district's assemblyman, Clarence Norman, has, however, also cooperated with the county organization and was recently elected county leader by a coalition of regular and insurgent blacks, white reformers, and the tacit approval of the Golden faction of the county organization.

2. Prime voters are those who have voted in one or more Democratic primaries in the past four-year presidential election cycle. For each AD, we selected a random sample of a list of prime Democratic voters purchased from a firm that specializes in compiling such data. This subset was matched with telephone numbers, and the survey firm of Schulman, Ronca, and Bucuvalas, Inc., administered a questionnaire prepared by researchers from the Wagner Institute to those who were in the resulting sample.

3. This was not an artifact of our sampling but represents the balance not only in registered voters but those going to the polls.

4. For Jones's autobiography, see J. Raymond Jones as told to John C. Walter, *The Harlem Fox: J. Raymond Jones and Tammany, 1920–1970* (Albany: SUNY Press, 1989).

5. James Q. Wilson, *The Amateur Democrat* (Chicago: University of Chicago Press, 1962).

6. Louis Harris and Bert Swanson, *Black-Jewish Relations in New York City* (New York: Praeger, 1970) show that this difference has existed for decades.

7. The standard deviation among the 60 ADs was 16.5.

8. For discussions of the stability of the vote decision in panel studies, see Angus Campbell, Philip E. Converse, William E. Miller, and Donald E. Stokes, *The American Voter* (New York: Wiley, 1960); D. Butler and Donald E. Stokes, *Political Change in Britain* (London: Macmillan, 1969); M. Kent Jennings and Richard G. Niemi, "The Persistence of Political Orientations: An Over-time Analysis of Two Generations," *British Journal of Political Science* 8 (1978): 333–96; Gregory B. Markus, "The Political Environment and the Dynamics of Public Attitudes: A Panel Study," *American Journal of Political Science* 23 (1979): 338–59; Philip E. Converse and Gregory B. Markus, " 'Plus ca change. . .:' The New CPS Election Study Panel," *The American Political Science Review* 73 (1979): 32–49; Michal Shamir and Asher Arian, "The Intifada and Israeli Voters: Policy Preferences and Policy Evaluations," in Asher Arian and Michal Shamir, eds., *The Elections in Israel—1988* (Boulder, CO: Westview 1990), 65–76.

9. Jews in this sample came from the liberal Upper West Side as well as the more conservative Midwood/Kings Highway section of Brooklyn.

10. These data are based on a count of respondents who mentioned any of the agents below.

11. Wilson, *The Amateur Democrat*.

12. Roy V. Peel, *Political Clubs of New York City* (New York: Putnam, 1935).

13. Norman Adler and Blanche Blank, *Political Clubs in New York* (New York: Praeger Publishers, 1975).

CHAPTER 8
NEW YORK CITY AND THE NATION—A COMPARISON

1. See William J. Wilson, *The Truly Disadvantaged: The Inner City, the Underclass, and Public Policy* (Chicago: University of Chicago Press, 1987), and *Annals of the American Academy of Political And Social Science* 501 (January 1989), special issue on the underclass.

2. NES was conducted by the Survey Research Center at the University of Michigan. NYCES was a project of the Robert F. Wagner, Sr., Institute of Urban Public Policy at the Graduate Center of the City University of New York. The telephone survey was implemented by the Survey Research Lab of the Center for Social Research at the CUNY Graduate Center. For a comparison of the NES and NYCES questions, see chapter 3 and Appendix A.

3. For the NES data, those claiming not to have thought much about the topics were excluded from the calculation, as were those who chose a center position (4 on the 1–7 scale). Only in four instances did this produce a data base of less than 60 percent of the total sample. For 1984 the data base for the ratio on reducing government services was 56 percent of the total sample; for 1984 and 1988 the data bases on the defense spending question were 59 percent and 57 percent respectively. In 1988 55 percent of the national sample claimed not to have thought much about the government's role in aiding minorities; in addition to the 10 percent in the middle category, the base for the ratio on that question was reduced to 34 percent of the sample.

4. The categories of urbanization in Table 9.2 were constructed as follows: New York City data from NYCES study; the remaining columns based on the 1988 data set with the New York City respondents removed. The specific categories using the *1988 NES Pre-Election Codebook* were constructed by recoding variable 32:

Other large city	code 11
Small city/small town	codes 30–34, 51–53
Suburban	codes 21–27, 41–46
Rural	codes 20, 40, 50.

5. Angus Campbell, Philip E. Converse, Warren E. Miller, and Donald E. Stokes, *The American Voter* (New York: Wiley, 1960); Otto A. Davis, Melvin J. Hinich, and Peter C. Ordeshook, "An Expository Development of a Mathematical Model of the Electoral Process," *American Political Science Review*, 1970 (64): 426–48; Mark A. Schulman and Gerald M. Pomper, "Variability in Electoral Behavior," *American Journal of Political Science* 19 (1975): 1–18; Herbert B. Asher, *Causal Modeling* (Beverly Hills and London: Sage Publications University Paper Series on Quantitative Applications in the Social Sciences, 1983).

6. For a good review of the efficacy of this model over time, see Herbert B. Asher, *Presidential Elections and American Politics* (Homewood, Ill.: Dorsey Press, 1980), 218–22.

7. For the impact of education on issue based voting, see W. Russell Neuman, *The Paradox of Mass Politics* (Cambridge, Mass.: Harvard University Press, 1986).

8. Asher, *Presidential Elections and American Politics*.

CHAPTER 9
LESSONS OF *CHANGING NEW YORK CITY POLITICS* *1988–89*

1. Raphael Sonenshein, "Biracial Coalition Politics in Los Angeles," in Rufus P. Browning, Dale Rogers Marshall, and David H. Tabb, eds., *Racial Politics in American Cities* (New York: Longman, 1990), 33–48; Harlan Hahn, David Klingman, and Harry Pachon, "Cleavages, Coalitions, and the Black Candidate: The Los Angeles Mayoralty Elections of 1969 and 1973," *Western Political Quarterly* 29 (1976): 521–30.

2. Paul Kleppner and D. Garth Taylor, "The Erosion of Washington's Voting Coalition," paper presented to the American Political Sciences Association, San Francisco, August 1990.

3. Mitchell Moss and Sarah Ludwig, "The Structure of the Media," in John Mollenkopf and Manuel Castells, eds., *The Dual City: Restructuring New York* (New York: Russell Sage Foundation, 1991), describes these patterns. WLIB is owned by Percy Sutton's Inner City Broadcasting, in which Dinkins and a number of other major black leaders were minority investors. WLIB has given a great deal of air time to militant black nationalists who might have attacked Dinkins for pandering to white

sentiment. During the campaign, they and WLIB performed a kind of self-imposed censorship. Dinkins put one potential troublemaker of this sort, Sonny Carson, on his payroll.

4. See Jim Sleeper, *The Closest of Strangers: Liberalism and the Politics of Race in New York* (New York: W. W. Norton, 1990).

BIBLIOGRAPHY

Abott, David W., Louis H. Gold and Edward T. Rogowsky, *Police, Politics and Race* (Cambridge: Harvard-MIT Joint Center for Urban Studies, 1969).

Adler, Norman and Blanche Blank, *Political Clubs in New York* (New York: Praeger Publishers, 1975).

Armstrong, Regina, "New York and the Forces of Immigration," paper presented to a conference on Future Shocks To New York, Citizens Budget Commission, January 24, 1989.

Asher, Herbert B., *Presidential Elections and American Politics* (Homewod, Illinois: The Dorsey Press, 1980).

Asher, Herbert B., *Causal Modeling* (Beverly Hills and London: Sage Publications University Paper Series on Quantitative Applications in the Social Sciences, 1983).

Bailey, Thomas, and Roger Waldinger, "The Changing Ethnic Division of Labor," in John Mollenkopf and Manuel Castells, eds., *Dual City: Restructuring New York* (New York: Russell Sage Foundation, 1991).

Bogen, Elizabeth, *Immigration in New York* (New York: Praeger, 1987).

Bookbinder, Bernie, *City of the World: New York and its People* (New York: Harry N. Abrams, Inc., 1989).

Butler, David, and Donald E. Stokes, *Political Change in Britain* (London: Macmillan, 1969).

Campbell, Angus, Philip E. Converse, William E. Miller and Donald E. Stokes, *The American Voter* (New York: John Wiley and Sons, 1960).

Converse, Philip E., and Gregory B. Markus, " 'Plus ca change . . . :' The New CPS Election Study Panel," *The American Political Science Review* 73 (1979): 32–49.

Davis, Otto A., Melvin J. Hinich, and Peter C. Ordeshook, "An Expository Development of a Mathematical Model of the Electoral Process," *American Political Science Review* 64 (1970): 426–448.

Downs, Anthony, *An Economic Theory of Democracy* (New York: Harper & Row, 1957).

Eichenthal, David, "Changing Styles and Strategies of the Mayor," in Jewel Bellush and Dick Netzer, eds., *Urban Politics New York Style* (Armonk, New York: M.E. Sharpe, 1990).

Enelow, James M., and Melvin J. Hinich, *The Spatial Theory of Voting: An Introduction* (New York: Cambridge University Press, 1984).

Fiorina, Morris P., *Retrospective Voting in American National Elections* (New Haven: Yale University Press, 1981).

Gerson, Jeffrey, "Building the Brooklyn Machine: Jewish and Black Succession in the Brooklyn Democratic Party Organization, 1919–1964," (Ph.D. Dissertation, Political Science Program, CUNY Graduate Center, 1990).

Glazer, Nathan, "A New Look At The Melting Pot", *The Public Interest,* Special Issue: Focus on New York, Number 16 (Summer 1969): 181–193.

Glazer, Nathan, and Daniel P. Moynihan, *Beyond the Melting Pot: The Negroes, Puerto Ricans, Jews, Italians, and Irish of New York City,* second edition (Cambridge: MIT Press, 1970).

Goldberg, Arthur S., "Discerning a Causal Pattern among Data on Voting Behavior" *American Political Science Review,* 60 (1966): 913–922.

Gordon, Diana R., *City Limits: Barriers to Change in Urban Government* (New York: Charterhouse, 1973).

Grant, Michael M., and Norman R. Luttberg, "The Cognitive Utility of Partisanship," *Western Political Quarterly* 40 (1987): 499–517.

Hahn, Harlan, David Klingman, and Harry Pachon, "Cleavages, Coalitions, and the

Black Candidate: The Los Angeles Mayoralty Elections of 1969 and 1973," *Western Political Quarterly* 29 (1976): 521–530.

Harris, Louis, and Bert Swanson, *Black-Jewish Relations in New York City* (New York: Praeger, 1970).

Jackson, John E., "Issues, Party Choices, and Presidential Votes," *American Journal of Political Science* 19 (1975): 161–185.

Jennings, M. Kent, and Richard G. Niemi, "The Persistence of Political Orientations: An Over-time Analysis of Two Generations," *British Journal of Political Science* 8 (1978): 333–396.

Key, V. O., Jr., *Southern Politics in State and Nation* (New York: Harper and Row, 1947).

Kleppner, Paul, and D. Garth Taylor, "The Erosion of Washington's Voting Coalition," paper presented to the American Political Sciences Association, San Francisco, August 1990.

Kornblum, William, and James Beshers, "White Ethnicity: Ecological Dimensions," in John Mollenkopf, J. ed., *Power, Culture, and Place: Essays on New York City* (New York: Russell Sage Foundation, 1988), pp. 201–221.

Kramer, Michael, "The City Politic: Racism and the Runoff," *New York Magazine,* 6 (June 25, 1973).

Lowi, Theodore, "Machine Politics—Old and New," *The Public Interest* (Fall, 1967): 83–92.

Maier, Mark H., *City Unions: Managing Discontent in New York City* (New Brunswick: Rutgers University Press, 1987).

Markus, Gregory B., and Philip E. Converse, "A Dynamic Simultaneous Equation Model of Electoral Choice," *American Political Science Review* 73 (1979): 1055–1070.

Markus, Gregory B., "The Political Environment and the Dynamics of Public Attitudes: A Panel Study," *American Journal of Political Science* 23 (1979): 338–359.

Markus, Gregory B., "Political Attitudes during an Election Year," *American Political Science Review* 76 (1982): 538–560.

Mollenkopf, John, and Manuel Castells, "Introduction," in Mollenkopf and Castells, eds., *Dual City: Restructuring New York* (New York: Russell Sage Foundation, 1991).

Mollenkopf, John, *A Phoenix in the Ashes: The Rise and Fall of the Koch Coalition in New York City* (Princeton: Princeton University Press, forthcoming).

Moscow, Warren, "The Mayors of New York City," *City Almanac* 8:1 (June 1973): 4.

Moss, Mitchell, and Sarah Ludwig, "The Structure of the Media," in Mollenkopf and Castells, eds., *Dual City: Restructuring New York* (New York: Russell Sage Foundation, 1991).

Neuman, W. Russell, *The Paradox of Mass Politics* (Cambridge, MA: Harvard University Press, 1986).

Newfield, Jack, and Wayne Barrett, *City for Sale: Ed Koch and the Betrayal of New York* (New York: Harper and Row, 1988).

Page, Benjamin E., and Richard A. Brody, "Policy Voting and the Electoral Process," *American Political Science Review* 66 (1972): 979–995.

Peel, Roy V., *Political Clubs of New York City* (New York: Putnam, 1935).

Rabinowitz, George, and Stuart Elaine Macdonald, "A Directional Theory of Issue Voting," *American Political Science Review* 83 (1989): 93–121.

Reeves, Richard, "Splitting the Jewish Vote," *New York Magazine,* 6 (June 18, 1973).

Reibstein, Regina, "Mayoralty Elections in New York City," *City Almanac,* 4:3 (October 1969).

Rieder, Jonathan, *Canarsie: Jews and Italians of Brooklyn Against Liberalism* (Cambridge: Harvard University Press, 1985).

Rogowsky, Edward T., Louis H. Gold and David W. Abbott, "Police: The Civilian Review Board Controversy," in Jewel Bellush and Stephen M. David, eds., *Race and Politics in New York City: Five Studies in Policy-Making* (New York: Praeger, 1971).

Sayre, Wallace, and Herbert Kaufman, *Governing New York City* (New York: W.W. Norton, 1965).

Schulman, Mark A., and Gerald M. Pomper, "Variability in Electoral Behavior," *American Journal of Political Science* 19 (1975): 1–18.

Shamir, Michal, and Asher Arian, "The Intifada and Israeli Voters: Policy Preferences and Policy Evaluations," in Asher Arian and Michal Shamir, eds., *The Elections in Israel—1988* (Boulder, CO: Westview, 1990), pp. 65–76.

Shefter, Martin, "New York City's Fiscal Crisis: The Politics of Inflation and Retrenchment," *The Public Interest* 48 (Summer 1977): 98–127.

Shefter, Martin, *Political Crisis/Fiscal Crisis: The Collapse and Revival of New York City* (New York: Basic Books, 1987).

Sleeper, Jim, *The Closest of Strangers: Liberalism and the Politics of Race in New York* (New York: W. W. Norton, 1990).

Sonenshein, Raphael, "Biracial Coalition Politics in Los Angeles," in Rufus P. Browning, Dale Rogers Marshall, and David H. Tabb, eds., *Racial Politics in American Cities* (New York: Longman, 1990), pp. 33–48.

Thompson, J. Phillip, "The Impact of the Jackson Campaigns on Black Political Mobilization in New York, Oakland and Atlanta," (Ph.D. dissertation, Political Science Program, CUNY Graduate Center, 1990).

Tobier, Emmanuel, "Estimating Population Change in the 1980's," (Urban Research Center, New York University, September, 1990).

Wade, Richard, "The Withering Away of the Party System," in Jewel Bellush and Dick Netzer, eds., *Urban Politics New York Style* (Armonk, New York: M.E. Sharpe, 1990).

Walter, John C., *The Harlem Fox* (Albany: SUNY Press, 1989).

Ware, Alan, *The Breakdown of Democratic Party Organization, 1940–1980* (New York: Oxford University Press, 1985).

Wilson, James Q., *The Amateur Democrat* (Chicago: University of Chicago Press, 1962).

Wilson, James Q., "The Mayors vs. The Cities," *The Public Interest* Special Issue: Focus on New York, No. 16 (Summer 1969): 25–37.

Wilson, William J., *The Truly Disadvantaged: The Inner City, the Underclass, and Public Policy* (Chicago: University of Chicago Press, 1987).

Wilson, William J., special editor, *The Annals of the American Academy of Political and Social Science* 501 (January, 1989), The Ghetto Underclass: Social Science Perspectives.

INDEX

INDEX

identification, 116–118, 119;
perceptions of candidates, 61–62, 109–112; presidential election 1988, 57, 58, 59, 63–68; presidential primaries 1988, 40, 44–50; primary and mayoral votes 1989, 119–120, 127–129, 157–164; registration campaign, 34; runoff election 1977, 23–28; state governor election 1982, 32; voting, 95–96, 133–134

Blumenthal, Al, 17, 18
Board of Estimate, 29
Bonfire of the Vanities, 144
Botnick, Victor, 70
Bowery Savings Bank, 71
Bradley, Tom, 77, 198
Bronx, 5, 11, 15, 23, 24, 32, 136, 145, 148
Brooklyn, 4, 11, 23–35, 32–33, 45, 75, 136, 137; regular Democratic organization, 138, 144, 146, 147
Brooklyn Heights, 139
Buckley, William F., 12
Buckley, Charles, 136
Burrows, Daniel L., 142
Bush, George, 60–63, 94, 104, 147–148, 187; presidential election 1988, 56–57, 58, 151–152; mayoral election 1989, 107–109, 130
Bushwick, 84, 138–142, 145–146, 148–175
Butts, Calvin, 36

Campaign activity, 167–171
Campaign Finance Board, 73
Campaign spending, 22, 26
Campbell, Angus, 186
Canarsie, 4, 24, 25, 93
Candidate Evaluation Differential (CED), 61, 186–196, 220, 221
Candidate Issue Differential (CID), 60, 221
Candidate attributes: presidential election 1988, 59–65; mayoral election 1989, 101–106; in United States and New York City, 186–196
Carey, Hugh, 18, 20, 22, 25, 26
Carson, Sonny, 107–109, 130
Carter, Jimmy, 144

Carver Democratic Club, 39, 142
Catholics, and Koch, 21, 25–26, 28–33, 121–122; by assembly districts, 139, 148–175, 199, 201; if Koch had run, 121–122; in US and NYC, 182–196; mayoral election 1965, 12; mayoral election 1981, 30, 31; mayoral election 1985, 36; mayoral election 1989, 89, 93, 97–106, 108–109, 114, 127–134, 198–205; mayoral primaries 1989, 76–78, 84–87, 153–156; party identification, 117–118, 119, 124–127; perceptions of candidates, 109–112; presidential election 1988, 57, 58, 63, 68; presidential primaries 1988, 46; primary and mayoral votes 1989, 119–120, 157–164; runoff election 1977, 22, 25, 26; voting, 133–134
CBS/*New York Times* exit poll, x–xi, 22, 50, 77, 95, 96, 104, 105, 109, 120
Central Park incident, 90
Chicago, 34, 89, 198, 202
City University of New York, x
Civilian Complaint Review Board, 13–15, 204
Coalition: against Koch, 34–38; biracial, 199–205; Dinkins 1989, 76; Giuliani 1989, 93
Coalition for a Just New York, 34
Communications Workers Union, 41
Communist party, 8, 142
Conservative Party, 8, 148
Conservatives, 27: and Koch vote 1977, 23; assembly district, 137, 147, 148–175 coalition, 2; in US and NYC, 182–196; mayoral primaries 1989, 69, 76; presidential primaries 1988, 51–56
Converse, Philip, 186
CORE, 13
Corruption, 39–40, 45, 70, 80–82, 97–100, 127–134, 204
Costikyan, Edward, 24
Crime, 80, 81, 97–100, 127–128, 130–134
Croker, Richard, 136
Crown Heights, 84, 136–137, 141, 142–144
Cunningham, Pat, 24
Cuomo, Mario, 20–23, 37: governor

INDEX

The City in the Twenty-First Century

The Robert F. Wagner, Sr. Institute of Urban Public Policy
The Graduate School and University Center of the City University
of New York

The Robert F. Wagner, Sr. Institute of Urban Public Policy supports the development of volumes on the City in the Twenty-First Century. The books seek to stimulate dialogue between policymakers and the research community and to provide a broad perspective on issues facing the modern city. Joseph S. Murphy, University Professor of Political Science and Chancellor of the City University of New York from 1982 to 1990, serves as general editor of the series. Asher Arian, Director of the Wagner Institute, is editor.

The Robert F. Wagner, Sr. Institute of Urban Public Policy was established at the Graduate School and University Center of The City University of New York in 1987. It uses the resources of the academic community to understand and address the pressing social problems facing New York City and other large urban areas. Its agenda includes the analysis of the social, legislative, and political legacy associated with Senator Robert F. Wagner, Sr., a key architect of the American welfare state during and after the New Deal.